The Fourteenth Amendment

The Fourteenth Amendment

From Political Principle to Judicial Doctrine

William E. Nelson

Harvard University Press
Cambridge, Massachusetts
London, England
1988

Library of Congress Cataloging-in-Publication Data

Nelson, William E., 1940–
   The Fourteenth Amendment: from political principle to judicial
doctrine / William E. Nelson.
      p. cm.
   Bibliography: p.
   Includes index.
   1. United States—Constitutional law—Amendments—14th—History.
2. Civil rights—United States—History.   3. Equality before the
law—United States—History.   I. Title.
KF4757.N45 1988
342.73'085—dc19   76772
[347.30285]   87–35226
   ISBN 0–674–31625–8 (alk. paper)   CIP

To Greg

Preface

I have been privileged in more than two decades of professional work to associate with many extraordinary people, most of whom have contributed to this book. I first became fascinated with the issues raised by the history of the Fourteenth Amendment when, as law clerk to Justice Byron R. White during the October Term 1970, I observed the Court deciding the case of *Oregon* v. *Mitchell*. My observations persuaded me that scholars who had addressed Fourteenth Amendment issues had produced only advocacy history and that a need accordingly existed for a history of the amendment more finely attuned to the contours of the past.

As soon as I left the Court, I began exploring the intellectual backgrounds of those who adopted the amendment in an effort to appreciate the problems they faced and the means by which they hoped to solve them. But I found the puzzles raised by the history of the Fourteenth Amendment intractable. Fortunately, my then colleague Bruce Ackerman persuaded me not to abandon the research I had done but to redirect it instead to a study of late nineteenth century legal and political theory in general, rather than of the amendment in particular. This led first to an article, "The Impact of the Antislavery Movement upon Styles of Judicial Reasoning in Nineteenth Century America," published in the 1974 *Harvard Law Review,* and ultimately to a book, *The Roots of American Bureaucracy, 1830–1900,* published in 1982 by Harvard University Press.

Teaching proved more productive. My efforts to bring coherence to takings and regulation jurisprudence in the first-year property course led me to find in late nineteenth-century cases a line of doctrine differentiating between legislative efforts to promote the public good, and partisan attempts to further narrow, sometimes even private interests. When I began teaching constitutional law in the late 1970s, the same distinction emerged in several opinions of Justice White, especially in *Washington* v. *Davis.*

At that point various pieces of the Fourteenth Amendment puzzle fell into place, as I identified a historical question about the framing and ratification of the amendment that other scholars had not yet addressed. The question was whether the people who adopted the amendment in the 1860s anticipated the distinction between public good and partisan interest that animated the Supreme Court's interpretation of the amendment less than a decade later. With this in mind I began in 1981 to undertake the specific research that has led to this book.

This research has been generously supported by the John Simon Guggenheim Memorial Foundation and by the Filomen D'Agostino and Max E. Greenberg Faculty Research Fund of New York University School of Law. A Guggenheim Fellowship enabled me to extend a sabbatical leave from one to two semesters. The Greenberg Fund provided a third semester of research time. In addition, it granted me several summer stipends and financed many weeks of travel to Washington, D.C., to work at the Library of Congress.

Not unexpectedly, the data I uncovered did not answer my initial questions in a clear, unidimensional fashion. As a result, my questions and hypotheses required continual rethinking and modification. Two individuals played especially vital roles in this process. Ronald Dworkin helped bring greater conceptual clarity to my analysis by sharing with me ideas that have since appeared in his recent book, *Law's Empire;* in particular, he explained why judicial protection of equality typically leaves legislatures greater leeway in making law than does judicial enforcement of a defined set of natural rights. Robert Kaczorowski provided another invaluable sounding board.

Over a period of several years we frequently discussed his work on the Fourteenth Amendment, which came to fruition before mine and arrived at a different conclusion. In consequence of those discussions, I was frequently compelled to reframe my own hypotheses in response to the growing subtlety of Kaczorowski's.

Many people have either read the manuscript or heard me present parts of it. Michael Les Benedict, Norman Cantor, John Phillip Reid, and Harvey Rishikoff made noteworthy contributions to my thinking. I am also indebted to J. Willard Hurst, Harold Hyman, and Robert Post for their helpful critiques of the final manuscript.

Two others deserve mention even though they have not read the manuscript: Bernard Bailyn, who taught me how to write history, and Edward Weinfeld, who embodies for me the highest aspirations of American constitutionalism as they have found representation in the Fourteenth Amendment. I am also grateful to the Harvard Law School Library for permission to quote from the James Bradley Thayer (1831–1902) Papers and the Harvard Law School Student Notebooks, to the Bentley Library of the University of Michigan for permission to quote from the Thomas M. Cooley Collection, and to the New Jersey Historical Society for permission to quote from the Joseph P. Bradley Papers. Special gratitude is due the staff of the Library of Congress for its consistently courteous and professional manner of facilitating access to large portions of the manuscript and newspaper materials in its custody.

Finally, there is my family. Elaine has waited through this book with her accustomed patience, while Leila has appreciated its connection to the bicentennial of the Constitution. Greg remains too young yet to have appreciated the book or to have shown much patience with its drafting, but he has always been at the center of my thoughts during the research and writing. The Fourteenth Amendment offers him, despite his birth abroad under conditions of deprivation and poverty, the hope of a decent life as an American.

CONTENTS

The Fourteenth Amendment

ARTICLE XIV

Section 1. All persons born or naturalized in the United States, and subject to the jurisdiction thereof, are citizens of the United States and of the State wherein they reside. No State shall make or enforce any law which shall abridge the privileges or immunities of citizens of the United States; nor shall any State deprive any person of life, liberty, or property, without due process of law; nor deny to any person within its jurisdiction the equal protection of the laws.

Section 2. Representatives shall be apportioned among the several States according to their respective numbers, counting the whole number of persons in each State, excluding Indians not taxed. But when the right to vote at any election for the choice of electors for President and Vice President of the United States, Representatives in Congress, the Executive and Judicial officers of a State, or the members of the Legislature thereof, is denied to any of the male inhabitants of such State, being twenty-one years of age, and citizens of the United States, or in any way abridged, except for participation in rebellion, or other crime, the basis of representation therein shall be reduced in the proportion which the number of such male citizens shall bear to the whole number of male citizens twenty-one years of age in such state.

Section 3. No person shall be a Senator or Representative in Congress, or elector of President and Vice President, or hold any office, civil or military, under the United States, or under any State, who, having previously taken an oath, as a member of Congress, or as an officer of the United States, or as a member of any State legislature, or as an executive or judicial officer of any State, to support the Constitution of the United States, shall have engaged in insurrection or rebellion against the same, or given aid or comfort to the enemies thereof. But Congress may by a vote of two-thirds of each House, remove such disability.

Section 4. The validity of the public debt of the United States, authorized by law, including debts incurred for payment of pensions and bounties for services in suppressing insurrection or rebellion, shall not be questioned. But neither the United States nor any State shall assume or pay any debt or obligation incurred in aid of insurrection or rebellion against the United States, or any claim for the loss or emancipation of any slave; but all such debts, obligations and claims shall be held illegal and void.

Section 5. The Congress shall have power to enforce, by appropriate legislation, the provisions of this article.

CHAPTER I

The Impasse in Fourteenth Amendment Scholarship

As Judge Henry Brannon wrote in 1901, it was "almost daily, in the federal and state courts, that the Fourteenth Amendment . . . [was] appealed to. . . . The supreme importance of that Amendment . . . [was] at once evident in theory and practice."[1] Indeed, William D. Guthrie thought that the nation's "constitutional history" during the last three decades of the nineteenth century "may be said to be but little more than a commentary on the Fourteenth Amendment."[2] As Brannon added in a statement that remains true today, the amendment's "importance is not waning, but growing."[3]

As a list of the Supreme Court's Fourteenth Amendment cases suggests, Brannon and Guthrie were surely correct. By the time they had published their books at the turn of the century, the Court had already decided the *Slaughter-House Cases*,[4] upholding state zoning and regulation of the business of butchering and selling animals; the *Civil Rights Cases*,[5] holding that the amendment applies only to state action; *Plessy* v. *Ferguson*,[6] upholding racial segregation; and *Allgeyer* v. *Louisiana*,[7] limiting the regulatory power of states over business. In the next three decades, the Fourteenth Amendment provided the basis for deciding *Lochner* v. *New York*,[8] which invalidated a New York statute setting maximum hours of work; *Muller* v. *Oregon*,[9] which sustained an Oregon statute setting maximum hours of work for women; *Coppage* v. *Kansas*,[10] which voided a Kansas act directed against "yellow dog" contracts; and *Adkins* v. *Children's Hospital*,[11] which declared a District of Columbia law setting minimum wages for women unconstitutional. In more recent decades, the Fourteenth Amendment has been implicated in *Brown* v. *Board of Education*,[12] dealing with racial segregation in public schools; in *Roe* v. *Wade*,[13] invalidating state antiabortion legislation; and in *University of California Regents* v. *Bakke*,[14] involving affirmative action for racial minorities. Most recently, however, the Court refused in *Bowers* v. *Hardwick*[15] to read the amendment as guaranteeing individuals autonomy to engage in whatever sorts of consensual sex they wish.

All these cases, along with many others applying the Fourteenth Amendment to a wide variety of legal and social issues, were highly controversial. On the one hand, claims were advanced about the need for federal judicial intervention to protect fundamental rights of individuals and minorities.[16] On the other hand, arguments were made that judges appointed to the bench with life tenure have no business overruling the policy choices of democratically elected legislatures and that the federal government has no business interfering in the internal governance of the states.[17]

Meanwhile, historians have been engaging in a debate which parallels that of the lawyers. The first full history of the amendment, by Horace E. Flack, concluded that the framers intended their handiwork to give the federal government broad powers to protect individual freedoms, including those enumerated in the Bill of Rights.[18] Almost half a century later, Jacobus tenBroek emphasized that the Republican legislators who framed and ratified the amendment had devoted two decades of their lives prior to the Civil War to the advancement of human rights and equality and implied that those legislators intended to achieve codification of their libertarian views through the Reconstruction amendments.[19] In a series of articles published at about the same time, Howard Jay Graham maintained that the Fourteenth Amendment was designed to protect equality and natural rights,[20] while in recent books Chester J. Antieau, Judith A. Baer, and Michael Kent Curtis have concluded that the amendment both applies the Bill of Rights to the states and guarantees equality together with other unspecified rights.[21] In addition, numerous articles urge that the framers drafted their amendment with sufficient breadth to prohibit racial segregation,[22] to grant blacks the right to vote,[23] and to protect blacks against private discrimination as well as against state action.[24]

This expansive reading of the Fourteenth Amendment's framing and ratification has not, however, gone unchallenged. In what still remain two leading articles, Alexander M. Bickel and Charles Fairman argued that the Fourteenth Amendment was not intended to prohibit states from segregating blacks in public schools or to render the Bill of Rights applicable to the states.[25] In recent articles, Earl M. Maltz has suggested that the amendment was not intended to give blacks the right to vote and that the concepts in section one—privileges and immunities, due process, and equal protection—had their origins in the antebellum period not only in radical antislavery thought but in proslavery Southern thought as well.[26] The most important history of the amendment to read the intentions of its authors and ratifiers narrowly is Raoul Berger's,[27] which also takes the view that section one had a "clearly understood and narrow compass"[28] and was not intended either to grant blacks voting rights, to eliminate segregation, or to bind the states to the provisions of the Bill of Rights.

The debate among legal historians about the purposes and intentions of the Fourteenth Amendment's framers is linked, in turn, to a more general historical controversy over the nature of Reconstruction. On one view, the Republican legislators who dominated the Thirty-ninth Congress and state legislatures throughout the North were idealistic statesmen who meant to concretize in constitutional law the right to equality and other rights for which they had struggled all their lives.[29] An alternative view is that the primary concern of mainstream Republican leaders during the course of 1866 was to hold the party together, retain political power, and thereby preserve a political climate in which the North's capitalist economy could continue to flourish and grow.[30]

Voluminous evidence has been presented in support of both the expansive and the narrow readings of the Fourteenth Amendment's history. Historians who read the amendment broadly point to statements made by its proponents that the rights specified in the first eight amendments, together with the right to vote, were among those included in the privileges and immunities of citizens that section one was designed to protect. They also point to the lifelong antisegregationist attitudes of many Republicans, as well as to the belief of the Forty-third Congress, only seven years after the Fourteenth Amendment's ratification, that the amendment gave it power to prohibit segregation in public facilities. An impressive book by Robert J. Kaczorowski shows that, throughout the late 1860s and early 1870s, federal officials in the South, acting under the authority of the Fourteenth Amendment, protected voting rights and First Amendment rights against infringement by private individuals as well as public officials.[31] Taken together, the evidence in support of a broad reading of the Fourteenth Amendment is quite substantial.

Equally cogent evidence has been mustered in favor of the narrow reading, however. Negrophobia, it has been shown, was rampant throughout the North, where, it is said, only a minority of voters truly cared about protecting black rights and guaranteeing black equality. Most Northern states maintained segregated schools, denied blacks the right to vote, and failed to give their citizens all the rights guaranteed by the Bill of Rights. Historians who read the Fourteenth Amendment narrowly point to statements made in Congress that the amendment would have no effect whatever in the North, as well as to the fact that legislatures ratified the amendment without expressing any concern that its passage would require them to change any of their practices, and to the further fact that, after the amendment's passage, no states altered their practices, apparently out of a belief that the amendment did not require them to do so.

Historical scholarship on the adoption of the Fourteenth Amendment is now at an impasse. The conflicting interpretations, all of them supported by impressive arrays of evidence, have left historians and lawyers wondering whether the Republicans who pushed the amendment through Congress and the state legislatures had any clearcut intentions as to what it should mean. Legal historians with viewpoints as divergent as Earl Maltz and Judith Baer agree only that the historical "evidence . . . is not entirely consistent" and often "is simply ambiguous;"[32] that "[c]onfusion and contradiction abound;" and that "the guarantees found" in section one of the amendment "are so broad and general that they could be used to support almost anything."[33]

Not only has this impasse in Fourteenth Amendment scholarship impoverished our understanding of constitutional history; it has also transformed the judicial search for framers' intentions into a sort of game, in which judges search for historical tidbits to support preconceived positions grounded in contemporary policy choices. Virtually everyone who plays this interpretivist game knows that specific intentions compelling judges to reach a particular result rarely exist in Fourteenth Amendment cases; historical arguments usually can be made in support of any result. Nonetheless judges and lawyers continue to search for specific intentions, with the perverse consequence that interpretivism has been transformed from a method for controlling discretion and dictating results into a device freeing judges to decide cases on whatever bases they prefer.

This study attempts to move historical scholarship on the Fourteenth Amendment beyond this present impasse. My argument proceeds in two obvious fashions: by examining primary source materials that most previous historians have ignored, and by asking questions about the sources that previous historians have not asked.

First, the sources. Nearly all the scholarship dealing with the adoption of the amendment which is addressed to lawyers[34] is based on a single set of source materials: the debates of Congress as reported in Benjamin B. Kendrick's *The Journal of the Joint Committee of Fifteen on Reconstruction*[35] and in the *Congressional Globe*. Only occasional references are made to other sources such as newspapers. Although historians like tenBroek and Wiecek, who have studied the antislavery antecedents of the amendment, and Kaczorowski, who has studied the enforcement of the amendment in Southern localities during the decade after its enactment, have looked outside the confines of the congressional materials, legal scholars who have examined the passage of the amendment itself have generally not done so.[36] This is not surprising. The debates of Congress recorded in the *Journal* and the *Globe* are an unusually extensive and rich body of materials; it is impossible to examine these materials without spending a great deal of time and obtaining a good deal of insight. But it is essential to move beyond the familiar sources. Accordingly I have also examined the state ratification debates, the private papers of congressmen, and some one hundred newspapers during the period when the Fourteenth Amendment was under consideration in Congress and in the states, as well as court cases and professional legal commentary during the years when the amendment was first being construed by the judiciary.

It is even more important to ask new questions than to examine more sources. The present impasse has resulted largely from the persistence of scholars in asking questions of twentieth-century significance that cannot be answered by historical inquiry, such as, for example, whether the framers intended section one to preclude states from enacting antiabortion legislation[37]—a question that never occurred to the Reconstruction generation and hence cannot be answered by examining records of its actual thought. More commonly, scholars have inquired about how the framers would have resolved issues they did consider but in fact never resolved. A classic issue of this sort concerns the impact of the amendment on voting rights—a question discussed incessantly during the congressional and ratification debates but never decided by either Congress or the state legislatures. In an effort to resolve it historians have tallied up the evidence and tried to identify the dominant or weightier view, but it is not surprising that different historians who have examined varying packages of evidence and assigned uneven weights to them have reached opposite conclusions. The problem, of course, is that history can never tell us how the framing generation would have resolved inconsistencies that it did not, in fact, resolve. The present impasse in Fourteenth Amendment scholarship results from continued efforts to accomplish this impossible task. If historical scholarship is to move forward, it must turn instead to identifying the meaning which the amendment had for its proponents, even if that meaning is not dispositive of the issues pending in the courts today.

I can best illustrate my difficulty with most of the existing scholarship by examining what I find to be the best single article yet written on the Fourteenth Amendment—the classic article on segregation by Alexander Bickel.[38] After considering the congressional debates—in which he found no evidence that anyone proposed to end segregation—together with the widespread existence of segregated schools and public facilities in the North, Bickel wrote that "[t]he obvious conclusion to which the evidence . . . leads is that section 1 . . . was meant to apply neither to jury service, nor suffrage, nor antimiscegenation statutes, nor segregation." He added that "[t]he evidence of congressional purpose [was] as clear as such evidence is likely to be."[39] My difficulties with this conclusion are twofold. One is that, because Bickel did not spend time examining newspapers systematically, he missed some of the evidence, which will be presented below, that cuts against his conclusion. But my fundamental difficulty is that he found it necessary to ask how the framers resolved the segregation issue when, in fact, they never did resolve it. Although Bickel did not end his analysis with his narrow finding about the framers' intent, but instead developed a powerful legal argument for reading the Fourteenth Amendment broadly enough to authorize the desegregation efforts of *Brown* v. *Board of Education,*[40] the key fact remains that he asked anachronistic questions and thereby failed to escape the lawyers' myopic vision of history.

My approach has been different. Although my reading of the many sources on the framing and ratification of the amendment has uncovered a rich debate on virtually every issue that would subsequently come before the Supreme Court, the participants in this debate never agreed on how section one would apply to those issues. The framers of the Fourteenth Amendment simply never took advantage of the many opportunities they had to specify its precise boundaries. But the ambiguities of the amendment for purposes of today's doctrinal issues should not lead to a conclusion that the amendment had no meaning for its supporters. It did have meaning. But the meaning the amendment had for them existed on a conceptual level different from the doctrinal level on which most scholars have tended to examine it, and this meaning can only be recovered through a more genuinely historical analysis than those scholars have employed.

Harold M. Hyman is the historian who has advanced farthest in this type of analysis. Hyman has made significant advances in recapturing the thought processes of Republican political leaders in the 1860s. In his view, Republicans in Congress had committed themselves to completing "the unfinished wartime work of emancipation" because they appreciated the need to make the labor systems of North and South more congruent, and thereby to heal the sectional divisions that had plagued America before the war.[41] But at the same time the Republicans remained dedicated to traditional values of federalism and did not, according to Hyman, want to undermine state power in any drastic fashion.[42] Substantial evidence supports both facets of Hyman's argument. Historians who have searched for an intention on the part of Republicans to provide blacks with full protection of their rights have found voluminous evidence of that intention, as have historians who have tried to show that the party did not wish to upset the existing balance of federalism.

Hyman's thesis, which reflects a sound historical insight that two inconsistent but well-documented interpretations of the past often are both partially correct, is the starting point of my analysis. He raises the fundamental question that I address in this book: how could the Republican party in 1866, and for that matter the bulk of the Northern electorate, have been committed simultaneously to federal protection of black rights and to preservation of the existing balance of federalism? Today the protection of individual rights, typically by the judiciary, appears hopelessly at odds with the free exercise of legislative power, especially by the states. But, as I hope to show, Republicans of 1866 had a political agenda and a historical past that kept them from experiencing as clearly as we do the conflict between the protection of individual rights and the preservation of state legislative freedom.

Those who adopted the Fourteenth Amendment did not design it to provide judges with a determinative text for resolving this conflict in a narrow doctrinal fashion. They wrote the amendment for a very different audience and purpose: to reaffirm the lay public's longstanding rhetorical commitment to general principles of equality, individual rights, and local self-rule. Conflict between these principles, though foreseeable, was not thought to be inevitable. Hence the framers and ratifiers of the Fourteenth Amendment could reasonably hope that conflict would not arise, rather than assume the contrary and proceed to work out whether and to what degree either the principle of rights or the principle of legislative freedom should have priority. The Supreme Court began to elaborate doctrines resolving issues of priority only when a flood of cases in the closing decades of the nineteenth century made the inevitability of conflict fully apparent. The Court then strove to elaborate doctrine faithful to the framers' design to protect both individual rights and legislative power.

The structure of the book flows from its thesis. The next chapter turns to the decades prior to the Civil War to examine how antebellum Americans, including opponents of slavery who would later become the main proponents of the Fourteenth Amendment, proclaimed and acted upon beliefs in the sanctity of rights, the maintenance of equality, and the preservation of state and local power. As we are about to see, no apparent conflict existed between the three sets of belief. Practices of local self-rule persisted during the half century preceding the Civil War and Reconstruction and were frequently employed by antislavery forces to promote their cause of individual freedom. Simultaneously, antislavery advocates utilized concepts of individual rights and equality during the prewar decades. None of this is new to scholars familiar with the Fourteenth Amendment's history, but it is essential background, as is the survey in chapter 3 of the events that culminated in the drafting, adoption, and ratification of the Fourteenth Amendment.

Chapter 4 turns to the debates on the Fourteenth Amendment to show how antebellum ideas of individual rights and equality were repeated by the amendment's proponents during the 1866–1868 period. The main point of the chapter is that the proponents used equality and rights principles exactly as they had used them before the Civil War: to articulate a moral posture and, by enacting their morality into law, to encourage others to abide by it. With the few exceptions that will be examined in chapter 6, supporters of the Fourteenth Amendment spent little time elaborating how it would apply to specific issues they faced. Ultimately, chapter 4 suggests that the framing generation understood constitutional politics as a rhetorical venture designed to persuade people to do good, rather than a bureaucratic venture intended to establish precise legal rules and enforcement mechanisms.

Chapter 5 turns to the rhetoric used by Democratic opponents of the amendment. It shows that the Democratic opponents permitted Republicans to assume a monopoly over the principles of equality and individual rights, which both camps had shared in the antebellum era. The Democrats were thereby left with only one significant argument: that the Fourteenth Amendment would seriously undermine the traditions of local self-rule that had been so important to the American polity during the first nine decades of its independent existence.

The heart of the book is its last two chapters, which examine how the rhetorical principles of the framers were translated into legal doctrine. Chapter 6 shows that the Republican proponents of the amendment agreed with the Democrats about the importance of preserving local autonomy. This agreement rendered it necessary for the Republicans to explain why the Fourteenth Amendment would not deprive the states of their legislative power. The explanation they most commonly offered was that the amendment did not remove fundamental individual rights from the sphere of state control; states would still retain power to regulate rights or perhaps even to cease recognizing them. The object of the amendment, in this view, was the limited one of outlawing arbitrary and unreasonable lawmaking on the part of states. Supporters of the amendment patiently explained that it would have no effect in states, like those in the North, that did not have arbitrary or unreasonable laws.

Of course, this explanation remained at a vague level of rhetorical abstraction: "arbitrary" and "unreasonable" are broad concepts that can mean almost anything. Although a few Republicans strove to give them more specific content during the congressional and state ratification debates on the amendment, the business of giving precise content to the Fourteenth Amendment was left, in large part, to the Supreme Court.

Chapter 7 examines the implementation of the Fourteenth Amendment by the Court in the last three decades of the nineteenth century. Although the framers may have intended the amendment to leave the states with plenary lawmaking power as long as they exercised the power reasonably, the breadth of even this narrow amendment became apparent to judges as soon as they entered upon the task of Fourteenth Amendment adjudication. In the *Slaughter-House Cases*,[43] the initial response of a five-man majority of the United States Supreme Court was to decline the power that the amendment thrust upon it, but within four years that majority had reversed itself and the Court had accepted the task of determining the reasonableness of state law. The Court concluded that reasonable laws were those that were equal, and it determined that states could enact whatever laws they deemed best for the public welfare provided they did not oppress or unjustly discriminate against any particular class. For some three decades thereafter, the Court gave specific content to the rhetorical principles of the framers by administering this extensive but nevertheless limited doctrine of substantive due process.

Lochner v. *New York*,[44] which is considered in a brief concluding chapter, marked the beginning of a new judicial approach, with its apparent declaration that freedom of contract was a federally protected right beyond any state regulation whatever. In the nearly century-long course of adjudication since *Lochner*, the Supreme

Court has persistently identified fundamental rights with which states may not interfere, and the Fourteenth Amendment has assumed a breadth that its proponents did not contemplate. At the same time, the Court and the commentators who analyze its work have lost the capacity to understand how the amendment could ever have been envisioned as a significant but at the same time only limited intrusion upon the power of legislatures.

The historical tale recounted in this book, apart from whatever value it may have purely as history, offers a start for thinking anew about contemporary Fourteenth Amendment adjudication. It directs judges to cease searching in the amendment's legislative history for specific binding resolutions of the particular issues they face. Instead the book's argument suggests that judges who wish to remain faithful to the general purposes of those who added the amendment to the Constitution should heed their dual command to protect rights and to leave legislatures unfettered to adopt laws for the public good. The final substantive chapter, which analyzes the first three decades of judicial application of the amendment, identifies equality as the master concept that best gives effect both to individual rights and to legislative freedom.

Despite its adumbration of a general approach to Fourteenth Amendment adjudication, this book offers no specific answers for individual cases. It takes no position on whether judges should strive to give effect to their obligation of neutrality by deriving law from the Constitution's text or the underlying intentions of its framers, or alternatively, from some other neutral source.[45] Nor does the book direct judges how to attain a specific balance between the protection of human rights and the preservation of legislative freedom,[46] or how to move from a general concept to more specific conceptions of equality.[47]

These tasks are beyond the ken of legal history. The essence of history is the identification of continuities and discontinuities between past and present; this book will identify one such discontinuity: between the constitutional world of Reconstruction, when statesmen of principle strove to transform the ethics of their fellow citizens by codifying moral symbols into constitutional texts, and the constitutional world of today, where judges protect minority interests by trumping legislative policy choices with doctrinal rules. Portraying this discontinuity will identify a gap that must be bridged before the intentions of the framers can control contemporary adjudication. It may even provide a blueprint for a bridge. But the bridge cannot be constructed in a single book, and, if it is ever to be constructed, work will be required from scholars in many disciplines.

CHAPTER II

Ideas of Liberty
and Equality in
Antebellum America

Whatever the reality,[1] a popular ideology of liberty and equality existed in antebellum America. This mid-nineteenth-century ideology, from which section one of the Fourteenth Amendment was ultimately derived, had an amorphous quality that imprecisely linked together several ideas, each with a quite different core content. Ideas about equality coexisted with ideas about rights derived from natural law or from the nature of republican society and with ideas about the importance of local self-rule. Historians have written extensively about these concepts and the ways in which they were deployed in political and social discourse during the decades preceding the Civil War,[2] and little that is new can still be added. Nevertheless it seems essential to survey these three sets of antebellum ideas and the diverse uses to which they were put in the rhetoric of the time. Only then will it be possible to appreciate fully the process through which constitutional doctrine ultimately emerged out of them.

▪ Equality in American Politics, 1830–1860

At a convention held in 1821 to draft a new constitution for the state of New York, one of the nation's most eminent conservatives,

Chancellor James Kent, argued that "[t]he notion that every man that works a day on the road, or serves an idle hour in the militia, is entitled as of right to an equal participation in the whole power of government, is most unreasonable, and has no foundation in justice." Kent believed instead that "[s]ociety is an association for the protection of property as well as of life, and the individual who contributes only one cent to the common stock, ought not to have the same power and influence in directing the property concerns of the partnership, as he who contributes his thousands."[3]

As one historian has observed, this "Federalist logic of power" soon "became a casualty of history."[4] Indeed, several delegates responded to Kent at the New York Convention. The comments of two seem especially relevant. Jacob Radcliff of New York City "thought there should be an equality" and that property rights did not require special solicitude, since "[p]roperty will always carry with it an influence sufficient for its own protection." Giving "it an artificial aid" might "be dangerous to the rights of the community."[5] Peter R. Livingston agreed that a property qualification would not "advance the cause of civil liberty" and also expressed concern about "the justice of withholding th[e] right" to vote from "fellow citizens" upon whom the state relied "in time of war."[6]

Within a decade of the New York Convention, ideas about equality had become a staple of American political rhetoric. Just one year after the convention Cornelius Blatchly, a Quaker and a medical doctor, wrote of society's obligation to "bestow her blessings and donations in the most wise, just, equal and social manner."[7] Seven years later Frances Wright, a radical follower of Robert Dale Owen, defined a republic as a polity in which "the rights of all are equally respected, the interests of all equally secured."[8] Ideas of this sort spread rapidly at the grass roots, as is evidenced by a resolution of a mass meeting in Racine County, Wisconsin, in the mid-1840s declaring that "all exclusive privileges and monopolies, whereby the few may be enabled to amass wealth at the expense of the many, are contrary to the spirit of a government of true equality."[9]

Concern for political equality led some people to strive for economic and social equality as well. For example, Mike Walsh, a radical Tammany Democrat who served in the New York Assembly, spoke of people's "equal right to the share of the means which nature provided,"[10] while New York workingmen endorsed the view that the precept of the Declaration of Independence—"[t]hat all men are created equal"—gave people a right "to the use of such a portion of the earth and other elements as are necessary for their subsistence and comfort."[11] When accused "of exciting the evil passions of the poor, against the rich" with such rhetoric, radicals responded that they "would destroy those evil passions . . . by destroying *poverty* itself." For "[t]o admit that the poor exist *in sufficient numbers, in this country,* in a degree to cause alarm to the rich, is the severest censure that could be passed on all our boasted institutions."[12]

A key element in the attack on economic and social inequality was an intense dislike of monopolies. Much of the antimonopoly rhetoric of the later radical Republicans went back to Andrew Jackson's contest as president with the Second Bank of the United States. Jackson's 1832 message vetoing the recharter of the bank is one of the earliest documents in American politics joining together the concept of equality and the concept of protection of the law. After observing how differences in wealth, talent, and education would produce "[d]istinctions in society," Jackson continued: "[E]very man is equally entitled to protection by law; . . . [and] when the laws undertake to add to these natural and just advantages artificial distinctions, . . . to make the rich richer and the potent more powerful, the humble members of society . . . have a right to complain of the injustice of their Government."[13]

Jackson, of course, was not alone in his indictment of the bank. A year before the veto message, Thomas Hart Benton had accused the bank of "tend[ing] to agravate the inequality of fortunes; to make the rich richer, and the poor poorer" and of becoming "too great and powerful to be tolerated in a Government of free and equal laws." He objected to the bank "on account of the exclusive privileges, and anti-republican monopoly" that it created.[14] Nor was the bank unique in its monopoly status. As Senator Benton noted, "the States abound[ed] with other monopolies, just as much at war with the Rights of the People as that great one was. . . . Chartered companies, with exclusive and extraordinary privileges," he added, were "the legislative evil, and the opprobrium of the age."[15] Radicals of the Age of Jackson agreed and accordingly sought the "Abolition of all Licensed Monopolies."[16] The antimonopoly position was best summed up perhaps in a memorandum written to President Jackson by Roger B. Taney shortly before he was appointed Chief Justice. It is somewhat paradoxical that Taney's language would become constitutional doctrine through the Fourteenth Amendment a half century later, when, as most observers then understood it, the Supreme Court had rejected most of what Taney had stood for. Taney's words merit full quotation:

> It would be against the spirit of our free institutions, by which equal rights are intended to be secured to all, to grant peculiar franchises and privileges to a body of individuals merely for the purpose of enabling them more conveniently and effectually to advance their own private interests. . . . The consideration upon which alone, such peculiar privileges can be granted is the expectation and prospect of promoting thereby some public interest.[17]

Ideas of this sort were passed directly from Jacksonian Democrats to later Radical Republicans. One can begin with Martin Van Buren, who wrote during his presidency that it was "only when the natural order of society" was "disturbed . . . that the wages of labor bec[a]me inadequate." The laboring classes, he concluded, would always be fairly compensated when "[l]eft to" themselves "free from the blighting influence of partial legislation, monopolies, congregated wealth, and interested combinations."[18] Next in this line of thinking was Amasa Walker, a Democrat who later became a Republican. According to Walker, "[c]orporations change the relation of man to wealth." Only if monopolies and corporations were eliminated and every man were left with "his property in his own hands, and manage[d] it himself," would he then be "responsible for the manner in which he . . . [used] it."[19] Finally there is the language of Republican Senator James M. Harlan, an Iowa radical, who wished to put the laborer "on a platform of equality [with others]—let him labor in the same sphere, with the same chances for success and promotion—let the contest be exactly equal between him and others; and if, in the conflict of mind with mind, he should sink beneath the billow, let him perish!"[20]

The egalitarian principles of the mid-nineteenth century, as we have just seen, were not the monopoly of any single political group or single section of the country. Radical members of the Democratic party of Jackson and Van Buren were not their only users. One of Van Buren's main opponents in New York politics was William H. Seward, who as governor of the state in 1837 led the fight for a general incorporation law—a statute enabling groups that did not enjoy the political favor of the legislature to obtain equal access to corporate privileges. Seward, a leading Whig during the 1830s and 1840s, frequently used egalitarian rhetoric. On one occasion, for example, he argued: "We should be degenerate descendants of our heroic forefathers did we not assail this aristocracy, remove the barriers between the rich and the poor, break the control of the few over the many, extend the largest liberty to the greatest number, and strengthen in every way the democratic principles of our constitution."[21] The American political system, according to Seward, was grounded upon the teaching that "all mankind are brethren, practically equal in endowments, equal in natural and political rights, and equal in the favor of the common Creator,"[22] and the Republican party, of which he later became a principal organizer, stood for "one idea . . . the idea of equality—the equality of all men before human tribunals and human laws."[23] Maine Whigs, it should be noted, agreed with Seward about the virtue of "*[e]qual rights, equal laws, and equal privileges* for all classes of the community,"[24] as did Lemuel Shaw, the Whig chief justice of Massachusetts, who believed in "[t]he great principle" that "all persons . . . are equal before the law."[25]

The rhetoric of equality was even put to use by political leaders in the South.[26] An early egalitarian was John Taylor of Caroline, who in arguing for economic as well as political equality took the position that "wealth, like suffrage, must be considerably distributed, to sustain a democratick republick."[27] Two decades later, John C. Calhoun was arguing that the American union "rest[ed] on an equality of rights and advantages among its members"[28]—an argument that in another twenty years developed into the following typical complaint on the part of the *Charleston Mercury:* "Has the principle of equal protection to slave property been carried out by the Government [in Kansas] in any of its departments? . . . In our opinion, had the principle of equal protection to Southern men and Southern property been rigorously observed by the General Government, both California and Kansas would undoubtedly have come into the Union as Slave States."[29] Ultimately this complaint would be given recognition in 1857 by the Supreme Court in *Scott* v. *Sandford*,[30] when Chief Justice Taney accepted the Southern claim that the "Government of the United States had no right to interfere" with slavery "for any other purpose but that of protecting the rights of the owner."[31]

However, the group that made use of concepts of equality in the manner most significant for the future Fourteenth Amendment consisted of the various antislavery political leaders who coalesced in 1854 to form the Republican party. The favorite document of these antislavery advocates was the Declaration of Independence with its ringing proclamation that all men are created equal. They contended that the Declaration "embodie[d] the fundamental elements and principles of American constitutional law"; compared to the Declaration, the Constitution was merely a vehicle "for the adjustment and proper application of the . . . great principles of constitutional law."[32] In view of the Declaration's principle of equality, they urged that "[n]o civil government" could "either authorize or permit one individual, or class of men to infringe the . . . equal rights" of others.[33] They therefore opposed, in the familiar language of mid-nineteenth century radicals, "[a]ll monopolies, class legislations, and exclusive privileges" as "unequal, unjust, morally wrong, and subversive of the ends of civil government."[34]

The most important contribution of the opponents of slavery to ideas underlying the Fourteenth Amendment was their elaboration of the concepts of equal protection used, on occasion, by radical Jacksonians and proslavery Southerners. The antislavery position was "that the benefit and protection of the . . . laws [should] be extended to all human beings *alike,* . . . and that all mankind [should] be allowed the *same* legal rights and protection without regard to color or other physical peculiarities."[35] The leaders of antislavery maintained that if a legislature had "no power to protect *one* man . . . it has none to protect another—none to protect *any*—and if it *can* protect *one* man and is *bound* to do it, it *can* protect *every* man—and is *bound* to do it."[36] All people, in short, should be given "impartial legal protection."[37] Antislavery advocates argued that "he who murders a black man [should] be hanged; that he who robs the black man of his liberty or property [should] be punished like other criminals."[38]

According to opponents of slavery, the factor that distinguished slaves from freemen was that slaves were not protected by the law: a slave, for example, could not sue when his master assaulted or otherwise committed a trespass against him. Thus they were convinced that once "impartial legal protection" was extended to blacks, slavery would disappear. "Give the slave," wrote Henry B. Stanton, "equal legal protection with his master, and at its first approach slavery and the slave trade [would] flee in panic, as does darkness before the full-orbed sun."[39] When slavery had disappeared, some hoped to raise blacks "to become free men with the whites, enjoying the same just, equal rights and privileges."[40]

Some Eastern abolitionists went well beyond mere antislavery, calling for "human brotherhood" and "the restoration of equality of rights, among men." In the Liberty party platform of 1844, these Eastern radicals "cordially welcome[d] our colored fellow citizens to fraternity with us" and promised to "carry out the principles of Equal Rights, into all their practical consequences and applications, and support every just measure conducive to individual and social freedom," even to the extent of repealing all racially discriminatory state laws.[41] Charles Sumner, who would become the most prominent of these Easterners, supported strikingly modern measures of equality at various times in his career, such as black suffrage, desegregation of public facilities, and even integration of public schools.[42]

Other antislavery advocates, in contrast, did not qualify at all as believers in racial equality. The Republican paper for Wisconsin, the *Wisconsin State Journal,* found that there was "a natural antipathy between . . . [the black] and the white race that we do not profess to have overcome,"[43] while the *New York Tribune,* edited by Horace Greeley, a longtime antislavery activist, found that "[a]s a class, the Blacks [were] indolent, improvident, servile and licentious."[44] The Philadelphia *North American* attributed the lowly economic position of blacks not to discrimination but to "something deeper . . . the constitution of the negro himself,"[45] and the *National Era* found that "the real evil of the negro race [was] that they are so fit for slavery as they are."[46] Even radical leaders like Joshua Giddings and William H. Seward would "not say the black man is, or shall be, the equal of the white man,"[47] but instead looked upon blacks as "God's poor; they always have been and always will be everywhere."[48]

Still other antislavery leaders took a middle position between these extremes—a position resting on two key assumptions. The first premise was that, even if blacks were not equal to whites genetically or socially, they were entitled to equal legal rights. Abraham Lincoln often voiced this assumption, "declar[ing] his opposition to negro suffrage, and to everything looking to placing negroes upon a footing of political and social equality with the whites;—but . . . assert[ing] for them a perfect equality of civil and personal rights under the Constitution."[49] Lincoln said of a black woman that "[i]n some respects she certainly is not my equal; but in her natural right to eat the bread she earns with her own hands without asking leave of anyone else, she is my equal, and the equal of all others."[50] Like Lincoln, Salmon P. Chase would not "proscribe men on account of their birth" or "make religious faith a political test."[51] His fellow Ohioan, John A. Bingham, joined other Republicans in speaking against the Oregon constitution of 1857 because it made entry into the state depend on the entrant's race.[52] Several years earlier antislavery political figures in Ohio had taken a similar stand in regard to their own state constitution, arguing that "while the colored people are voluntary residents in the State," they should "enjoy the protection of its laws,"[53] even though, as Chase later recognized, "[a] majority of the people of Ohio unquestionably desire a homogeneous population and would gladly see such provision made for the colored race in more congenial latitudes as would supersede the necessity of their emigration to northern states."[54]

The moderate antislavery insistence that blacks be protected equally in their rights was joined to a second assumption, which underlay the moderate position—that once blacks were so protected, they might rise economically and socially. One antebellum New York moderate thought it "nonsense to talk about the inferiority of the negro race, whilst at the same time they are kept in a state of degradation, which renders mental and moral improvement an impossibility."[55] A Minnesotan agreed that "the temporary condition of a people" was not evidence of their longterm prospects,[56] while an Ohioan, Benjamin F. Wade, told blacks in 1852 that after they had been granted their rights, they would "attain . . . intelligence and independence," followed by "social and political rights."[57] Lincoln took a similar stance, demanding that every man be given "the chance—and I believe a black man is entitled to it—in which he *can* better his condition."[58] Antislavery advocates argued throughout the 1850s that blacks should be allowed to take advantage of any homestead legislation, so that they could "have the opportunity to prove . . . [their] equality with the whites, or make . . . [their] inequality manifest beyond controversy."[59]

The concept of equality, in short, had quite different meanings for different groups in the antislavery movement. Indeed, the concept of equality had an even larger number of meanings for different groups in mid-nineteenth-century American society at large. Some of these meanings, moreover, were not consistent with each other. To some mid-nineteenth-century Americans equality had reference only to political rights. To others, in contrast, the concept had reference to economic power and social place; to some of these others, equality was associated with an old antimonopoly tradition. To Southerners, the concept of equality was a weapon for use in the defense of slavery, whereas for advocates of antislavery in the North it was the principal bulwark of their movement. To some within the antislavery movement, blacks would gain only legal rights once they received the equal protection of the laws. But to others, equal protection would bring in its wake political, economic, and ultimately social equality.

Equality was thus a vague, perhaps even an empty idea in mid-nineteenth-century America.[60] But it was the very emptiness and vagueness of the concept that made it so useful and popular. Equality could mean almost anything, and hence it could be used by almost any group in antebellum America to defend almost any position. The use of more precise arguments in support of a political program might tend to drive off potential support, but no one could be driven away by an argument for equality, since everyone believed in it.

▪ Liberty in American Politics, 1830–1860

The second main theme of American political rhetoric in the three decades prior to the Civil War was that the nation was specially blessed with liberty. Libertarian talk assumed three distinctive forms, each of which will be considered in turn: first, claims that people obtained their liberty through natural law from God; second, analysis of how liberty flowed from the nature of republican government; and third, discussion of the relationship between liberty and practices of local self-government formalized in the federal system.

Liberty as a Product of Higher Law

Many Americans of the mid-nineteenth century professed a deep religiosity that proclaimed immutable moral principle as the source of all human law and the basis of all human governance. For many religious enthusiasts of the era, truth was a fixed, permanent law which a person accepted when God worked a revelation in his soul and "the spirit" aroused his "conscience and [made] it pierce like an arrow."[61] As Theodore Parker, one of the great religious intellects of the period, warned in addressing the relationship between politics and higher law, a "nation, like a man, is amenable to the law of God; suffers for its sin, and must suffer till it ends the sin."[62] Another minister explained that it was not merely "my right" but "my duty . . . to obey [God] in using my political influence, my elective franchise, in his service, by placing those in political office who, I believe, will be faithful in his cause;—in other words, I am bound to act in behalf of morality through political instrumentalities."[63] Many Americans of the mid-nineteenth century probably agreed with the sentiments of a minor party platform in the mid-1840s that "a principle of universal morality [is] that the moral laws of the Creator are paramount to all human laws: or, in the language of an Apostle, that 'we ought to obey God rather than men.' "[64]

Recent historical scholarship has analyzed the importance of higher law ideas to most of the men in the antislavery movement—those who would later constitute the Republican majorities in Congress and the state legislatures that would engraft the Fourteenth Amendment onto the Constitution.[65] Antebellum antislavery leaders spoke constantly about the conformity of their cause to the law of God.[66] In the words of Theodore Dwight Weld, for instance, the cause of antislavery was "the cause of *changeless eternal right;*" Weld added that "God ha[d] decreed its ultimate triumph."[67] Two decades later the founders of the Republican party were similarly observing that "the great central truth of Christianity is the great central truth of our movement as a party," whose "high and holy mission and duty [is] to redeem America."[68] As one of their leaders, the future Chief Justice Salmon P. Chase observed, there was "such a thing as natural rights, derived not from any constitution or civil code, but from the constitution of human nature and the code of heaven."[69] Among "[t]he primary and essential rights of humanity" was "the right . . . to wield, at discretion, the powers conferred by the Creator . . . in any manner not inconsistent with the exercise of the same rights in others."[70]

Higher law arguments were used not only by opponents, but also by defenders of slavery. Higher law had a quite flexible content in mid-nineteenth-century America, as different people came to understand the law and commands of God and nature in quite different ways. Thus, Southerners were able to argue that "[n]o human institution . . . [was] more manifestly consistent with the will of God, than human slavery"[71] and that slavery had been "intended by our Creator for some useful purposes."[72] Southerners also spoke of their "duty" to prevent blacks from acquiring power in any form; that duty was "paramount to all laws, all treaties, all constitutions." It arose "from the supreme and permanent law of nature, the law of self-preservation."[73] Higher law defenders of slavery, it should be noted, made arguments not only about duties imposed on them by God but also about "the rights which God and nature ha[d] given" them.[74]

Like arguments about equality, higher law arguments, especially in relation to the issue of slavery, thus possessed an imprecisely defined, multisided quality in the antebellum United States. Included within the concept of higher law were duty-based claims—claims that God or nature required that people and their governments behave in particular ways. But there was also room within the concept of higher law for right-based claims—claims that God or nature had conferred privileges upon individuals that government could not take away. Both sorts of argument, moreover, could be and were in fact used by proponents as well as opponents of slavery.

Higher law in the antebellum period was not, in short, a species of legal doctrine that dictated or even pointed toward certain and specific results on any of the questions to which higher law arguments were addressed. Such arguments were, instead, a form of political rhetoric occasionally addressed to courts but more frequently addressed to legislative bodies or to the people themselves. It was precisely the flexibility and multisidedness of the arguments that made them attractive for the purpose of political debate: all politicians, whatever practical positions they advocated, could use higher law arguments to connect their positions to a set of popularly held beliefs without compelling them to reach any particular substantive result. While higher law arguments were often advanced in support of libertarian claims, there was nothing internal to the higher law concept dictating that result.

Liberty as a Product of Citizens' Rights

Higher law arguments of a rights-oriented sort must be distinguished from another sort of argument made quite frequently in the antebellum period. This second argument was that people who live under a republican form of government possess rights arising out of the very nature of the political and social system. These rights, like the rights granted by God or nature, are often labeled natural rights. Even though it might be better to use a concept of citizens' rights in talking of rights adhering to the residents of a republican or free society, faithfulness to the rhetoric of the mid-nineteenth century requires that we also refer to these rights as natural rights, as people of the time did.

The natural or citizens' rights tradition can be traced back at least to the early days of the American republic. One early statement came from Supreme Court Justice Samuel Chase in the 1798 case of *Calder v. Bull.*[75] In an opinion concurring in the disposition of the case, Chase wrote that "[a]n Act of the Legislature (for I cannot call it a *law*), contrary to the *great first principles* of the *social compact,* cannot be considered a *rightful exercise* of *legislative* authority."[76] Twelve years later Chief Justice John Marshall in an opinion for the Court in *Fletcher* v. *Peck*[77] similarly struck down a Georgia statute as contrary to "general principles which are common to our free institutions."[78] The early statement of the citizens' rights approach that was most frequently quoted, however, both in the period 1830–1860 and in the debates on the adoption of the Fourteenth Amendment, was Justice Bushrod Washington's dictum in the circuit court case of *Corfield* v. *Coryell.*[79] In defining the privileges and immunities clause of article IV, section 2, Washington referred to rights

> which are, in their nature, fundamental; which belong, of right, to the citizens of all free governments; and which have, at all times, been enjoyed by the citizens of the several states which compose this Union, from the time of their becoming free, independent, and sovereign. What those fundamental principles are, it would be more tedious than difficult to enumerate. They may, however, be all comprehended under the following general heads: Protection by the government; the enjoyment of life and liberty, with the right to acquire and possess property of every kind, and to pursue and obtain happiness and safety; subject nevertheless to such restraints as the government may justly

prescribe for the general good of the whole. The right of a citizen of one state to pass through, or to reside in any other state, for purposes of trade, agriculture, professional pursuits, or otherwise; to claim the benefit of the writ of habeas corpus; to institute and maintain actions of any kind in the courts of the state; to take, hold and dispose of property, either real or personal; and an exemption from higher taxes or impositions than are paid by the other citizens of the state; may be mentioned as some of the particular privileges and immunities of citizens, which are clearly embraced by the general description of privileges deemed to be fundamental; to which may be added, the elective franchise.[80]

The precepts of citizens' rights continued to be used after 1830. For example, in *Wilkinson* v. *Leland*,[81] authored in that year by Justice Joseph Story, the Court explained:

> The fundamental maxims of a free government seem to require, that the rights of personal liberty and private property should be held sacred. At least no court of justice in this country would be warranted in assuming, that the power to violate and disregard them; a power so repugnant to the common principles of justice and civil liberty; lurked under any general grant of legislative authority, or ought to be implied from any general expressions of the will of the people. The people ought not to be presumed to part with rights so vital to their security and well-being.[82]

Nine years later the Supreme Court of Maryland similarly referred to the "fundamental principle[s] of right and justice, inherent in the nature and spirit of the social compact, (in this country at least) . . . that rise . . . above and restrain . . . and set . . . bounds to the power of legislation."[83]

For some mid-nineteenth-century Americans, rights also sprang out of "the common law," which was "the grand element in the United States' Constitution." Indeed, all of the "*fundamental* provisions" of the Constitution were "instinct with its spirit."[84] "The main business of civil government," some argued, was "to 'DO JUSTICE and execute judgment'—upon the maxims of Common Law—that 'no human laws have any validity if contrary to this' and that all enactments 'contrary to reason are void.' "[85] One common law principle, in particular, was thought to be an essential element of all free government. That principle, which was derived from *Calvin's Case*,[86] was that any person who gave allegiance to a government was entitled, in return, to protection from that government. "*[A]llegiance* and *protection*" were said to be "inseparable"—a "doctrine . . . so well established" that it was "almost universally acknowledged."[87] It was "an axiom of the civilized world, and a maxim even with savages, that allegiance and protection [were] reciprocal and correlative."[88]

Like the concept of natural law, concepts about rights derived from the nature of the nation's political system were put to use on both sides of the great issue in mid-nineteenth-century American politics, the issue of slavery. Opponents of slavery argued, for example, that a legislature in a republican government had "no more power to make a slave than to make a king; no more power to institute or establish slavery, than to institute or establish a monarchy."[89] They found "the entire system of slavery at war with the rights of man"[90] and believed that if they gave "ground a single inch" in "the great trial now pending between LIBERTY and DESPOTISM," there would be "no stopping place."[91] "[A] people who ha[d] declared, 'That *all* men are by nature *equally free* and *independent*,' and ha[d] made this declaration the first article in the foundation of their government" could not tolerate slavery and expect their government to endure.[92]

Southern supporters of slavery made like arguments. Thus the South Carolina legislature resolved that the state intended to "adhere to a system, descended to them from their ancestors, and now inseparably connected with their social and political existence."[93] South Carolinians also argued that slavery enjoyed a status based on the "inherent principles of the national compact."[94] As the South Carolina Court of Appeals declared in *Ex parte Boylston*[95] in 1846, " 'every endeavor to extend to . . . [a slave] positive rights, is an attempt to reconcile inherent contradictions,' " for the "very nature" of slavery made a slave "subject to despotism."[96] Such despotism was essential, moreover, to protect slaveholders' right of property—a right "as inviolable as the right of the owner of any property whatever,"[97] according to an amendment added to the Kentucky Constitution in 1850. Similar arguments against "THE ABROGA-TION OF VESTED RIGHTS"[98]—arguments not unlike that of Justice Story in *Wilkinson* v. *Leland*[99] noted above—were made by conservative Southerners in other antebellum contexts.

Although arguments about the nature of citizens' rights in the American polity were more often made by or addressed to courts than were arguments about higher law, they were still, in essence, a form of political rhetoric rather than legal analysis. And, like higher law rhetoric, arguments about citizens' rights did not dictate or point toward certain and specific results. Citizens' rights arguments were multisided and could be used to advocate many different practical positions, some of them inconsistent with each other. Although the equivocal nature of citizens' rights arguments would render them, together with equality and higher law arguments, problematic when examined by twentieth-century legalists who seek to give precise meaning to Reconstruction provisions such as the Fourteenth Amendment, this ambiguity was the very strength that made them so useful and commonplace in antebellum America.

Federalism as a Bulwark of Liberty

Historians typically agree about the centrality of state governments in the public life of antebellum America. States built and subsidized a transportation infrastructure, set money and banking policies, established a legal structure for business growth, defined and punished crime, alleviated poverty, and determined the extent of people's moral and religious freedom. The federal government, in contrast, had little impact on people's daily lives.[100]

But historians have tended to ignore another aspect of antebellum federal-state relations: whether the states or the federal government possessed ultimate coercive power.[101] Today it seems clear that if Congress enacts a statute or the federal courts render a judgment, military power is sufficient to insure its enforcement. No state can interpose its power to prevent enforcement. Until the Union victory in the Civil War, however, the national government's ultimate enforcement powers were untested and uncertain. Antebellum Americans of all political stripes expected that state governments would provide them, in the words of Alexander Hamilton, with "security against invasions of the public liberty by the national authority,"[102] and state governments did not disappoint them. Even the alleged nationalists who authored the Fourteenth Amendment had, prior to the Civil War, shared familiar expectations about the importance of state power for the preservation of liberty and, on occasion, successfully called on state power to block the execution of proslavery federal programs.

During the first seven decades of the national government's existence, the states, usually acting through their courts, nullified federal law with some frequency. One technique of nullification was for state courts to refuse obedience to mandates from the Supreme Court. Some state courts explicitly repudiated the Court's mandates, but that approach only called forth declarations from the Justices reaffirming the validity of their mandates.[103] More subtle was the approach of Massachusetts' highest court, which conceded the "authority" of the Supreme Court but nonetheless declined "to be considered as a mere machine, to execute the decrees of the Supreme Court of the United States, without power to inquire into the grounds of their proceedings, in order to ascertain whether they may not inadvertently have made a mistake."[104]

Another common state judicial practice was to grant writs of habeas corpus on behalf of prisoners in federal custody.[105] This power, which in the view of the leading scholar of early habeas corpus was designedly left in state court hands,[106] impeded federal officials in their enforcement of federal policies by making it impossible to coerce obedience from citizens who had the support of local governing bodies. Federal officials were also hampered by liability to civil suit in state courts, where local juries hostile to national policies had power to impose damage judgments on them.[107]

On at least three occasions between 1789 and 1860 state efforts to invalidate federal law generated highly visible political controversies. The first occurred between 1798 and 1800, when the legislatures of Kentucky and Virginia published resolutions declaring the Alien and Sedition Acts unconstitutional and urging other states to join with them to render the federal statutes unenforceable. Even though Kentucky and Virginia failed to secure support from their sister states and the Adams administration succeeded for two years in enforcing its restrictive legislation, the efforts of the Kentucky and Virginia opposition were not without significance: in 1800 Thomas Jefferson, the leader of the opposition, won the presidential election and upon assuming office permitted the offending legislation to expire. The first major confrontation between state and federal authorities was thus something of a standoff: federal authorities were able to enforce partially some unpopular legislation, but state authorities were able to proclaim their opposition and ultimately to secure the expiration of the legislation.[108]

A second politically charged confrontation between federal and state power involved South Carolina's efforts to nullify the Tariff of 1832. Upon passage of the tariff, the South Carolina legislature met in special session and declared the congressional act void and unenforceable in the state, specifying particular legal procedures that were to be used to render the act a nullity. President Andrew Jackson responded with a ringing statement of his intention to enforce federal law, and Congress responded by adopting the Force Act, which strengthened the hands of federal authorities by giving them, among other things, the right to remove suits brought against them in state court into federal court. Thus federal power and state power were pitted against each other. The confrontation again ended in a standoff, however, with neither side testing its weapons or resolve, as representatives in Congress reached a compromise that left national law in force but lowered import duties to a level more acceptable to South Carolinians.[109] Federal power was thereby vindicated, but so too was state opposition.

A third confrontation between federal and state power ended only slightly differently. It began with Congress's declaration of war against Great Britain in 1812. Until the final battle of New Orleans the war went badly and opposition to it mounted, especially in New England, where it had always been unpopular. Throughout the war the Madison administration had difficulty enforcing federal law in New England. Ultimately New England's opposition culminated in the Hartford Convention, which attacked federal policies, sought constitutional amendments to preclude the adoption of similar policies in the future, and ultimately threatened secession. But a final confrontation between federal and state power never materialized, as Andrew Jackson's victory at New Orleans and the signing of a peace treaty with Britain ended both the war and the opposition.[110] As a result, neither state nor federal power emerged triumphant: both had been asserted and both had enjoyed some success, but neither had vanquished the other.

Beneath these political ambiguities lay important military realities. Until the Civil War, the federal government possessed a minuscule army, numbering only about 8,000 men as late as the mid-1840s.[111] This force, which was charged with fighting Indians and guarding the nation's borders, could not be massed in sufficient numbers to enforce federal law against determined resistance by any state or states. For purposes of domestic law enforcement on occasions such as the Whiskey Rebellion, government depended upon the militia.[112]

The militia, however, was under state command, and, although the president had authority under the Militia Act of 1792[113] to call militiamen into federal service when specified conditions existed, the president's power was less than fully effective. During the War of 1812, for example, the governors of Connecticut, Massachusetts, and Rhode Island refused to place their militias into federal service. The governors claimed that they rather than the president had jurisdiction to determine whether the conditions warranting federalization existed, and since in their view the conditions did not exist, the president was without power over their troops.[114]

Fifteen years later the issue of the president's power to federalize state militias came before the Supreme Court in *Martin v. Mott.*[115] *Mott* arose when a militiaman was sued for a penalty for refusing to report for federal duty. His defense was that no emergency warranting federalization of the militia existed. The defense was rejected, and the Court held that a presidential declaration of emergency was final and could not be called into question by any other authorities. But even the *Mott* decision did not transform the militia into an effective instrument for enforcing federal law against recalcitrant states. During the nullification crisis six years after *Mott,* when South Carolina raised an informal army to obstruct federal law enforcement, President Jackson did not even try to federalize the South Carolina militia but instead encouraged pro-Union leaders to raise their own informal army.[116]

Even if the federal government had had a substantial number of soldiers at its command, the War for Independence and Napoleon's unsuccessful invasion of Russia had illustrated the difficulties that armies faced as they attempted to invade and retain control over a large, hostile countryside. As late as 1860, the seceding Confederate states assumed that they would win their independence because no Northern armies would be able to penetrate and then retain control over the Southern countryside.[117] Prior to the development of railroad and telegraph lines and of new weapons technology that first came into use during the Civil War, some people believed that a disciplined and determined militia could stand up to a professional army—that citizens could function as the military equals of soldiers.[118] And, as long as the federal government did not possess plainly superior military power, there was no reason to expect it to possess plainly superior political power.

Patterns of local self-rule persisted in this fashion in antebellum

America because people believed they promoted liberty. At least since the 1780s American political thinkers have worried about how to prevent majorities from oppressing minorities. Madison's view, for example, is familiar: less danger of minority oppression existed in an extended than in a small republic because majorities in a large republic would lack cohesion; such majorities would be coalitions of factions, any one of which could become a minority and all of which would therefore have an interest in establishing nonoppressive patterns of governance.[119] The Antifederalists, of course, disagreed: in their view, majorities could be prevented from oppressing minorities only in small republics, where all citizens had like interests and so never became divided into majority and minority factions.[120] But the important fact, however much the Federalists and Antifederalists disagreed about how to keep majorities from oppressing minorities, is that they did agree that preventing such oppression and thereby preserving liberty was the main task of constitutional government.

This same concern informed the opposition of Kentucky and Virginia to the Alien and Sedition Acts. The Kentucky Resolutions, for example, objected that aliens living "under the jurisdiction and protection of the laws" of Kentucky were subject to deportation at the command of the president. With "the barrier of the Constitution thus swept away," it appeared that

> no rampart now remain[ed] against the passions and the powers of a majority of Congress, to protect from a like exportation or other more grievous punishment the minority of the same body, the legislatures, judges, governors, and counselors of the States, nor their other peaceable inhabitants who may venture to reclaim the constitutional rights and liberties of the State and people, or who for other causes, good or bad, may be obnoxious to the views or marked by the suspicions of the President, or be thought dangerous to his or their elections or other interests, public or personal.[121]

Minorities would be saved from oppression only if the provisions of the Constitution designed for their protection were enforced, not as Rhode Island urged in its reply to Kentucky and Virginia, by judicial review of allegedly unconstitutional acts in the Supreme Court of the United States,[122] but by the parties to the Constitution itself—that is, by the states. Kentucky's analysis, drafted by Jefferson, bears quotation in full:

> That to this compact each State acceded as a State, and is an integral party, its co-States forming, as to itself, the other party: That the government created by this compact was not made the exclusive or final judge of the extent of the powers delegated to itself; since that would have made its discretion, and not the Constitution, the measure of its powers; but that as in all other cases of compact among parties having no common Judge, *each party has an equal right to judge for itself, as well of infractions as of the mode and measure of redress.*[123]

The same concern motivated the delegates who attended the Hartford Convention. They objected to what they perceived as "[a] deliberate and extensive system for effecting a combination among certain states, by exciting local jealousies and ambition, so as to secure to popular leaders in one section of the Union, the controul of public affairs in perpetual succession,"[124] all of which would lead to the oppression of minority regions like New England. The remedy proposed at Hartford was not all that different from the one proposed by Kentucky and Virginia. By requiring that important national actions, such as a declaration of war, be taken only with the concurrence of two-thirds of each house of Congress,[125] the Hartford Convention would have enabled a third of the states plus one or a third of all House districts plus one to block a majority's policies.

South Carolina's nullification ordinance seventeen years later was no different. The concern of the South Carolina legislature was that the 1832 tariff gave "bounties to classes and individuals engaged in particular employments, at the expense and to the injury and oppression of other classes and individuals."[126] Because Congress had "violated the true meaning and intent of the Constitution, which provides for equality in imposing the burdens of taxation upon the several States and portions of the Confederacy," the legislature acting for the people declared that the tariff was "unauthorized by the Constitution of the United States, and violate[d] the true meaning and intent thereof" and was thus "null, void, and no law, nor binding upon this State."[127] Like the efforts of Kentucky and Virginia in 1798 and of New England in 1815, the South Carolina effort of 1832 sought invalidation of federal law, not because it failed to meet some objective standard of constitutionality applied by a neutral Supreme Court, but because the minority could not "cheerfully . . . surrender its opinion to a majority of its sister states" in respect to "momentous regulations . . . which so vitally wound[ed] the best rights of the citizen." As Kentucky had earlier noted, although it would be prepared to yield to the majority's will "in matters of ordinary or doubtful policy,"[128] it could not so yield when fundamental constitutional rights were at stake.

The position that minorities should ultimately possess power to decide whether law made by majorities would bind them was brought to its ultimate theoretical fruition by John C. Calhoun. Like everyone else, Calhoun began with the premise that the task of a constitution is "to prevent any one interest or combination of interests from using the powers of government to aggrandize itself at the expense of others." This task could be accomplished only by "prevent[ing] any one interest or combination of interests from obtaining exclusive control of the government," which in turn could be accomplished by giving "each interest or portion of the community a negative on the others." This "mutual negative" would place "the rights and safety of each" interest where they could alone "be securely placed, under its own guardianship." A negative would compel government to function not by *"force"* but through *"compromise."* It would also tend

> to unite the most opposite and conflicting interests and to blend the whole in one common attachment to the country. By giving to each interest, or portion, the power of self-protection, all strife and struggle between them for ascendency is prevented. . . . Each sees and feels that it can best promote its own prosperity by conciliating the good will and promoting the prosperity of the others.[129]

Although twentieth-century Americans have rejected it, the political theory of South Carolina and the Hartford Convention—of Calhoun and Jefferson—was hardly frivolous. It made sense to antebellum Americans of many political colorations. Prior to the Civil War Americans had not yet considered the possibility of using neutral and objective bureaucratic standards as a device for protecting rights.[130] Nor had they grown accustomed to an active national government which frequently needed to compel citizens to obey its laws. The danger that majorities might oppress minorities thus could be addressed sensibly by allowing minorities to nullify laws that they perceived as threatening to their basic interests.

Many groups in pre-Civil War America were prepared to tolerate nullification of federal law in order to protect minority rights. But for purposes of understanding the background of the Fourteenth Amendment, the advocates of antislavery were the most important such group.

For three decades prior to 1860, antislavery activists effectively used the power of Northern state governments to harass slaveowners and federal officers working to protect slaveholders' rights. In response to antislavery demands, legislatures in Northern states enacted personal liberty laws for the stated purpose of preventing slavecatchers from kidnapping free black citizens and selling them South as slaves; in practice, the personal liberty laws were also used to obstruct enforcement of the federal Fugitive Slave Act of 1793.[131] Opponents of slavery also brought proceedings in state courts to harass Southern slaveholders who brought their slaves with them to the North either for temporary stays or while in transit between two slave states.[132] The result by 1860 was that only five Northern states—California, Illinois, Indiana, New Jersey, and Oregon—accorded any protection to the property rights of slaveowners traveling with their slaves.[133]

The most notorious example of how antislavery forces tried to use state power to nullify proslavery federal law came before the Supreme Court in *Ableman* v. *Booth*.[134] The case arose out of a federal criminal prosecution of Booth for aiding and abetting a fugitive slave to escape from a federal deputy marshal. When Booth was brought before a federal magistrate and charged with the offense and later, after he had been indicted and convicted, Booth went into state court for a writ of habeas corpus directing the federal marshal to release him from custody. In affirming the issuance of the writ,[135] the Wisconsin Supreme Court acted in precisely the fashion in which state courts had acted throughout the first half of the nineteenth century in using habeas corpus to limit federal coercive power. Even more striking, however, was the reasoning of one of the Wisconsin judges to justify the writ's issuance.

Each judge on the Wisconsin Supreme Court wrote an opinion in the *Booth* case. The opinion of Judge Abram D. Smith,[136] however, came directly out of the writings of John C. Calhoun. "The states," according to Smith, had "never yielded to the federal government the guardianship of the liberties of their people." On the contrary, they had "reserved the power to prescribe the rules of civil conduct, and continued upon themselves the duty and obligation to protect and secure the rights of their citizens."[137] Smith then continued, "But it may be said, if this be so, our system is not perfect, and there can be no uniform will to guide its operations. So indeed is the truth. But, it should be remembered that where one will rules, there can be no freedom for the many. The *imposition* of uniformity is but another name or process for usurpation or tyranny."[138] Like Calhoun, Smith found state and federal governments "coequal and coordinate" and understood that neither could "be subjected to the other without endangering the very object of its institution and endowment."[139] He then turned to the question whether the equality of state and federal governments would produce "troublesome collision[s]." He found

> little danger. . . , so long as each shall be willing to measure its functions by the standard created for the guide of both. But, if to avoid collision, an absolute unquestioning submission on the one hand is requisite, and on the other, a perfect immunity to claim and usurp all powers, and to be the sole and ultimate judge of the extent and validity of its own claims; and to enforce its decisions upon the states, then collision is the preferable alternative. . . .[140]

Smith then planted himself firmly in the state sovereignty camp of Jefferson and Calhoun with his observation that " '[c]ollisions' of this kind" were "by no means new in this government" and were, indeed, "rightful and healthful operations of those necessary checks and balances which are indispensable . . ." The usual result of "such 'collisions' " was "the awakening of inquiry, . . . a recurrence to primary and fundamental principles, and . . . a return of the erring to the constitutional sphere."[141]

When the Supreme Court in 1859 reversed Judge Smith and his Wisconsin colleagues in *Ableman* v. *Booth*,[142] it began a nationalizing trend that would ultimately make the states-rights views of the first half of the nineteenth century seem unreal. But the nationalist transformation did not take place overnight. For example, the holding of *Ableman* had to be reiterated by the Court thirteen years later in *Tarble's Case*[143] before state courts were convinced that it was good law. Older states-rights ideas did not die out immediately during the decade following *Ableman*, when, among other things, the Fourteenth Amendment was being debated. Those ideas remained alive not only among Southern secessionists but also among the antislavery Republicans who would procure congressional passage and state ratification of the amendment. They remained alive because

Americans of all political viewpoints could use them in ways they thought important to the preservation of their liberty.

▪ Ideas in Combination, 1830–1860

The principles of liberty and equality that we have been considering were capable of being used in political discourse to support any practical position desired by some significant group in the American social and political spectrum. Moreover, the strands of egalitarianism, natural law, citizens' rights, and federalism were not kept carefully separate by those who used them. The rhetoric we have been considering was typically not the learned and theoretical discourse of the classroom or the courtroom, but the speech of political and sometimes religious leaders aimed at ordinary lay people, many of whom had little, if any, formal education. Those who used the discourse of equality, natural law, natural rights, and federalism in the three decades before the Civil War generally were not concerned with intellectual coherence or precision, but with persuading those to whom their rhetoric was addressed. Sometimes, in their efforts to persuade, they pursued a single, coherent theme to its logical conclusion. But at other times, when it suited their purposes of persuasion, the political and religious rhetoricians of the mid-nineteenth century mixed together and often confused the logically discrete concepts of equality, higher law, citizens' rights, and local self-rule.

It was especially difficult to preserve a distinction among concepts first, of duties imposed on government by higher law; second, of rights granted to people by God; and third, of rights which people derived from the very meaning of republicanism. As fine a lawyer as Salmon P. Chase, in an argument before a court, confused the concepts when he spoke about "such a thing as natural rights, derived . . . from the constitution of human nature and the code of Heaven, . . . proclaimed by our fathers in the Declaration of Independence to be self-evident, and reiterated in our state constitution as its fundamental axiom."[144] Other antislavery leaders similarly confused discrete concepts when they observed that their cause was "embodied in the self-evident truths of the Declaration of Independence, and in the Golden Rule of the Gospel—nothing more, nothing less"[145] and was consistent with "the principles of the Declaration of Independence, and . . . the law of nature."[146] "[F]reedom" was both "the natural right of man" and required by "the spirit of our confederated government,"[147] and "constitutional law" had to be "consistent with natural law, and man's natural rights."[148] Governments having a republican form—that is, "governments deriving their just powers from the consent of the governed"—were required "to secure all those inalienable rights of life, liberty, and the pursuit of happiness with which . . . [people] are endowed by their Creator."[149] Even Southern political leaders agreed that law must be consistent with "the principles of natural justice and of the social compact."[150]

The idea of equality was also conflated with concepts of higher law and citizens' human rights. Salmon P. Chase, for example, thought that the most "fundamental" of "natural rights" was the "axiom, that all men are born equally free."[151] Similarly, an antislavery party platform in 1846 maintained that the purpose of government was "to secure and preserve the natural and equal rights of all men."[152] The various concepts we have been discussing were most exquisitely conjoined, however, by Congressman John A. Bingham, the future draftsman of section one of the Fourteenth Amendment, in a speech he delivered to the House in 1857. According to Bingham, the "charm" of the Constitution

> lies in the great democratic idea which it embodies, that all men, before the law, are equal in respect of those rights of person which God gives and no man or State may rightfully take away, except as a forfeiture for crime. Before your constitution, sir, as it is, as I trust it ever will be, all men are sacred, whether white or black, rich or poor, strong or weak, wise or simple. Before its divine rule of justice and equality of natural rights, Lazarus in his rags is as sacred as the rich man clothed in purple and fine linen; the peasant in his hovel, as sacred as the prince in his palace, or the king on his throne.[153]

Concepts of equality and individual rights were also employed in conjunction with ideas about federalism and local self-rule. The ideas were mixed together, for example, in South Carolina's nullification of the Tariff of 1832, which, it was urged, "violate[d] the eternal principles of natural justice,"[154] including the "right[s]" to "the free and unrestricted use of the productions of our industry"[155] and to "bear an equal share of the burthens, and . . . enjoy an equal share of the benefits of the common government."[156] John C. Calhoun likewise used all the ideas in combination in his *Disquisition on Government,* where he invented the idea of the "concurrent majority" as a device for protecting local interests from national majorities[157] and also spoke of "the Infinite Being,"[158] "liberty,"[159] and "equality."[160]

At the opposite end of the political spectrum, all the ideas discussed in this chapter were yoked together in the service of antislavery in the lower court opinion of Judge Smith in *Ableman v. Booth*. At one point in his opinion, Smith spoke of "a paramount law; the *fundamental* law,"[161] a reference apparently to natural law. But the most interesting point at which the various concepts crossed came when Smith spoke of the need "to secure beyond contingency personal liberty, and to protect and preserve, as far as practicable, the independence and sovereignty of the respective states," because he was convinced that "the American people" could "no longer enjoy the blessings of a free government, whenever the state sovereignties shall be prostrated at the feet of the federal government, nor the proud consciousness of equality. . . ."[162]

Thus, as they embarked upon the task of framing and ratifying the Fourteenth Amendment, the American people had at hand rhetorical principles dealing with equality, liberty, and federalism which they had used for more than three decades. The ambiguity and malleability of the principles had proved to be their most useful quality in the three decades before the Civil War, when different strands of principle had been used separately and in combination in support of all political positions. Ultimately, the adoption of the Fourteenth Amendment would require the transformation of this political rhetoric, which had been used in antebellum America in a symbolic fashion to convert people into moral citizens who would pursue the public good,[163] into legal doctrine, which could be used in an instrumental fashion to control citizens who had not been converted. The transformation would begin during the framing and ratification debates themselves, when it would become apparent that the various strands of principle could be used more effectively in support of some positions than of others. But the congressmen and state legislators who had been schooled in the imprecise modes of antebellum thought did not transform their discourse overnight. They continued to make fuzzy use of the old antebellum ideas, in part, perhaps, because the old imprecision had the same value to them during Reconstruction that it had had before the Civil War: it enabled them to retain the support of political coalitions whose individual members shared an agreement only about vague ideas, not about specific programs. It was only after the Fourteenth Amendment was turned over to the courts, which had a set of institutional obligations different from those of Congress and the state legislatures, that the vague rhetorical principles of the antebellum era were transformed into a more precise and consistent body of legal doctrine.

CHAPTER III

The Drafting
and Adoption
of the
Amendment

The Thirty-ninth Congress assembled in Washington on December 4, 1865, to begin the task of reconstructing the Union following the North's victory in the Civil War. In essence, Reconstruction required the restoration of self-government in the South under the direction of leaders willing to accept the results of the war and the readmission to Congress of Southern representatives similarly willing to accept the war's outcome. The attitudinal changes that would be required to bring Reconstruction about made the task formidable indeed, given the North-South mistrust and even enmity that developed prior to the war, and the commitment that most white Southerners had made to achieving their independence. Hindsight—the knowledge that, in large part, Reconstruction was completed within a decade—should not make us discount the difficulties of the task.

A persistent theme in the correspondence of congressmen during the early months of 1866 was the difficulty of securing Southern loyalty. As Brigadier General J. W. Sprague wrote to Senator John Sherman in April 1866, "[s]entiments the most disloyal and treasonable are constantly expressed," and it was "made apparent everywhere that northern men are not welcome in the South."[1] A South

Carolinian similarly warned Thaddeus Stevens, the Republican leader of the House, not to be

> deluded by these men. I beseech you, if you value the safety of the government, and the peace, freedom and happiness of the people, trust them not, though they be willing to swear fealty and devotion morning, noon and night! They want office—power, — *all they ever wanted,* and they are vile enough to secure these ends, *in any way possible.* . . . [C]ertainly those traitors who still *hate* the government can afford to wait. . . . Nothing should be done hastily. . . . *Presume nothing upon the loyalty of any one here.*[2]

John Kirkwood of Little Rock asserted that most white Southerners "are more out & out rebels than they were in 1861. They having been whiped [sic] in the Field, have simply changed their base for a fresh attack."[3] In New Orleans, according to one correspondent of Senator Sherman, secession was "rampant again" in December of 1865,[4] while Jesse Shortess of Springfield, Missouri, "just recently on tour to the South," told Sherman that Southerners were "determined to do by policy what they had failed to do with arms."[5] Another of Senator Sherman's correspondents gave him details about the extent of disloyalty in Kentucky:

> [T]he state courts including the appellate court have decided that any trespass to person or property (including arrests made for disloyal conduct, and property taken for the use of the Government forces) by a federal soldier can be punished both civilly & criminally by the state laws and that the Act of Congress . . . authorizing the removal to the federal courts of all cases brought in the state courts against persons in the federal service . . . is void. To these rulings of our courts, . . . add the teachings of our politicians that the passage of certain acts of Congress which have passed the present session gives the people of the state as good cause for rebellion as the colonies had in 1776, and to all this add the declaration of the leading men in the legislature that the acts of Congress should be resisted by the bayonet.[6]

In view of the information they received from their correspondents, it is not surprising that key Republicans in Congress doubted the loyalty of white Southerners. Representative Benjamin F. Butler's speech of August 1866 expressed the common Republican understanding that Southerners in 1861 had left their seats in Congress "for the purpose of destroying this government. . . [;] they now desire to return to their seats for the same purpose."[7] An important Senate Republican, Lyman Trumbull, chairman of the Judiciary Committee and author of the 1866 Civil Rights Act, wrote to a Mrs. Gary in the same vein, saying that it was impossible to restore to "authority and control the very men who causelessly inaugurated a civil war and brought upon the land, North and South, unnumbered evils—the very men who, although overcome by force of arms, are still as hostile as ever in their hearts to the Union."[8] And the Joint Committee of Fifteen included prominently in a March 1866 report on the state of affairs in the South the testimony of the Union military commander in Virginia that "[t]he feeling on the part of Secessionists toward Unionists . . . is hostile."[9]

Southern intransigence took several forms. One was the persecution of white Unionists, both through private violence and through the machinery of the law. Unionists, according to the commander in Virginia, were not "secure in the enjoyment of their rights in a Secession community; they could not rely upon the State Courts for justice."[10] Furthermore, Senator Trumbull thought Mrs. Gary could "not be ignorant of the fact that in many parts of the South Union men, whether natives of the state or from the North, are . . . now without protection to person or property except as it is afforded by the military."[11] A constituent of Senator Sherman agreed "[t]hat should the Freedmens Bureau and the Army be withdrawn, no Union man from either north or south would be safe."[12] Since "[o]ne of the main objects for which the loyal people of the North . . . [had] fought . . . was to secure the enjoyment of the whole country for themselves and their children,"[13] congressional action to protect Unionists was essential.

Southern intransigence also took the form of denying freedom of speech to those who attacked Southern ways. As another of Sherman's correspondents wrote, it was "notorious" that "Northern men have been subjected to the *Gun knife* the *pistol* the rope & tar & feathers for opinion sake all over the South" and that such persecution would prevent "employment" of "[a] multitude of people" in "teaching & preaching in the South."[14] Representative Butler observed that a Southerner "knows that he can go to any part of the North and speak his sentiments freely," whereas Northerners could not go South and "argue the principles of free government without fear of the knife or pistol, or of being murdered by a mob."[15] As one Joseph Bailey wrote to Secretary of War Stanton, when a Union convention met in New Orleans in the summer of 1866, "the mayor and city police [did not] protect that meeting. No. But on the other hand fell upon it like savages and butchered a number of the delegates in cold blood."[16]

A third form of Southern intransigence was hostility toward blacks. Although some Southerners recommended that blacks be treated with justice and kindness, most did not. According to the Union commander in Virginia, most Southern whites wished to reduce blacks

> to a condition which will give the former masters all the benefits of slavery, and throw upon them none of its responsibilities . . . I do not think it would be safe to leave the great body of freedmen to the care of the local authorities or of the State Legislatures. I think there would be danger that the blacks would be so treated that they would commit those acts which an oppressed people, sooner or later, commit against their oppressors.[17]

Most Southern states demonstrated that the Union general's fears were well founded by enacting the infamous black codes, which imposed a second-class status just short of slavery on blacks.[18]

Public opinion in the North would not tolerate this intransigence. Northerners thought "the South can not yet be trusted to govern even themselves, much less the negros."[19] Loyal citizens like William Draper Lewis were not willing to have "unrepentant traitors"[20] and "Southern rebels resume their place in our National Councils until we have from them an assurance of good behavior."[21] They insisted that "*Loyal* men [,] . . . who *can take the oath,* . . . be found to elect *loyal* representatives in loyal Legislatures."[22] Most Northerners also demanded "the protection of the freedmen,"[23] while the freedmen themselves argued that it was the "solemn duty" of the federal government to provide "for our protection" until it "grant[s] us the right to protect ourselves by means of the ballot."[24]

It would thus "take a good deal of whitewash to cover the blood that ha[d] been shed."[25] "The great mass of the northern people," according to the New York *Evening Post,* were simply "determined that lawful liberty shall be secured in all the states of the Union, and to all the people, white and black alike," and they were "very earnest" in their determination.[26] "[T]he loyal sentiment of the Country" demanded that the "brave boys who offered their lives upon the Altar of their country" not be "sacrificed . . . in vain."[27] As

Samuel Craig wrote to his Congressman, Thaddeus Stevens, he had "lost some of . . . [his] best friends in the late rebellion & . . . [his] son spent 4 years in our army & was wounded several times in it." All this would be in vain "unless you do justice to the coloured people," for without justice "we will never have a permanent peace."[28] A correspondent of a Boston newspaper urged that, if blacks did not receive their full rights, "*[t]he agitation of the question will be continued,* . . . until at last the decision shall be in favor of human liberty,"[29] while a correspondent of Senator John Sherman agreed that if the South were "reconstructed upon the principle that the rights of any class . . . depend upon *race* or *color,* we may well expect that the two opposite principles will produce constant agitation and struggle for supremacy, until it culminates in a resort to arms."[30] This position, which was nothing more than a restatement of antebellum ideas like those in Lincoln's house-divided speech, was endorsed by the Union Party of Ohio in a June 1866 resolution calling for the reestablishment of peace "upon such stable foundations that rebellion and secession will never again endanger our National existence."[31]

The task confronting the Thirty-ninth Congress was to devise a formula, in which the South would acquiesce, "to secure in a more permanent form the dear bought victories achieved in the mighty conflict."[32] In the words of Massachusetts Senator Henry Wilson, the task was to put an end to "the power" of aristocratic Southern slaveholders "which caused the war. . . , to the end that the curse of civil war may never be visited upon us again."[33] This task of transferring power from a Southern to a Northern political elite in a manner acceptable to both was one from which ordinary politicians would shrink, but the leaders of the Thirty-ninth Congress were no ordinary men.

Nearly every one of them had been fighting the antislavery battle against overwhelming odds for several decades, and they understood that their victory in that battle had created an unparalleled opportunity to enact their goals into law. Many Republicans had a sense that "*now* is the time to take our guarantees. If we don't do it now, we never will have them."[34] As publisher A. M. M'Clure warned Stevens, "*Do not let the power pass away.*"[35]

The era of Reconstruction was so important because it was an "age of rapid progress."[36] According to Indiana Congressman George W. Julian, the 1860s were revolutionary days. Whole generations of common time are now crowded into the span of a few years. Life was never before so grand and blessed an opportunity. The man mistakes his reckoning, who judges either the present or the future by any political almanac of bygone years. Growth, development, progress, are the expressive watchwords of the hour. Who can remember the marvelous events of the past four years, necessitated by the late war, and then predict the failure of further measures, woven into the same fabric, and born of the same inevitable logic?[37]

In recommending to the New York legislature that it ratify the Fourteenth Amendment, Reuben E. Fenton, the state's governor, agreed with Julian that "[p]rogress in human affairs" normally was "of slow growth, except in periods ... which form epochs in history."[38] The 1860s were such an epoch. They were a "day of growing liberty."[39] Even more important, the 1860s were a time when law seemed capable of transforming social reality: when it would be possible, for example, to enact laws that would

> educate, improve, enlighten, and Christianize the negro; to make him an independent man; to teach him to think and to reason; to improve that principle which the great Author of all has implanted in every human breast, which is susceptible of the highest cultivation, and destined to go on enlarging and expanding through the endless ages of eternity.[40]

The Republican proponents of the Fourteenth Amendment appreciated fully the importance of their work. They knew they were "framing an amendment of our fundamental law, which may exist for centuries without a change."[41] More pointedly, they realized they were "making history, and laying foundations for our future national building,"[42] and they assured each other that they would not "falter before taking th[e] last step."[43] Their constituents felt "the greatest interest in the Reconstruction measures."[44] As one of them wrote, "I know that the opinion of an obscure citizen on such intricate questions as these, is of little worth, except to myself, but as we have a constitutional right to enjoy an opinion, we also have the right to give one."[45] Thousands of others agreed, as they organized[46] and responded to[47] petition campaigns and wrote innumerable letters to their congressmen about proposed constitutional amendments. Hundreds of those letters are still preserved today.

The special, history-making character of Reconstruction was affirmed twelve days after Congress had assembled, when Secretary of

State William H. Seward proclaimed the ratification of the Thirteenth Amendment, which abolished slavery and, in the view of many Congressmen and other people of the time, conferred equal rights on blacks.[48] "[A] great oversight" occurred, however, "when the Great Amendment was passed," in "that a clause was not coupled with it, adjusting the rule of representation."[49]

This oversight vastly complicated the already difficult task of Reconstruction. The number of seats which a state posseses in the House of Representatives and the number of votes to which it is entitled in the Electoral College, it will be recalled, are based on population. An important compromise of the original Constitution, it will be further recalled, had counted a slave as only three-fifths of a person for purposes of enumerating population. With the Thirteenth Amendment's abolition of slavery, however, the black population of the South would be counted in full for purposes of determining the region's representation in Congress and votes in the Electoral College. Thus the somewhat perverse result of the Civil War, which had been fought, at least in part, to end Southern dominance of the national government, was that it increased the danger of such dominance.

Republicans in the fall of 1865 had calculated quite precisely the impact that abrogation of the three-fifths compromise would have.[50] They perceived a real danger that readmission of a solidly Democratic South would imperil Republican and hence Northern control of the federal government. This concern about a possible Democratic resurgence was not, however, a concern merely about partisan advantage. Most Republicans believed that their electoral victory of 1860 had prevented an encroaching Southern slaveocracy from destroying Americans' freedom and democracy and that the North's subsequent victory on the battlefields of the Civil War had preserved the American nation itself. More appeared at stake than partisan control of the apparatus of government; the stake which the Republicans perceived—the stake for which 364,511 Union troops had lost their lives[51]—was the future of liberty in the United States and, perhaps, in the world. As one Republican wrote, he was "willing to sacrifice almost anything to keep the democratic party out of power—thirty years warfare with the party ha[d] led . . . [him] to treat it with a holy hatred." Above all, he did not "want to see it in power again while I live."[52] In the words of the *Springfield Republican,* it was the "duty" of the party "to retain power as long as it can by honorable means, for the good of the country."[53]

These strong feelings did not stem primarily from a desire to hold office. As another Republican who held what he called "a little office" explained, officeholding was not important. In his words, he "had rather the office would sink than to . . . sacrifice all the practical benefits in our reach."[54] The Republicans strove to retain power because they saw themselves as "the party of progress."[55] The party's "great struggle," the seeds of which went back more than three decades into the early days of antislavery, would "go on until it is completed." Republicans thus urged that "all men in the country . . . who love liberty and justice; all who are for peace and prosperity; all who wish to see the country rapidly advance in prosperity, power, and glory, adhere more firmly than ever" to the program that would "lift the nation upward and carry it forward."[56]

Something accordingly had to be done to insure that the Civil War did not increase the political power of the disloyal groups that had brought the war about. One solution was to confer the franchise on Southern blacks. It was expected that blacks would vote in favor of those who had given them their freedom and that, in areas where blacks constituted a majority or even a substantial minority of the population, their votes would bring about the election of loyal candidates to Congress and the state legislatures.

A second solution was to deny political rights—both the right to vote and the right to hold office—to some or all who had participated in the rebellion against national authority. This scheme would increase the number of districts in which white Union loyalists had a majority or at least some power to tip the electoral balance in favor of loyal candidates.

A third solution was to alter the basis of representation: to base a state's number of representatives in the House and hence its votes in the Electoral College not on total population but on the number of people eligible to vote. Thus, if a state excluded blacks from the right to vote, they would not be counted in determining its representation in Congress and its vote in the Electoral College. The end result would be that the abolition of slavery and the end of the three-fifths compromise would reduce Southern political power in Congress unless Southern states gave blacks the right to vote and hence substantial power to participate in the election of loyal officials and the creation of loyal governments.

As the Thirty-ninth Congress progressed, another significant problem also came to its attention. In the period between Lee's surrender at Appomattox and the opening of Congress, most Southern states had enacted black codes that discriminated against former slaves in numerous ways. Early in the congressional session, the Republican leadership proposed legislation to override the black codes and protect black rights. Although the legislation was ultimately enacted as the Civil Rights Act of 1866, the enactment occurred only after long debate. Its proponents found constitutional sanction for the legislation in the newly adopted Thirteenth Amendment, which, they claimed, not only freed the slaves but gave Congress power to legislate on their behalf as well.[57] Democrats and occasional Republicans like John A. Bingham questioned the reach of the new amendment, however, and President Andrew Johnson vetoed the proposed act, in part, he contended, because the Constitution entrusted the protection of civil rights to the states. Although the Republican proponents of the Civil Rights Act mustered the necessary two-thirds vote to override the veto, some residual doubt about the power of the federal government to protect civil rights nonetheless remained.[58]

Taken together, the problems connected with the restoration of the South to the Union and the protection of freedmen's rights called for yet another constitutional amendment. It was open to doubt whether Congress had power to grant suffrage to blacks or otherwise to protect black rights under the Thirteenth Amendment or any other existing constitutional provision. Meanwhile, the Constitution determined the basis of representation in the House in a way that, in the absence of black suffrage, was unacceptable to most people of the North. Only some further constitutional change could resolve these matters in an acceptable way.

The Joint Committee on Reconstruction, established by concurrent resolution of the House and Senate in the opening days of the Congress,[59] took charge of the matters and attempted to put the possible solutions into some sort of order. This fifteen-man committee consisted of five Republicans—William P. Fessenden, J. W. Grimes, Ira Harris, Jacob M. Howard, and George H. Williams—and one Democrat—Reverdy Johnson—from the Senate, and seven Republicans—John A. Bingham, Harry T. Blow, George S. Boutwell, Roscoe Conkling, Justin S. Morrill, Thaddeus Stevens and Elihu B. Washburne—and two Democrats—Henry Grider and Andrew Jackson Rogers—from the House.[60] The committee was jointly chaired by Stevens of the House and Fessenden of the Senate.

At the third meeting of the Joint Committee on January 12, 1866, Bingham submitted a proposal for a constitutional amendment that would give Congress "power to make all laws necessary and proper to secure to all persons in every State within this Union equal protection in their rights of life, liberty and property."[61] The proposal was referred to a subcommittee, which eight days later returned it to the Joint Committee in the following form: "Congress shall have power to make all laws necessary and proper to secure to all citizens of the United States, in every State, the same political rights and privileges; and to all persons in every State equal protection in the enjoyment of life, liberty, and property."[62] On the same day, January 20, the subcommittee also presented to the full Joint Committee a proposal basing representation in the House on population, but further providing "[t]hat whenever the elective franchise shall be denied or abridged in any State on account of race, creed or color, all persons of such race, creed or color, shall be excluded from the basis of representation."[63]

Except for the addition of section three, which barred certain Confederate supporters from holding office, and section four, which guaranteed payment of the national debt and precluded payment of the Confederate debt, the package before the Joint Committee on January 20 was an embryonic form of the Fourteenth Amendment. The package contained an early variant of section one, protecting certain specified privileges of citizens together with the equal right of all persons to life, liberty, and property—a collapsed version of the equal protection together with, perhaps, the due process clause. There was also an early form of section two, depriving states of representation if they denied the franchise to blacks. Finally there was the grant of enforcement power to Congress, which ultimately reappeared as section five.

But the January 20 package differed from what ultimately became the Fourteenth Amendment in one important respect: it was clear and unambiguous. The guarantee of the same political rights and privileges to all citizens obviously gave Congress power, which it might or might not choose to exercise, to protect the right of blacks to vote and their privilege to hold office. Equal protection of life, liberty, and property gave Congress similar power with respect to black civil rights. And the amendment depriving states of representation if they denied blacks the franchise fit into the scheme as a constitutionally guaranteed remedy that took effect automatically in the event Congress otherwise failed to legislate against denials of black suffrage.

The Joint Committee did not, however, present the January 20 package to Congress as a coherent whole. It made two significant changes. First, it presented the two parts of the package separately. On January 22, the House received an amendment reducing the representation of states denying the franchise to blacks,[64] which it proceeded to pass nine days later by the required two-thirds vote.[65] But the Senate, after debating the amendment for over a month, killed it by an indefinite postponement.[66] An amendment protecting rights was presented to the Senate on February 13,[67] where it was never further discussed, and to the House on February 26,[68] only to die two days later when its Republican oppone ts and proponents agreed to a six-week postponement of consideration.[69]

The second change was in the phraseology of the amendment protecting rights. After debating the phraseology for two weeks, the Joint Committee finally agreed on February 3 to the following language:

> The Congress shall have power to make all laws which shall be necessary and proper to secure to citizens of each state all privileges and immunites of citizens in the several states (Art. IV, Sec. 2); and to all persons in the several States equal protection in the rights of life, liberty and property (5th Amendment).[70]

Ultimately, this provision would be transformed into the present section one, with its separate privileges and immunities, due process, and equal protection clauses.

The effect of these two changes was to introduce ambiguity and possible redundancy into the Joint Committee's proposals. What became section two had originated as a remedy if a state deprived blacks of the right to vote—a right specifically protected, in turn, by the original version of section one. But when the remedy was presented as a freestanding proposition, it appeared instead as an implicit grant of power to states to discriminate in respect to suffrage; the freestanding provision became "a dodge to get rid of the suffrage problem,"[71] which gave states a choice of either full representation with universal manhood suffrage or lesser representation with a restricted suffrage.[72] Of course, the proponents of the amendment urged that it had no such effect. They took the position that, if some other provision of the Constitution authorized congressional protection of the right to vote, the freestanding amendment should be understood to offer a remedy for violations of the right, and that, if no federally protected right existed, then the amendment should be understood as an effort to achieve a broader suffrage through indirection.[73] This argument, however, could not fully eliminate concerns that the phrasing of the eventual section two authorized what radicals believed the Constitution already prohibited: the denial of suffrage to blacks.

Even when section two was rejoined to section one in the final text of the Fourteenth Amendment, the ambiguity did not disappear, since section one itself was no longer clear. If the ambiguous section one were understood, as the *Portsmouth Journal* had understood it when it was first presented as a separate amendment, "to give Congress power to enforce civil and *political* rights,"[74] then section two could be interpreted as a remedy for infringements of the rights. However, if section one were understood to have nothing to say about suffrage, then section two could be read as an authorization to states to limit voting rights in return for reduced representation. Indeed, a majority of a committee of the Massachusetts legislature so read section two and accordingly urged that it not be ratified.[75] Alternatively, an interpreter could begin his analysis of the ambiguities in the two sections by looking at section two, concluding that it authorized states to deny suffrage to blacks, and then deciding that section one must have nothing to do with voting since a contrary reading would render it inconsistent with section two's authorization of suffrage restrictions.[76]

The greatest source of ambiguity, however, lay in the changes in language which the Joint Committee introduced into what ultimately became section one. The original proposal was clear: in addition to securing "to all persons . . . equal protection in the enjoyment of life, liberty, and property," it secured "to all citizens . . . the same political rights and privileges." The committee, however, substituted the word "immunities" for the words "political rights," thereby leaving Congress with power to secure "all privileges and immunities of citizens." With this substitution, a key question in Fourteenth Amendment jurisprudence became: what are the privileges and immunities of citizens and how, if at all, do they differ from "the rights of life, liberty, and property?"

Neither the Joint Committee nor its members left any record of why they changed the language of their amendment. But at least three explanations are available, each of which is consistent with one aspect of the cultural-political-legal context in which the Thirty-ninth Congress functioned. The first is that the draftsmen of section one, who were accustomed to thinking and speaking in the amorphous, moralistic, rhetorical categories of liberty and equality that had brought them to power in 1860, cared less about the section's precise substantive content than about its well-rounded phraseology. Their concern was that the Constitution contain a declaration about protecting fundamental rights in a language inspiring respect for them, but they had never worked out precisely what the fundamental rights were and accordingly could not provide an exact list of them.

A second explanation is that the committee omitted the language about political rights because the opposition to granting those rights was too great: the draftsmen, according to this explanation, substituted a phrasing that was sufficiently broad so that those who favored federal protection of political rights could construe it to provide such protection, and sufficiently innocuous so that those who opposed giving such power to the federal government could be reassured that the amendment did no such thing. Given the political situation of the Republicans in 1866, which centered on their need to retain the support not simply of a majority but of an overwhelming majority of the Northern electorate, their leaders may well have drafted a provision that would prevent the fragmentation of their precarious coalition.

The third interpretation focuses on the distinction in the proposed amendment between equal protection in the rights of persons, on the one hand, and security for the privileges and immunities of citizens, on the other. Under this interpretation, what ultimately became section one was designed to give constitutional stature to a basic distinction in mid-nineteenth-century American law between the rights of aliens and the rights of citizens. All persons, both aliens and citizens, possessed certain basic rights, including the rights to bodily integrity, to protection of reputation, and to enjoyment of the fruits of their labor. Citizens, however, possessed additional rights. Political rights, such as the right to vote and hold office, were the most important of these, but they were not the only added rights: citizens also possessed the right to serve on juries, the right to serve in the militia, the right to obtain a passport, and in some states the right to own real property.

Awareness of these distinctions suggests that the Joint Committee may have selected its language in order to address issues of legal doctrine. Such an awareness explains the need to distinguish between the rights of all persons and the special rights of citizens. Congress could not simply be given power to secure equal rights to all because some people, namely citizens, possessed greater rights than others. Nor was it adequate, as the subcommittee first suggested to the full Joint Committee, to identify those greater rights as political ones because, even though the most significant of the greater rights of citizens were political, some were not. More general language was needed to describe the special rights of citizens, and the Joint Committee's change in language can be understood as a response to that need for generality.

The draftsmen of the forerunner of section one may have chosen their language for any of these reasons or for some combination of them. Their need to distinguish between the rights of persons and of citizens may, for example, have led them to abandon the phrase "political rights" while their imprecision of thought led them to use the vague word "immunities" in its place. Nor, of course, would anyone have raised practical political objections to the choice of the vague word. All historians can do, however, is speculate. We can never know why the language of the two forerunners of the Fourteenth Amendment was changed, and, in any event, by early March 1866, both proposals had come to nought.

The defeat of the Joint Committee's two proposals produced consternation among the party faithful. One party member, for instance, warned Representative Henry Dawes that if the Republicans did not develop a program to "reconstruct the country, pretty soon, the country will soon reconstruct that party."[77] Senator William M. Stewart agreed that "if no plan is presented by Congress we shall have anarchy, or we shall have to adopt the plan of the President."[78] As a third Republican wrote to Senator John Sherman, "We cannot afford to divide the Union party & in this way place the copperheads in power."[79]

Compromise of some sort was thus essential. One of his constituents advised Senator Sherman to "counsel *moderation* and insist on a union of views," lest the party "lose *all* the results of our success."[80] Since "the *most important interests are at stake*," E. B. Sadler urged Sherman "to do any thing for harmony in the Union party that will not lead to a sacrifice of right or endanger our safety as a people."[81] Compromise could be facilitated by the fact that the groups within the Republican party were "not hostile as regards the ends to be obtained, but only as to the means of achievement."[82] The New York *Evening Post* agreed that differences in the party were "not concerning ends but concerning means."[83] Many radical members of the party also felt comfortable with compromise because of their confidence that progress was on their side and that they could "afford to wait the rapid course of events."[84] One correspondent of Lyman Trumbull, for example, was prepared to let the party "fight itself out" and to leave some of his goals to "a future amendment."[85] Likewise, Senator Henry Wilson explained that one radical proposal was tabled in one session of Congress "in the full conviction that . . . the growth of public sentiment—which was great every day then, and has increased every day since and will grow stronger in the days to come —would enable us to carry a clean bill" in a later session.[86] Clearest of all in the conviction that compromise would bring victory in the future was Thaddeus Stevens who, after declaring the final version of the Fourteenth Amendment an "imperfect . . . proposition" produced by "[m]utual concession," stated his willingness to "take what we can get now, and hope for better things in further legislation; in enabling acts or other provisions."[87] Possible compromises were widely discussed, and many were suggested to Congress. The flavor of the discussion and the suggestions is apparent in the following letter of March 12, 1866, from R. P. L. Barber to Senator John Sherman:

> I think since the general *break down* on the Fessenden Constitutional amendment and the evident fact that neither wing can crush the other except by the destruction of the party, that a compromise may be effected by a series of measures, upon which all reasonable Union men may agree. . . . I have heard the following programme favorably discussed. *First,* Invest the Federal Courts with jurisdiction to protect the rights of the Freedmen, under the clause abolishing slavery. Our people[,] while a unit that these rights must be protected by constitutional laws[,] don't relish the trying of men without a jury in time of peace. *Second* —Pass the Constitutional Amendment for representation on the basis of voters who are *citizens of the United States.*[88]

In essence, Barber proposed that Congress adopt the two propositions from the Committee of Fifteen it had previously rejected.

Another proposal came from Robert Dale Owen, Jr., the son of the renowned English radical and a recent immigrant to the United States.[89] Its first section prohibited "discrimination . . . as to the civil rights of persons because of race, color, or previous condition of servitude." Its second section explicitly prohibited similar discrimination as to voting rights after 1876, and its third section reduced the representation of states if, prior to 1876, they denied blacks the vote. Section four prohibited the payment of Confederate war debts, and section five granted enforcement power to Congress.[90]

One noteworthy feature of this proposal, from which the Fourteenth Amendment was ultimately derived, was its apparent adoption of the suggestion of Representative Giles W. Hotchkiss of New York that any new constitutional provision be framed as a self-executing guarantee of rights, and not merely as a grant of power to Congress to legislate for the protection of rights. Hotchkiss had made his suggestion in response to the original Bingham amendment, which it will be recalled, merely authorized congressional legislation for the protection of life, liberty, and property. Hotchkiss agreed with Bingham about the need for protecting these "privileges," but he "want[ed] them secured by a constitutional amendment that legislation cannot override." Although Hotchkiss, like nearly all others who participated in the adoption of the amendment, expected that "laws of Congress" would be the primary instrument "for the enforcement of these rights," he wanted to be certain that the rights would be enforced by the judiciary even if Congress fell under Democratic control.[91]

What is even more remarkable about the Owen proposal is its clarity. Thus its first section explicitly guaranteed blacks equality of civil rights, and after 1876, its second section conferred equality of voting rights as well. It also dealt with the debt issue and granted enforcement powers to Congress. But ambiguity entered when the Joint Committee, on the motion of Bingham and with only two Democrats in opposition, agreed to tack an additional section five onto the Owen proposal. The new section, in what is now familiar language, read as follows:

> No state shall make or enforce any law which shall abridge the privileges or immunities of citizens of the United States; nor shall any state deprive any person of life, liberty or property without due process of law, nor deny to any person within its jurisdiction the equal protection of the laws.[92]

Presumably this section, which unlike the earlier Bingham amendment was cast in the self-executing language of Owen, added something to the civil rights and voting rights sections of the Owen proposal. It might, for example, have been designed to protect against nonracial discriminations, as, for example, discriminations on religious or political grounds. Or it might have been designed to give Congress, by virtue of its enforcement authority in the final section of the Owen amendment, immediate power to legislate in reference to political as well as civil rights.[93] A third possibility is that Bingham meant not merely to secure an equality of rights, as Owen did, but to protect some rights absolutely. If such was Bingham's intention, the change in language was important: a constitutional restriction in favor of equal property rights, for example, would not bar government from seizing private wealth as long as it seized everyone's wealth equally, but an absolute protection of property rights would render all seizures invalid.

The adoption of Bingham's language may have wrought significant changes in the developing Fourteenth Amendment. On the other hand, Bingham's additional section may merely have been redundant. Indeed, it may have been this redundancy which led the committee, only four days after accepting the Bingham language, to delete it from the proposed Fourteenth Amendment by a 7–5 vote.[94]

The Owen proposal, however, was to undergo a final transformation before being presented to Congress, and in that transformation the Bingham language reappeared. The key change was the omission of Owen's sections two and three, guaranteeing voting rights to blacks after 1876 and reducing the representation of states which denied blacks the vote prior to that date. In their place, the committee adopted the present section two, reducing the representation of states that did not allow blacks to vote, and a harsh section three, barring many white Southerners from the franchise. With the explicit wording granting black suffrage omitted, Bingham then moved to substitute his broad section one for the narrow Owen formulation dealing only with equality in civil rights. His motion was adopted by a 10–3 vote, with a combination of radical and moderate Republicans in opposition and a similar combination of Republicans, together with three Democrats, in support.[95]

The substitution of Bingham's language transformed the Owen plan. With the substitution, the Owen plan comprehended the two earlier proposals from the Joint Committee that had stalled in Congress; all that was left of the plan was its use of self-executing language for the protection of rights coupled with the grant of enforcement powers to Congress. In this new form, the Owen plan was approved by the Joint Committee on April 28 and reported on April 30 to both the Senate and the House.[96]

This omnibus measure differed from the original Owen plan and the committee's earlier proposals in several additional respects. The differences require examination because they tended to incorporate important ambiguity into the Reconstruction measure. The greatest ambiguity lay in section one. The new section one did not adopt either the clear "civil rights" phraseology of Owen's section one or the equally clear "political rights and privileges" wording of the committee's January 20 proposal. Instead it retained the hazy "privileges and immunities" language first introduced before the committee on February 3. Moreover, the committee introduced further uncertainty when it substituted the current due process and equal protection clauses for the earlier clause providing "equal protection in the rights of life, liberty, and property." The reasons for this change, which took place behind closed doors, are not apparent. Neither the records of the Joint Committee's deliberations nor the papers of its members provide any explanation of why the change was made. Perhaps the committee made its change for purely rhetorical reasons. Or its purpose may have had substantive import. An obvious possibility is that the committee decided to introduce the concept of due process into section one in order to guarantee that, in regard to fundamental personal rights, state law would be procedurally fair as well as substantively equal. But a further possibility is that the committee intended to incorporate a concept of substantive due process into the Fourteenth Amendment. That concept had been adumbrated in *Scott* v. *Sandford*[97] and in several state cases[98] prior to 1866, and there is no way of knowing whether the draftsmen of section one meant to incorporate it.

Other changes must also be noted. The provision reducing the representation of states that denied the right to vote to males over the age of twenty-one no longer appeared as a freestanding proposition but had been rejoined to section one as part of a coherent package. However, in view of the ambiguities that had been introduced into section one, the addition of section two did not render the latter section clear. Depending upon the interpretation given to section one, section two could still be interpreted either as a remedy for state violations of voting rights protected by section one or as an authorization for the denial of voting rights to blacks.

The omnibus measure of April 1866 also contained some new provisions. A new section three deprived all persons who had voluntarily supported the Confederate cause of the right to vote in federal elections prior to 1870. Section four guaranteed payment of the Union war debt, prohibited payment of the Confederate debt, and barred the payment of compensation to former slaveowners for their loss of their slaves. Finally, section five, giving Congress power to enforce the other four sections, was separated from section one, of which it had once been a part, and placed last in the overall amendment.[99] This change, as we have already seen, had two effects: first, it made section one self-executing and rendered the rights contained in it enforceable in the courts even if Congress failed to adopt legislation protecting them, and second, it extended Congress's enforcement power to the other three sections.

The omnibus amendment passed the House as proposed,[100] but it faced difficulties in the Senate. When it emerged from the Senate on June 8, it had been changed in two further respects. One of the changes added to section one a definition of citizenship and thereby avoided placing "reliance . . . upon judicial decisions" which might be "against freedom."[101] Of much greater importance was the weakening of section three: instead of disfranchising all those who had supported the Confederacy, it merely barred from federal office those Confederate supporters who prior to the Civil War had taken an oath to support the Constitution.[102] After the House had concurred on June 13 in the Senate's changes,[103] the amendment was sent to the states.

Republicans were, in general, pleased with the product of Congress's deliberations. "The main features of the plan" were "acceptable to most Union men"[104] and would "no doubt thoroughly unite . . . all the Union element in the country."[105] The *Cazenovia Republican* thought the amendment would "form . . . a rallying point for all who desire to see the Union restored."[106] It was a "*scheme*" on which Republicans could "*go into the election*"[107]—"as good a platform as can be desired for the fall *Campaign*."[108] Indeed, some found the Fourteenth Amendment "one of the best platforms our party can have to fight the copperheads at the coming elections."[109]

The amendment was, in fact, a central issue in the congressional elections in the autumn of 1866, and the Northern electorate gave it a hearty approval. Although the Republicans lost six seats in the House in the mid-term elections, they retained a nearly three-to-one majority, with a total of 143 seats as against 49 for the Democrats. They retained their 42 seats and their four-to-one majority in the Senate, where there were only 11 Democrats.[110] The Fourteenth Amendment was so successful that, in recommending ratification to the state legislature shortly after the fall elections, New York's Governor Fenton remarked: "Never before in the history of the Government, upon any great question affecting our national interests has there been such unanimity in the expression of the popular will . . . There is no other plan before the people, and the verdict of the ballot-box implies that no other plan is desired."[111] Indeed, the fact that the amendment had been discussed during the 1866 campaign "from every stump and school house" and that "the people ha[d] voted for it"[112] led many Republican state legislators to feel it in "the line of duty"[113] to support the amendment as having been "ratified by the imperial will of the . . . people."[114] As one Pennsylvania legislator explained, he

> had hoped and believed that when these resolutions came before the House, they would have been brought to a vote without debate. . . . These questions had been openly discussed and submitted to the people, sitting as a jury to determine whether they were right, or whether they were wrong. From the pine-clad forests of Maine to the broad plains of Kansas, yes, even to the golden shores of California, this great jury have brought in their overwhelming verdict in favor of these constitutional amendments.[115]

Meanwhile, on June 25, only twelve days after the amendment had passed Congress, Connecticut became the first state to ratify. Five additional states ratified the amendment in 1866, and eleven added their ratifications in January 1867. By June of 1867, one year after the amendment had been sent to the states, a total of twenty-two had ratified it.[116] Ratification by six more states was needed, however, and that did not occur until July 1868.[117] But by that time two of the states that had previously ratified the amendment—New Jersey and Ohio—had voted to withdraw their assent.[118] Nonetheless Congress ruled that their ratifications survived the subsequent effort at withdrawal and remained valid. On July 28, 1868, Secretary of State Seward accordingly proclaimed the Fourteenth Amendment part of the Constitution of the United States.[119]

The process by which the Fourteenth Amendment became part of the Constitution produced extensive debates in the Joint Committee, on the floor of Congress, in the state legislatures, in newspapers, and among the public at large. The debates that occurred in the Joint Committee have not been preserved, but voluminous material covers the debates in Congress, in the legislatures, and in the newspapers. Many public speeches given by congressmen and letters from citizens to members of Congress also exist. In all, the existing archival material suggests that, during the winter and spring and even into the autumn of 1866, questions connected with the adoption of the Fourteenth Amendment were the central political concern of the American people. Section one itself was not seen as a trivial matter designed merely to remove doubts about the constitutionality of the Civil Rights Act, but rather as a declaration of fundamental principle that made necessary and thereby justified the new scheme of representation contained in section two. As a declaration of fundamental principle—of the meaning of American citizenship and nationality—section one was in the center of public discourse.

But the debate on section one, both in Congress and in the later contest over ratification, assumed a puzzling form. As this chapter has shown, the wording of the section was ambiguous. As one radical newspaper indicated, after noting the amendment's "great value for national security and national justice," it would have "prefer[red], to prevent evasion, more definiteness of expression in the first section."[120] The ambiguity is deeper, however, than poor choice of language or even than the failure of section one to address issues, such as the legitimacy of racial segregation, that have been central to twentieth-century constitutional law. Section one simply fails to specify at all the particular rights to which it applies. What is puzzling about this failure is that the proponents of the section were perfectly capable of specificity: the earliest draft of what became section one stated clearly that it applied to political rights, while a later draft applied explicitly only to civil rights. But this clear language was omitted in favor of vague language about privileges and immunities. Perhaps the draftsmen had such recourse to vague language in order to hide from the public the reach of the Fourteenth Amendment and its radical effect on the existing constitutional structure, so as not to jeopardize ratification.[121] If that was the purpose of the draftsmen, however, it is even more puzzling that the opponents of the amendment did nothing to reveal it; although the opponents often claimed that the amendment would radically transform the Constitution, they failed during the debates in both houses of Congress to introduce a single provision that would either limit section one's scope or reveal through clarification of its language the extent of the section's reach.[122] Moreover, as we have just seen, radical supporters of the amendment, who would have been among the chief conspirators, were displeased by section one's indefiniteness of expression.

It simply will not suffice for historians to search for section one's meaning through speculations about the reasons for its ambiguous language. Nor is there much point to inquiring how the framers intended the section to resolve issues ranging from voting rights, through a state action limitation, to matters of family autonomy that have plagued the Supreme Court since the 1870s. Some of these issues were discussed during the debates on the amendment and others were not, but the massive quantity of material in the *Congressional Globe*, in congressmen's papers, in the state ratification debates, and in the newspapers makes it clear that the amendment's proponents reached no agreement even on the issues they did consider.

But the vagueness and ambiguity of section one's language and the failure of the framing generation to settle how it would apply to a variety of specific issues should not lead those who must interpret the Fourteenth Amendment to conclude that the section has no meaning. Meaning can be found once interpreters of section one recognize that the resolution of specific legal issues, such as who should possess the right to vote, was not the *raison d'être* of the Fourteenth Amendment. While many Americans cared deeply about the suffrage issue, its resolution in 1866 was not mandatory. What was politically essential was that the North's victory in the Civil War be rendered permanent and the principles for which the war had been fought rendered secure, so that the South, upon readmission to full participation in the Union, could not undo them. The Fourteenth Amendment must be understood as the Republican party's plan for securing the fruits both of the war and of the three decades of antislavery agitation preceding it.

Once the purpose of the amendment is so understood, there will be nothing odd in the failure of its proponents to resolve specific legal issues. Indeed, one should expect the debates about section one to be cast in terms of the moralistic libertarian and egalitarian rhetoric through which the supporters of the amendment had attained national political power, and for which they had fought and won the war. When we examine the debates in detail, the familiar precepts of liberty and equality will surface frequently.

But in some important ways these familiar arguments during Reconstruction differed from their antebellum predecessors. Before the Civil War, the principles of higher law, citizens' rights, and equality could be used by different political spokesmen to advance various, sometimes contradictory programs ranging from proslavery to antislavery. During the debates on Reconstruction, however, these principles lost their multisided quality and instead became aphorisms used by those who led the effort for the Fourteenth Amendment to communicate with others already convinced of its wisdom and merits. Opponents of the amendment had to turn to a new rhetoric of opposition.

As the old rhetoric of higher law, citizens' rights, and equality began to be put to use during the post-Civil War era only in support of the Fourteenth Amendment's program of equal rights, its meaning also began to lose some of its ambiguity and imprecision. The concepts of higher law, citizens' rights, and equality still overlapped. Moreover, they remained a species of political rhetoric, without clear content and clear limits, used by politicians to inspire moral reformation. But occasionally these concepts began to be used in a more legalistic or doctrinal manner. When opponents of the Fourteenth Amendment asked how the principles of human rights and equality applied in specific contexts or how much weight should be given to those principles when they were placed in competition with other values, they were asking the sorts of questions that would come before the courts as soon as the Fourteenth Amendment became law. In response, the proponents of the amendment, many of them lawyers, began the task of giving the amendment legal meaning and creating the constitutional doctrines that still underlie much of the Supreme Court's Fourteenth Amendment jurisprudence. It is in the framing generation's incomplete efforts to transform the principles of human rights and equality into constitutional law that historians must begin to find the Fourteenth Amendment's meaning.

But history can only begin the task of finding meaning with the framing and ratification of the amendment because the framers and ratifiers themselves only began the creative task of transforming constitutional rhetoric into constitutional law. The debates on the Fourteenth Amendment were, in essence, debates about high politics and fundamental principles—about the future course and meaning of the American nation. The debates by themselves did not reduce the vague, open-ended, and sometimes clashing principles used by the debaters to precise, carefully bounded legal doctrine. That would be the task of the courts once the Fourteenth Amendment, having been enacted into law, was given over to them to reconcile its ambiguities and its conflicting meanings.

CHAPTER IV

The Use of
Antebellum Rhetoric
in the
Amendment Debates

Both in the debates in Congress during which the Fourteenth Amendment was framed and in the ratification debates in the states, proponents of section one, most of them veterans of the antislavery movement, referred to the same libertarian and egalitarian principles that they had commonly used during the three previous decades. They had recourse, that is, to concepts of rights derived from a higher law, to notions of the rights possessed by citizens of a free society, and to ideas of equality before the law. In many respects the debates on the Fourteenth Amendment amounted to little more than a rhetorical replay of antebellum antislavery arguments. However, as the amendment's supporters used familiar antebellum ideas, they began in some slight but significant ways to transform them.

- The Higher Law Tradition
  in the Adoption of the Amendment

Like the people who became involved in the antislavery movement, many of those who participated in the debates on the Fourteenth Amendment were deeply religious. While the decades after the Civil

War would witness a decline in the evangelical fervor of many American Protestants, people living in the years immediately after the war, the years during which the Fourteenth Amendment was framed, were not yet far removed from antebellum religious values.[1]

The link between religious values and the Fourteenth Amendment emerges most clearly, perhaps, in letters which quite ordinary Americans wrote to their senators and representatives while the amendment was under consideration in Congress. As one self-proclaimed *"radical"* wrote to Ohio's Senator John Sherman, "a *just* God, can't permit a nation to [reject?] these just inalienable rights, without measuring but sooner or later the *penalty.*"[2] A constituent of Senator Lyman Trumbull of Illinois likewise was aware of the connection between religion and Reconstruction when he wrote that "Congress has the power [to resolve Reconstruction issues] and is responsible to God and Man for the right use of it."[3] In a similar vein a correspondent of Chief Justice Salmon P. Chase wrote that "Congress should remember Justice; for God and Humanity are on the side of the negro—oppression and wrong are on the other side."[4] It was obvious to lay correspondents of this sort that Reconstruction must occur "in accordance with the principles of eternal Justice;"[5] *"absolute right* must prevail, tis demanded by God."[6] A fear was expressed that, if the Republican party did not act in accordance with "men[']s honest convictions and sense of justice," it would lose "its moral advantage."[7]

Newspapers in localities across the North echoed similar sentiments. Thus *The Right Way*, published in Boston and distributed free to over 50,000 readers across the nation, did not "doubt that the Golden Rule . . . is the right way in all human affairs,"[8] while the *National Anti-Slavery Standard* in New York named "the church" as the "power to whom appeal should ever be pertinent in behalf of truth and righteousness."[9] Similarly, the Huntington *Long Islander* spoke of liberty and equality as "two vital principles belong[ing] to those divine statutes which are graven on the heart of universal man."[10] The *Long Islander* further argued against "sacrifice [of] principle for policy."[11] It continued: "Policy, like the devil in Eden, is deceptive in its appearance, and is the author of and father of lies. It degrades itself by surrendering principle to expediency, and showing the cloven-footed craven, when truth and justice raises its voice to protect the weak and the innocent from harm."[12] The *Wisconsin State Journal* agreed when it commented favorably on a message of Governor Fairchild recommending ratification of the Fourteenth Amendment on the ground that " '[t]he day for doing that which is right in itself has come . . . and until we have done the right, and done it for all time, we have shamefully failed in our duty.' "[13] Even Republican papers in the South took note of "the eternal truths proclaimed and revitalized by the reconstruction acts of Congress."[14]

In view of the hold that antebellum higher law ideas retained on the popular mind, it is not at all surprising that the people's representatives in Congress often used higher law language. Henry Wilson, the junior senator from Massachusetts, made clear the connections between religion, his constituents, and his own actions on the Senate floor. In a speech in support of the Freedmen's Bureau Bill, Wilson observed that "we who fill these seats, and those who sent us here, believe, *religiously believe*," in the sentiment that " '[y]ou cannot degrade any portion of your population.' "[15] Wilson continued that he wanted everyone, including "the men of the rebel States, to understand that we who are here, and those whom we represent, believe in that sentiment as we believe in the commandments of Almighty God."[16]

Many other proponents of the Fourteenth Amendment used the somewhat less explicit, but more familiar higher law principles of the antebellum antislavery movement. For example, John A. Bingham, the author of section one, defended the amendment on the floor of the House by urging that it was needed in order to protect "the inborn rights of every person,"[17] while Thaddeus Stevens, the floor manager of the amendment for the House, spoke of the need to "fix the foundations of the government on principles of eternal justice."[18] Senator Lyman Trumbull similarly referred to the principles "which the great Author of all has implanted in every human breast."[19] Even Edgar Cowan of Pennsylvania, a Conservative Republican who eventually voted against the final version of the Fourteenth Amendment in the Senate, had earlier indicated that he would support a provision such as section one that "secure[d] to all men of color and of every race and of every condition their natural rights, the rights which God has given them."[20] Or as Senator Yates, who was at the opposite end of the political spectrum within the Republican party, said in support of the question of universal manhood suffrage, "[n]o question of finance, or banks, or currency, or tariffs, can obscure this mighty moral question of the age."[21]

Republican believers in higher law ideas did more, however, than merely reiterate the commonplace precepts of the antebellum era; they also put the precepts into practice by applying them to the new problems and opportunities that arose out of the Civil War and Reconstruction. Henry Wilson, for instance, speaking in 1864 in favor of abolition of slavery in the District of Columbia, observed:

> No religion which recognizes God's eternal attribute of justice and breathes that spirit of love which applies to all men the sublime commandment, "Whatsoever ye would that men should do unto you, do ye even so to them," can ever be allowed free exercise where slavery curses men and defies God. No religious denomination can flourish or even be tolerated where slavery rules without surrendering the choicest jewels of its faith into the keeping of that infidel power which withholds the Bible from the poor.[22]

Similarly, Ebon C. Ingersoll, a Republican congressman from Illinois, spoke as follows in support of the Thirteenth Amendment:

> I am in favor of the adoption of this amendment because it will secure to the oppressed slave his natural and God-given rights. I believe that the black man has certain inalienable rights, which are as sacred in the sight of Heaven as those of any other race. I believe he has a right to live, and live in state of freedom. He has a right to breathe the free air and enjoy God's free sunshine. He has a right to till the soil, to earn his bread by the sweat of his brow, and enjoy the rewards of his own labor. He has a right to the endearments and enjoyment of family ties; and no white man has any right to rob him of or infringe upon any of these blessings.[23]

These applications of higher law ideas to the problems of Reconstruction would eventually lead to the refinement and elaboration of the principles. However, before turning to this transformation of higher law ideology, we must first examine how concepts of citizens' rights and equality were used during the Reconstruction debates.

▪ The Citizens' Rights Tradition in the Adoption of the Amendment

As was true in the case of appeals to a higher law, ideas about the rights of citizens in a free republic were carried over from antebellum debates about slavery into debates after the Civil War about reconstructing the Union. Republicans who found themselves in power during Reconstruction continued to use the ideas and principles which had come so naturally to them for some three decades. Language about citizens' rights can be observed in letters written to political leaders, especially to members of Congress; in newspaper discussion of the Fourteenth Amendment and other Reconstruction matters; and in debates in Congress and the state legislatures about the amendment and related legislation.

One especially lengthy and detailed letter about the Fourteenth Amendment was written to Ohio's Senator John Sherman by J. H. Martindale, the attorney general of New York. Martindale urged Sherman to take the "question of suffrage away from the strife which is raging in Congress" and to "plac[e] . . . it as a judicial question before the Courts of the Country, and ultimately the Supreme Court of the United States." He was convinced that the Courts would find "the right to vote . . . a constitutional right appertaining to native, national citizenship." Martindale reasoned as follows:

> [W]here is the Constitutional power to *classify* American citizens, giving to one class and *their posterity*, exclusive & perpetual political rights & government, and denying them *utterly* to the other class & their posterity? A Govt under which a dominant class is invested with political rights, withheld from another and inferior one, is not the system of Govt of the United States. . . . Monarchical and European Govts are founded on this division of the inhabitants into classes. . . . The entire absence of the power to make this classification of our people & citizens is the peculiar and distinguishing feature of the systems of Govt in the United States.

"These truths," according to Martindale, were "founded in the deepest philosophy, and [were] all-pervading in our system of government."[24]

Other correspondents of Senator Sherman, with less education and political skill, spoke in similar language. One James Auten in a brief letter requested Sherman to "discharge your duties carry out the principles of the Constitution of Life liberty and the pursuit of happiness to every person that has a place in the bounds of American possession and give by your laws the rite of sufferage" to the freedmen.[25] Thomas Richmond similarly advised him that "the *spirit* of *liberty* and of *justice, living elements*, in the great public heart" all dictated that "*absolute right* must prevail, tis demanded by . . . the spirit of the people."[26] Even Simeon Nash, who urged Sherman to take a more conservative stance and restrict voting rights to men of European descent, argued in similar terms. Because the preservation of American liberty depended upon the preservation of the American social order, he did "not want the pagan elements of Africa and Asia to be incorporated into our social organization;" as he explained, "[a] turk cannot live with us, because his social system is in conflict with ours; what we deem wrong and punish, he deems right and practices."[27]

Other laymen agreed with Nash that the extent of individual rights depended on the structure of a society and its government. But they did not necessarily adopt his view that voting rights should not be extended to non-Europeans. For example, the Union League Club of New York favored "securing to all the people the rights and immunities consonant with republican government."[28] Similarly, a correspondent of Illinois Senator Lyman Trumbull looked with favor upon plans "to secure to the freedman protection & a reasonable enjoyment of the rights of a free man."[29] For all these people, specific individual rights were implicit in concepts of freedom and republican government. As another citizen wrote, "[a] Republican form of govmnt as expressed in this Constitution is intended to mean a govmnt of equal and universal franchise," and he proposed that Congress adopt a constitutional amendment to that effect.[30]

These same ideas were echoed by the press. According to the *Rochester Democrat*, "[t]his republic was founded on the recognition of the rights of man, on principles of justice, freedom and equality,"[31] while the Huntington *Long Islander* spoke of liberty and equality as "the two vital principles of a Republican government, without which a government, though republican in name, cannot be republican in fact."[32] The *Worcester Daily Spy* took the same position when it proclaimed that "the theory of democratic institutions" demanded "that the elective franchise shall be regulated according to certain laws of universal application, and not by rules merely arbitrary, capricious, and personal."[33] The *Portland Transcript* agreed that with the abolition of slavery, the black man was entitled to full citizenship. It contended that "[t]here is no intermediate place for him—in our system of government there can be none."[34] Class-based distinctions and inequality simply could not exist in a republican society.

Given the pervasiveness of ideas about the rights of citizens in a republic, it was natural that men in Congress would use them not only in their public rhetoric, but even in correspondence with each other. For instance, Samuel Shellabarger, a congressman from Ohio, sought to obtain Senator Lyman Trumbull's support for a bill that " 'declares' and defines (and does not of course create) what are the 'fundamental' . . . rights of national citizenship."[35] In a letter to Horace Greeley, Senator James A. Doolittle of Wisconsin similarly sought Greeley's support for a bill which would "secur[e] . . . all rights which the federal courts shall adjudge to follow the change of a slave into a freeman."[36] Likewise, Charles Sumner spoke of "[e]quality" as "the master principle of our system, and the very frontispiece of our constitution,"[37] while Thaddeus Stevens, in a draft of a speech, argued that, "according to the fundamental law of this country," there is "no reason, to exclude any man, living in it, on account of his race, from full citizenship."[38] Of course members of Congress also used ideas about citizens' rights in their speeches on the floors of the Senate and the House. They were, for example, fond of quoting the language of *Corfield* v. *Coryell*[39] to the effect that the privileges and immunities clause of Article IV, Section 2 referred to "those privileges and immunities which . . . belong, of right, to the citizens of all free governments."[40] In arguing for his Civil Rights Bill, Senator Lyman Trumbull made reference to the same concept of rights inherent in the concept of freedom when he spoke of the rights to contract, to own property, to sue and be sued, to testify, and to enjoy the protection of the laws as "fundamental rights belonging to every man as a free man."[41] Jacob Howard, the senator from Michigan, made the same point in his defense of the Trumbull bill on the Senate floor, when he asked: "And what are the attributes of a freeman according to the universal understanding of the American people? Is a freeman to be deprived of the right of acquiring property, of the right of having a family, a wife, children, home? What definition will you attach to the word 'freeman' that does not include these ideas?"[42]

The same idea—that the concept of freedom entailed the recognition that individuals possess certain rights—also appeared in the course of the congressional and state ratification debates on the Fourteenth Amendment. Thus Frederick E. Woodbridge, a Republican congressman from Vermont, indicated that he supported the

Fourteenth Amendment because it would "give to a citizen of the United States the natural rights which necessarily pertain to citizenship."[43] Woodbridge's colleague from Vermont, Senator Luke Poland, likewise looked to the due process and equal protection clauses as "the very spirit and inspiration of our system of government, the absolute foundation upon which it was established."[44] In recommending ratification, Ohio's conservative governor, Jacob D. Cox, also understood that section one would protect citizens' rights, especially the right to "freedom of discussion" and other "immunities of this kind, which are of the very essence of free government."[45]

As the foregoing sampling of citizens' rights rhetoric suggests, its most common characteristic during Reconstruction, as in the earlier antislavery era, was its vagueness and imprecision. Users of the rhetoric made it clear that citizens possessed rights guaranteed by the Constitution, but they never specified the precise content of those rights. The vagueness of rights principles would, of course, bedevil the judges of a later era striving to give the concept specific doctrinal content. In the 1860s, on the other hand, the vagueness of the concept gave it greater power in the hands of proponents of the Fourteenth Amendment, who, by promising to protect rights, offered to many Union citizens federal support for whichever ones they valued most.

■ The Equality Tradition in the Adoption
of the Amendment

Another characteristic of Reconstruction rhetoric, like that of the antebellum antislavery movement, was the tendency of its users not to keep their ideas about rights derived from higher law separate and distinct from their ideas about rights dependent on living under a republican form of government. Republican Orris S. Ferry of Connecticut suggested, for instance, that "the fundamental principle on which our system rests, that all governments derive their just powers from the consent of the governed," was "recognized" in the Declaration of Independence. He then continued:

> Democrats sneer nowadays at the Declaration of Independence.
> But the words are not true merely because they are contained in

that instrument. They have an older origin than that. They go back through eighteen centuries to the time when He who spake as never man spake first proclaimed the principles of human brotherhood and human equality to the rude Galilean peasants.[46]

The Huntington *Long Islander* agreed when it declared that the "natural and inherent right of the people to govern themselves" was "founded on an immortal principle" and was "exemplified in American institutions, honored, admired, respected throughout the world."[47] A correspondent of Senator John Sherman took a like position in arguing that adherence to principle was "demanded by God, and the spirit of the people."[48]

Republicans like John A. Bingham imprecisely conflated "the rights of citizenship" with "the sacred rights of human nature"[49] not because they were careless, but because they understood that the demands of higher law overlapped or, perhaps, even coincided with the rights of citizens living under a republican form of government. The view that the American system of government was based on higher law and accorded protection to precisely those rights derived from higher law was especially persuasive when Reconstruction Republicans focused on the right of supreme importance to their generation—the right to equality.

Not surprisingly, the leading Republican spokesman in the House, Thaddeus Stevens, linked together ideas about higher law, citizens' rights, and equality. In a draft of a speech entitled, "Some Remarks on Reconstruction," Stevens observed that "[a]*ll* men . . . created by the laws of nature and nature's God [were] equally endowed with the inalienable rights of life, liberty and the *pursuit* of happiness" and further that "the fundamental laws of this country" barred the exclusion of "any man, on account of his race, from full citizenship."[50] Later, in a campaign speech, he pointed to the need "[t]o rebuild a shattered empire . . . fit to bear the proud temple of universal Freedom; to plant deep and solid the corner-stone of eternal Justice, and to erect thereon a superstructure of perfect equality of every human being before the law; of impartial protection to every one in whose breast God had placed an immortal soul."[51]

Charles Sumner, the leading Republican radical in the Senate, likewise spoke of "[e]quality" as "the master principle of our system,"[52] while William Windom, a Republican from Minnesota who served during Reconstruction in the House and later in the

Senate and the Cabinet, also tied the concept of rights granted by nature to the other concepts. As he put it,

> A true republic rests upon the absolute equality of rights of the whole people, high and low, rich and poor, white and black. Upon this, the only foundation which can permanently endure, we professed to build our Republic; but at the same time we not only denied to a large portion of the people equality of rights, but we robbed them of every right known to human nature.[53]

In a later debate, Illinois Senator Richard Yates agreed that the Declaration of Independence, the cornerstone of American government, "proclaimed the great doctrine which we stand maintaining to-day, that all men are created, not by man but by God himself, equal and entitled to equal rights and privileges."[54] Pursuant to this doctrine, rights and privileges under the Constitution could not be "accorded only to citizens of 'some class,' or 'some race,' or 'of the least favored class,' or 'of the most favored class,' or of a particular complexion, for these distinctions were never contemplated as possible in fundamental civil rights, which are alike necessary and important to all citizens."[55]

The derivation of the principle of equality from concepts of higher law and citizens' rights was continually reiterated during the years of Reconstruction. Only two more statements made on the floor of Congress need be noted. First are the remarks of John Bingham when he presented his early version of section one to the House in January 1866. He then commented that "[t]he spirit, the intent, the purpose of our Constitution is to secure equal and exact justice to all men" and that "the divinist feature of your Constitution is the recognition of the absolute equality before the law of all persons."[56] Second was the eloquent speech of Jacob Howard presenting the Fourteenth Amendment to the Senate:

> It establishes equality before the law, and it gives to the humblest, the poorest, the most despised of the race the same rights and the same protection before the law as it gives to the most powerful, the most wealthy, or the most haughty. That, sir, is republican government, as I understand it, and the only one which can claim the praise of a just Government. Without this principle of equal justice to all men and equal protection under the shield of the law, there is no republican government and none that is really worth maintaining.[57]

Likewise the Huntington *Long Islander* called equality one of "the two vital principles of a Republican government"—"principles belong[ing] to those divine statutes which are graven on the heart of universal man,"[58] while the Boston *Daily Evening Voice*, the official organ of the Boston Workingman's Assembly, thought there could be "no safety to free principles but in universal or manhood suffrage."[59] The *Portland Transcript* agreed that "the great distinguishing doctrine of Christianity is the unity and equality of the human race" and that "[t]his great truth our fathers recognized in the Declaration of Independence,"[60] while *Harper's Magazine*, quoting a speech of Benjamin F. Butler, spoke of the "true Democratic principle" of "equal rights to every man" as "God's Government."[61]

The overlap between the concepts of higher law, citizens' rights, and equality was also echoed in letters written to political leaders. Thus one correspondent of John Sherman maintained that Americans had "built a government based on the idea that *man* had *equal inalienable rights*" and that "[a] *just* God, can't permit a nation to undo these just inalienable rights."[62] A second correspondent agreed that a government was not republican in form if it did "not protect all men in the right to life liberty and property . . . [a]nd give equal and exact justice to all men,"[63] as did a constituent of Lyman Trumbull, who urged action upon the *"principle"* of "the *civil equality* of the people in the rebel states." More specifically, he urged that the constitution be amended to provide explicitly that "[a] Republican form of govnmnt as expressed in this Constitution is intended to mean a govnmt of equal and universal franchise."[64]

Letters to members of Congress from their constituents emphasized the centrality of equality to Republican thought during the era of Reconstruction. For instance, one of Thaddeus Stevens' constituents, A. H. Wood, expressed his views about the importance of the equality principle when he inquired about a candidate for the governorship of Pennsylvania, "[I]s he . . . right on the great question of the day [:] Does he go in for the equality of all men before the law?"[65] Jesse Baldwin, a constituent of Ohio's Senator John Sherman, also declared his preference for *"general, universal, equal laws"* and urged Congress to take *"permanent* action" to insure that "[a]ll citizens shall have *equal civil rights* and all adult male citizens filling the prescribed qualifications for interest & intelligence by the State, *equal political rights.*"[66]

Other correspondents of Senator Sherman expressed like sentiments. Thomas Richmond of Chicago thought that the Southern
states should not be restored to the Union without a guarantee "that
equal rights before the law shall be secured to all adults of whatever
colour."[67] J. H. Martindale, the attorney general of New York,
likewise maintained that, as a consequence of the Thirteenth Amendment, there did "not remain a logical argument on which to rest the
exclusion of the native born black man from all the civil and political
rights inherent in citizenship." As a result, Martindale thought that
"[n]o states" had a "constitutional right to classify . . . & degrade" a
black person "because he is black, any more than they have the
constitutional right to classify and degrade white men."[68]

Reuben E. Fenton, the governor of New York, made the same point
to Lyman Trumbull, chairman of the Senate Judiciary Committee,
when he expressed his "gratitude" for Trumbull's "dignified and
masterly vindication of the right of all men to equal rights before the
law."[69] Such equality was important not only to blacks but also to
Southern whites who were loyal to the Union, as a Virginian, T. J.
Pretlow, reminded Trumbull. According to Pretlow, nothing "could
do more to bring the secessionists to their senses" than "courts where
we can get even-handed justice,"[70] and he accordingly urged Trumbull to back "general legislation to enable all citizens to seek their just
rights in the federal courts."[71] Governor Paul Dillingham of Vermont
agreed on the need to "secure to the original Union men of the South
equal rights and impartial liberty."[72] Similarly, Abner Twining of
New Haven sent Trumbull a copy of a memorial which he and
twenty-three other residents of New Haven had sent to President
Johnson, urging the adoption of laws "to protect the freedmen *in
their civil rights and their equality before the law with other
freemen.*"[73] Memorials of this sort were apparently the product of an
organized campaign among citizens, for one can find in the archives
unexecuted printed petitions urging Congress to prohibit all "legislation, within the United States or Territories, against any civilized
portion of the inhabitants, native born or naturalized, on account of
race or color."[74]

Even some Southerners recognized that blacks must be treated
equally. In a formal petition to Thaddeus Stevens in his capacity as
chairman of the Joint Committee on Reconstruction, three Floridians
who had been elected to serve in the House and Senate expressed their

hope "that impartial justice tempered with kindness will be administered to all persons belonging to the Colored race" and that "all the inhabitants . . . shall enjoy the rights of person and property without distinction of color." In support of this belief they took note of state legislation giving blacks the rights to own property, make contracts, sue and be sued, and give testimony. They also pointed toward Florida's decision to establish an educational system for black children.[75]

Congressmen were not the only officials in Washington to receive letters in support of the equality principle. We have already seen that President Andrew Johnson received such correspondence.[76] So too did Chief Justice Salmon P. Chase; among others, there was a letter from the veteran abolitionist John Jay urging the Supreme Court to put the equality principle into practice:

> The decision which I most wish to see pronounced by your Court is that the adopting of the Amendment abolishing slavery has destroyed the only exception recognized by the Constitution to the great principle of the Declaration of Independence, and that from the date of the adoption of the Amendment all persons black & white stand upon an equal footing, that all state legislation establishing or recognizing distinctions of race or color are void. This is a proposition easy to be understood & I think capable of easy demonstration. It would give a broad national policy on which to reconstruct the Union.[77]

Newspapers also placed emphasis on the importance of equality. Thus the New York *Commercial Advertiser* supported an early version of the Fourteenth Amendment because it "recognize[d] the political equality of all people" and was "a step toward making this land a land of equal laws and of equal rights." The *Commercial Advertiser* wanted "no class, or caste, or color legislation, but instead, general laws applicable to all."[78] The Boston *Daily Evening Voice* agreed on the need for "a government which shall support the weak against the strong, and protect the high against the low—preserving a counterpoise between the forces of society, and securing the greatest good . . . of the whole country and of every individual."[79] The *Voice* wanted "no privileged class."[80]

From this it was easy to urge, as did the Huntington *Long Islander*, that blacks were entitled to "*equality before the law.*"[81] Similarly, the *Portland Transcript* took the position that the Civil War had established "the great fundamental doctrine of equal rights" and required "[t]he broad aegis of the constitution . . . [to] be extended over all classes of citizens—one flag, one law for all."[82] The issue was put best by the *Albany Weekly Journal*, as follows:

> The negroes must be protected. Whenever their rights are assailed by local legislation, by the customs and prejudices of communities, and by the decisions of State Courts, it becomes imperative that the safeguards of the Constitution shall be thrown around them—if essential by employing the resources of power at command of the Government. We have declared the slaves free. That declaration will be enforced. It is not enough to simply abrogate the legal declaration of existing Slavery, if those most concerned are left to suffer under arbitrary class and caste distinctions, which assume their inferiority before the laws, and deny them privileges which others enjoy without question. . . . In other words, unless the Constitution is to be nullified and the faith of the people broken, there cannot be one set of rules for the whites and another for the blacks.[83]

The issue was so important that the "whole time and thoughts" of some people in 1866 were "taken up discussing the subject of equality."[84]

The rhetoric of political leaders, of course, reflected the ideas present in the society at large, and hence congressmen talked incessantly about equality, especially about equality for the recently freed blacks. Henry Wilson, the radical senator from Massachusetts, argued that "[a]n equal and exact observance of the constitutional rights of each and every citizen, in each and every State, is the end to which we should cause the lessons of this war to carry us."[85] "Our great purpose," Wilson continued on another occasion, "is to make the citizens of the United States equal in rights and privileges."[86] Illinois Congressman Isaac Arnold likewise believed that a "new nation" was "to be born from the agony through which the people are now passing. This new nation," he added, "is to be wholly free" and *"equality before the law* is to be the great corner-stone."[87] Thaddeus Stevens, the Republican leader of the House, indicated that he would introduce a proposition to lay the cornerstone—a proposition that "[a]ll national and State laws shall be equally applicable to every citizen, and no discrimination shall be made on account of race or color,"[88] while Illinois Congressman Henry P. M. Bromwell drafted a resolution "[t]hat the Constitution should be so amended, as [to] prevent the existence of any law imposing any disability on any class of persons by reason of color or descent, or imposing any forfeiture, penalty or punishment whatever on any class or race of persons different from those imposed on the most favored class or race."[89] Senator Charles Sumner agreed that it would be necessary to assert by constitutional amendment "the *equality of all persons before the law.*"[90]

John A. Bingham, the author of section one of the Fourteenth Amendment, was the most eloquent spokesman for equality on the floor of Congress. "The law in every State," he believed, "should be just; it should be no respecter of persons."[91] In order "that hereafter there shall not be any disregard of that essential guarantee of your Constitution," Bingham proposed "simply adding an amendment to the Constitution . . . giving to Congress the power to pass all laws necessary and proper to secure to all persons—which includes every citizen of every State—their equal personal rights" and to "the Federal Judiciary . . . the power to take cognizance of the question, and assert those rights by solemn judgment."[92] By adopting what ultimately became the Fourteenth Amendment, Bingham "want[ed] the American people . . . to declare their purpose to stand by the foundation principle of their own institutions, the absolute equality of all citizens of the United States politically and civilly before their own laws."[93] He concluded his speech in support of what later became section one as follows:

> Representatives, to you I appeal, that hereafter, by your act and the approval of the loyal people of this country, every man in every State of the Union, in accordance with the written words of your Constitution, may, by the national law, be secured in the equal protection of his personal rights. Your Constitution provides that no man, no matter what his color, no matter beneath what sky he may have been born, no matter in what disastrous conflict or by what tyrannical hand his liberty may have been cloven down, no matter how poor, no matter how friendless, no matter how ignorant, shall be deprived of life or liberty or property without due process of law—law in its highest sense, that law which is the perfection of human reason, and which is impartial, equal, exact justice.[94]

Congressmen thought the equality principle was important because, as Fernando Beaman, a Republican congressman from Michigan explained, "no man can be sure of the preservation of his own rights unless every other man is also protected. The practice of wrong upon one man implies that injustice may be done to another. If a man may be ignored because he is black, another man may be treated in the same manner because he is poor. Every man's safety consists in the maintenance of laws that shall protect every other man."[95] Congressman George S. Boutwell agreed that "the Constitution is for all people or it is for none of them,"[96] as did Senator Charles Sumner, who reminded his colleagues that "you cannot do injustice to the colored race without injuring that white race which you desire to favor."[97]

As it was finally adopted by Congress and ratified by the states, section one of the Fourteenth Amendment accomplished, at least in vague, general terms, what Bingham and others sought to have done. In introducing the amendment to the House, Stevens observed that the Constitution, as it then existed, protected individual rights only against federal but not state action. "This amendment," he continued, "supplies that defect, and allows Congress to correct the unjust legislation of the States, so far that the law which operates upon one man shall operate *equally* upon all."[98] Representative Henry J. Raymond, a Conservative Republican who had wavered throughout most of the first session of the Thirty-ninth Congress between loyalty to the party and support of President Johnson, indicated that he would support the amendment because he "was in favor of securing an equality of rights to all citizens of the United States."[99] Senator Luke Poland of Vermont thought that the language of section one encapsulated "the very spirit and inspiration of our system of government" and that it was "desirable that no doubt should be left existing as to the power of Congress to enforce principles lying at the very foundation of all republican government."[100] After the Fourteenth Amendment had been ratified by most Northern but by few Southern states, Senator Timothy Howe of Wisconsin declared that what it would "really" accomplish was "to remit to the Government of the United States the power to protect classes against class legislation."[101] Howe and other Republican congressmen, in short, had no doubt about their "constitutional right and duty to protect citizens of the United States against unjust and oppressive state laws."[102]

The state legislatures that ratified the Fourteenth Amendment also understood that, at least in a vague, general sense, the amendment guaranteed equality, particularly equality for blacks. One of the earliest proponents of ratification was Governor Brownlow of Tennessee, who in calling a special session of the Tennessee legislature to ratify the amendment took note of the fact that it provided "[e]qual protection of all citizens in the enjoyment of life, liberty and property."[103] Similarly, the New Hampshire legislature ratified the amendment on the basis of a committee report which recognized that section one conferred "fixed and well defined rights of citizenship applicable to all . . . born or naturalized on American soil,"[104] while in Wisconsin a Democratic state senator was reported during the ratification preceedings to have "unqualifiedly placed himself in the ranks of those supporting equal rights to the black men" when he announced that he favored the amendment. Blacks, he said, "had nobly earned the right to the same privileges enjoyed by himself and other American citizens."[105]

As was true with the rhetoric about higher law and citizens' rights, most of the rhetoric of equality preached by the Republican supporters of the Fourteenth Amendment never went beyond vague generalities such as these. Republicans agreed that all people, including blacks, were entitled to equal rights. However, an element of that agreement—an element essential to creating the supermajorities needed to incorporate the equal protection concept into the Fourteenth Amendment—was its ultimate emptiness. Americans of 1866, like Americans of today, could all agree upon the rightfulness of equality only because they did not agree on its meaning, and their political leaders, unlike the managers of the modern bureaucratic state, were content to enact the general principle rather than its specific applications into law.[106]

■ The Transformation of Antebellum Ideas

The Republican proponents of the Fourteenth Amendment were not able, however, to avoid all discussion of the specific applications the amendment might have. Their understanding that concepts such as liberty, equality, and republican form of government had an operative meaning which conferred rights on individuals made some discussion of specifics inevitable. Their agreement with Senator Richard Yates of Illinois, who insisted "that there were no idle words in the Constitution of the United States; that they meant something,"[107] ultimately compelled some proponents of the amendment to elaborate what the words they were adding to the Constitution did mean.

At times, their elaboration took the form of a quotation from *Corfield* v. *Coryell*,[108] which had listed the privileges and immunities, or fundamental rights, of Americans as follows:

> What these fundamental principles are, it would perhaps be more tedious than difficult to enumerate. They may, however, be all comprehended under the following general heads: Protection by the government; the enjoyment of life and liberty, with the right to acquire and possess property of every kind, and to pursue and obtain happiness and safety . . . The right of a citizen of one state to pass through or reside in any other state, for purposes of trade, agriculture, professional pursuits, or otherwise; to claim the benefit of the writ of habeas corpus; to institute and maintain actions of any kind in the courts of the state; to take, hold and dispose of property, either real or personal; and an exemption from higher taxes or impositions than are paid by the other citizens of the state, may be mentioned as some of the particular privileges and immunities of citizens, which are clearly embraced by the general description of privileges deemed to be fundamental: to which may be added the elective franchise.[109]

Jacob Howard, in presenting section one of the Fourteenth Amendment to Congress, was prepared to add to *Corfield's* list

> the personal rights guarantied and secured by the first eight amendments of the Constitution; such as the freedom of speech and of the press; the right of the people peaceably to assemble and petition the Government for a redress of grievances, a right appertaining to each and all the people; the right to keep and to bear arms; the right to be exempted from the quartering of soldiers in a house without the consent of the owner; the right to be exempt from unreasonable searches and seizures, and from any search or seizure except by virtue of a warrant issued upon a formal oath or affidavit; the right of an accused person to be informed of the nature of the accusation against him, and his right to be tried by an impartial jury of the vicinage; and also the right to be secure against excessive bail and against cruel and unusual punishments.[110]

Those who spoke of natural rights and citizens' rights during Reconstruction also made some attempts at definition beyond merely listing what constituted the particular rights of citizens. Proponents of a rights approach occasionally found it necessary to differentiate among the various sorts of rights that individuals might possess: rights derived from some transcendent source, rights dependent upon the nature of the political and social order, and rights derived from state law or congressional legislation.

A further elaboration of higher law ideas occurred when Senator Lyman Trumbull suggested that the consistency of legislation with moral precepts could affect the legitimacy of stringent enforcement and procedural provisions contained in the legislation. He took this position in response to a claim that the Civil Rights Act of 1866, which contained provisions analogous to those contained in the 1850 Fugitive Slave Act, must therefore be equally "odious and wicked and wrong."[111] Trumbull answered:

> Sir, that does not follow at all. A law may be iniquitous and unjust and wrong which undertakes to punish another for doing an innocent act, which would be righteous and just and proper to punish a man for doing a wicked act. We have upon our statute-books a law punishing a man who commits murder . . . and the party who does it forfeits his right to live; but would it be just to apply the law which punishes a person for committing murder to an innocent person who had killed another accidentally, without malice? That is the difference. It is the difference between right and wrong, between good and evil. True, the features of the fugitive slave law were abominable when they were used for the purpose . . . of punishing white men who aided to give the natural gift of liberty to those who were enslaved. Now, sir, we propose to use the provisions of the fugitive slave law for the purpose of punishing those who deny freedom, not those who seek to aid persons to escape to freedom. The difference [is] too clear . . . to justify me in taking further time in alluding to it.[112]

An equally important elaboration of antebellum libertarian ideas occurred when the proponents of the Fourteenth Amendment conceded that rights derived from higher law or from the nature of citizenship in a republic were not absolute but were subject to reasonable regulation by government, including the states. This concession became necessary in order to prevent section one of the amendment from being construed to give the federal government plenary jurisdiction over all subjects of law. Representative Samuel Shellabarger of Ohio showed great sensitivity to this issue. On one occasion, for example, he discussed the issue whether, once the rights to property and to the enjoyment of the fruits of one's labor had become federally protected, states could change the age at which an apprentice attained his majority. The problem, of course, was that, if a state raised the age of majority, it would restrict the right of the individual who was temporarily serving as an apprentice to enjoy the fruits of his own labor; if, on the other hand, it lowered the age of majority, it would cut down the master's property right in his apprentice. Shellabarger put the issue as follows:

> Now, the inquiry I wish to make is this: suppose that at the time of taking a statutory apprentice, or at the time of the birth of a child, the age of majority for the child and the expiration of the apprenticeship is fixed by the law of this District, or of any of the States, at the age of twenty-one years; and suppose the State, or the Legislature of this District, in the exercise of municipal legislation, should change the law so as to terminate the minority and the apprenticeship at eighteen instead of at twenty-one years, and thus should take from the parent and from the master three years of service, would that be a depriving the citizen of property without due process of law within the meaning of Magna Carta or of the Constitution of the United States? Is not the property in these personal relations within the full control of the municipal legislation of every supreme legislature?[113]

The plain answer to Shellabarger's rhetorical question was that the states did possess power to adopt such a legislative change—a point made by James F. Wilson, chairman of the House Judiciary Committee, in the debate on the Civil Rights Bill, which he understood would protect "rights in respect to those things which properly and rightfully depend on State regulations and laws."[114]

Clearest of all, perhaps, was Senator Richard Yates of Illinois who sought to explain how legislatures could regulate the citizen's right to vote. He believed that

> To define the length of residence necessary to enable a man to vote, to say what his age shall be, is one thing; and to say that he shall not vote at all because he is black or white, is an entirely different thing. In the latter case, color is made the disqualification, just as race would be if Germans were excluded from the ballot-box. The State may preserve a right; it may fix the qualifications; it may impose certain restrictions so as to have that right preserved in the best form to the people; but it is not legitimately in the power of the State, it is not in the power of the Congress of the United States, it is not in any earthly power to destroy a man's equal rights to his property, to his franchise, to his suffrage, or to the right to aspire to office—I mean according to the true theory of a republican government. That is the one thing, that in this country, the Government cannot do.[115]

Congressman John H. Broomall tried to specify even more precisely the ways in which states could and could not restrict suffrage. He thought that a government might be republican in form even when only one-tenth of the population possessed the right to vote. That would be true, however, only

> if that tenth be so selected as fairly to represent the interests of the remaining nine tenths ... but if that tenth be selected according to some rule which would make them antagonistic to any of the remaining tenths—as if they be taken only from the learned professions or only from the manufacturers, the merchants, or the farmers, or if they be taken exclusively or largely from geographical divisions containing a minority of population, so as to represent land rather than people—it is obvious that the whole people would not be represented, and that the government would be that of a class only, an aristocracy and not a republic.
>
> To constitute the required form of government, therefore, it is necessary that every citizen may either exercise the right of suffrage himself, or have it exercised for his benefit by some one who by reason of domestic or social relations with him can be fairly said to represent his interests.[116]

Yates himself did not agree, though, with Broomall's formulation. He argued instead that the legitimacy of a restriction on a recognized right depended on the background of and reasons for the restriction. He thought, for example, that the legitimacy of a minimum voting age of forty-five would depend on who had established it. He asked:

> Were all men, of all races and colors permitted to vote on the question whether that limitation should be put on all alike? If he means that in the State of New York, where only a portion of the people can vote, that that portion of the people have a right to impose such a limitation on others who have no voice in making the limitation, then most clearly such a provision would be anti-republican. My answer to him is, that such a provision as he mentions, would establish an oligarchy.[117]

Still a third possibility was adumbrated by Representative Frederick E. Woodbridge, who suggested that government must guarantee absolutely "the inalienable rights of life and liberty," but need only grant to a citizen "that protection to his property which is extended to the other citizens of the State."[118] Congressman Bingham apparently agreed that "[t]he rights of life and liberty are theirs whatever States may enact," but that "[a]s to real estate, every one knows that its acquisition and transmission under every interpretation ever given to the word property . . . are dependent exclusively upon the local law of the States" and hence that the Fourteenth Amendment would protect only those property rights that state law conferred.[119]

In being put to use in the debates on the framing and ratification of the Fourteenth Amendment, libertarian ideas derived from the antislavery movement thus underwent some degree of transformation and legalization. This occurred because those who used libertarian ideas during Reconstruction found themselves facing different circumstances and operating in a different forum than had been the case in the antebellum period. Before the Civil War, the advocates of antislavery had not enjoyed majoritarian status in national politics. Hence they had not possessed power to legislate, but had strived instead to maintain and increase the power base they did possess. Before the Civil War higher law arguments had not often been advanced in support of pending legislation having a serious chance of passage or in forums where the arguments were needed to convince marginal members of a potential majority to support legislation. Higher law arguments had then served a largely rhetorical function of keeping the faithful committed to the antislavery cause and of attracting new converts to the fold. Frequent reiteration of vague and open-ended higher law themes had generally served that function well.

During Reconstruction, on the other hand, those who accepted higher law ideas were part of working majorities in Congress, or at least had some capacity to assemble working majorities. Higher law ideas were thus being advanced in support of legislation likely to win enactment. Opponents of Reconstruction legislation, in turn, attacked it by showing that the vague and open-ended thrust of the libertarian arguments advanced in its support would give the legislation too broad a scope and lead to its application in unpopular ways. They suggested, for example, that, when carried to its logical extreme, the thrust of higher law antislavery ideology would produce political equality and social intermixture among blacks and whites. In order to keep their majorities in line, Republican supporters of liberty had to show why their ideology would not produce such results when it was codified in enactments such as the Civil Rights Act and section one of the Fourteenth Amendment. In doing so, they elaborated, refined, and transformed their old ideas.

But the transformation was far from complete and did not result in an agreed upon definition of the specific rights secured to individuals. No consensus or majority formed in support of any single idea; instead, different congressmen threw out different ideas to be picked up and used later by whoever found them attractive. Many odd views were advanced during the congressional and state ratification debates, such as the view of Senator Jacob Howard, who drew a distinction between rights conferred by "natural law and national law."[120] Another unusual view was expressed by a Democratic member of the Joint Committee on Reconstruction, Congressman Andrew J. Rogers of New Jersey. Rogers agreed with many Republicans that "[t]here are really but two kinds of rights, natural rights and civil rights." He also agreed that a natural right was "a right which God gives us," whereas a civil right was one "derived from the Government and municipal law, as laid down in the organism of a State, and to extend to such persons as it may see fit." The disagreement came when Rogers identified what constituted natural rights; he named only one: "the right of self-defense, the right to protect our lives from invasion by others."[121] In articulating a narrowly limited category of natural rights Rogers thereby suggested that most rights were created by and were subject to the control of government.

In the course of the debates on the Fourteenth Amendment, then, some change in antebellum libertarian ideology began to occur as that ideology was applied to concrete legal issues demanding legislative solution. The libertarian scope began to grow somewhat narrower and more precise, but not significantly so: the greatest ambiguity in the ideology of rights—the ambiguity about the specific rights that people possessed—remained.

Change also began to occur in the concept of equality as the Republican proponents of the Fourteenth Amendment were pressed to specify what they meant when they said that section one would protect all people, especially the recently freed blacks, in their right to equality. Equality, according to Republican House leader Thaddeus Stevens, did not mean that every person was "equal in strength, height, beauty, intellectual and moral culture, or social acquirements."[122] Nor was the equality principle implicated in "[t]he imaginary evils that people see in the distribution of wealth and in the distribution of honors and all that kind of thing," at least not in the view of Pennsylvania's Senator Edgar Cowan.[123] In claiming that blacks were equal to whites and were entitled to equal treatment under law, the Republican proponents of the Fourteenth Amendment did not mean that blacks either had or should have the same socio-economic position in the South as whites.

In what senses, then, did the proponents of the amendment understand blacks to be the equal of whites and entitled to equal treatment? There was, again, no one answer to this question that all Republicans accepted. Some of the more radical members of the party took the view that blacks, as a race, possessed the same intellectual capacity as whites. "[I]ntelligence and virtue," according to Senator Adonijah S. Welch, were "not the distinctive characteristics of races; they are not peculiar to any race; they are not monopolized by nor wholly excluded from any people on the round earth. Intelligence and virtue are individual possessions, inconstant qualities varying *ad infinitum* among the individuals of every people."[124] Similarly a letter in the papers of Senator John Sherman tells how the writer's *"mind in the last few years has undergone some change in regard to the intellect of the negro. I find the negro child just as apt in learning their alphabet as the white and why not anything else."*[125] One of Sherman's correspondents was of the view "that the slaves as a Class or Race were far more Intelligent than the Class called *poor White Trash* at the South,"[126] while a correspondent of Lyman Trumbull thought blacks "as well qualified as ... foreigners,"[127] many of whom were granted all the rights of citizenship, including the right to vote, after only a brief residence upon a mere declaration of their intention to become citizens. As Pennsylvania's Senator Simon Cameron concluded, he favored equal suffrage because it "invites into our country everybody; the negro, the Irishman, the German, the Frenchman, the Scotchman, the Englishman, and the Chinaman." Cameron "welcome[d] every man, whatever may be the country from which he comes, who by his industry can add to our national wealth."[128]

Not every Republican in Congress, of course, agreed with Cameron that blacks should exercise the franchise. For some, the lack of educational attainment by most blacks justified the exclusion of all blacks from the political process. Others, however, urged that the low educational level of most blacks, since it was the consequence of slavery, should not be an obstacle to equal rights, including the right to vote. They urged that "the franchise" should be given "to *all* on a basis of intelligence"[129] as reflected in some readily ascertainable fact such as a literacy or an educational qualification[130] or the ownership of some minimum amount of property.[131] Perhaps such a limitation on the right to vote would work against immediate enfranchisement of nearly all blacks, but even opponents of equal suffrage, such as the New York *Sunday Mercury*, assumed that in time blacks would satisfy the limitation and thereby gain voting rights.[132] And, by bestowing the right to vote on even some blacks, Pennsylvania Congressman Glenni W. Scofield argued, Congress would "awaken the hope and ambition of the whole race throughout the country" and thereby hasten the day of full racial equality.[133] "[T]he ballot itself," according to New Jersey's Senator Frederick T. Frelinghuysen, "is a great education; . . . by its encouraging the citizen, by its inspiring him, it adds dignity to his character and makes him strive to acquire learning."[134]

There were two respects other than intelligence in which some proponents of the Fourteenth Amendment argued blacks were equal. According to radicals, blacks were surely equal if not superior to Southern whites in their patriotism. As one of Lyman Trumbull's constituents wrote, "it would be safer to trust 4,000,000 loyal negroes than 8,000,000 disloyal whites" with the ballot in the South.[135] The same point was made in more extended fashion on the floor of the Senate by Adonijah Welch:

> The crowning virtue of American citizenship is patriotism. Nothing is more clearly written in the history of the immediate past than that intellect becomes the instrument of treason when patriotism is wanting. Just here the southern negro appears to decided advantage. He possesses this indispensable virtue. Intellectually and socially below the dominant class, but equal, at least, to the poorer class of southern whites, he is, if we except the southern loyalists, who are limited in number, infinitely superior to them all as a patriot; and I weigh my words well when I say that if his ignorance were as rayless as the darkest midnight, if he never had a dozen thoughts in all his life and never changed their course, his steady, unflinching love of this Union would render him a far safer depository of the right of suffrage than he who has compassed all knowledge and all science and hates his country.[136]

Blacks were also the equal of whites in their need for protection by government and the legal system, and granting blacks the right to vote was understood to be a means of insuring that government would function in their interest. "[S]uffrage," according to the New York *Evening Post* was "one of the most effective guarantees of the citizen's right; his means of protecting himself from the encroachment of others."[137] Southern whites, according to one of John Sherman's constituents, could not be relied upon to "do justice by the blacks; their prejudices and education will not let them do it."[138] Thus, even if blacks were not yet ready for the vote, another constituent "never could see how the freedmen could be protected without it."[139] According to a correspondent of Lyman Trumbull, "Negroes" were "no fools[:] they know who will do them justice;" moreover, he urged, they "must have protection," which they could "get . . . at the ballot box."[140] There was simply no "other effectual remedy for all" than "the ballot for all."[141]

The Republican proponents of the Fourteenth Amendment all agreed that race was not a legitimate reason to treat people differently in respect to their civil rights—that a black man and a white man, even though they occupied a different socio-economic position, must receive the same treatment from the law. Similar views were widespread among many, though not all, Republicans in respect to political rights. In what contexts, however, other than the context of race, did the proponents of the new amendment think it might apply?

Except for their statements about race, the framers and ratifiers of the Fourteenth Amendment had little reason to define further what equality meant or on whose behalf the concept should be invoked. The framers and ratifiers understood their task in office to be the moral one of proclaiming vague principles of civic reformation, not the academic or bureaucratic one of engaging in precise conceptual definition, and accordingly they made no coherent effort to formulate any systematic definition of equality. They were forced, however, into some degree of further definition. Opponents of the Fourteenth Amendment, chiefly Democrats, paraded a bag of horribles before Congress and the public during 1866, 1867, and 1868, listing all the unwanted consequences to which adoption of the amendment might lead. Republicans had to respond to these Democratic arguments, and their responses gave somewhat greater meaning to their amendment. In the next chapter we shall examine the Democratic objections to the Fourteenth Amendment, and in the chapter that follows focus on the Republican response.

Nonetheless, the Fourteenth Amendment emerged from the process of adoption and ratification as a still vague charter for the future. It began to receive real meaning only when the Supreme Court took hold of the charter in the *Slaughter-House Cases* and in the next three decades made section one into the single most important text in constitutional adjudication.

CHAPTER V

Objections
to the
Amendment

In presenting a variety of objections to the Fourteenth Amendment during the course of the congressional and later the state ratification debates, the opponents of the amendment never questioned its premise that the law should treat all people equally. Equality, as we have seen, was a premise which all political groups—Jacksonian and Southern Democrats as well as Republicans—had accepted in antebellum America. In the aftermath of the Civil War, Americans of all political stripes continued to believe in equality as a general principle, even though they may have understood the concept in diverse ways.

As President Andrew Johnson said succinctly in his December 1865 State of the Union message, "the American system rest[ed] on the assertion of the equal right of every man to life, liberty, and the pursuit of happiness." The president continued:

> Monopolies, perpetuities, and class legislation are contrary to the genius of free government, and ought not to be allowed. Here there is no room for favored classes or monopolies; the principle of our Government is that of equal laws and freedom of industry ... We shall but fulfill our duties as legislators by according "equal and exact justice to all men," special privileges to none.[1]

In March of 1866, when he had broken with and become the center of opposition to the Republican party in Congress, Johnson still retained his commitment to equality. As he wrote in his veto of the Civil Rights Bill, the action that made the break irreparable, he remained ready to "cooperate with Congress in any measure that may be necessary for the protection of the civil rights of the freedmen, as well as those of all other classes of persons throughout the United States, by judicial process *under equal and impartial laws*."[2] Alexander H. Stephens, former vice president of the Confederacy, agreed in a speech sanctioned by the Georgia legislature that "full protection should be secured" to the freedmen "so that they may start equal before the law in the possession and enjoyment of all rights of personal liberty and property,"[3] while Pennsylvania's Senator Edgar Cowan, a Republican who would oppose the Fourteenth Amendment, also indicated his support for the principle of "equality before the law."[4]

Support for the equality principle was echoed in newspapers opposed to the Fourteenth Amendment. The *Little Rock Daily Gazette*, for example, was "in favor of the protection of the civil rights of the negroes, and of giving them fair play in all things,"[5] while the *Memphis Daily Post* thought it essential for white Southerners to recognize that blacks "remember, reflect, form opinions, and communicate" and that to "move a negro, you must go at him, not as an ox or a machine, but . . . as a man."[6] The Jackson *Daily Clarion* favored educating blacks,[7] and the New York *Commercial Advertiser* found an equal suffrage bill "in principle correct for it banishes all distinctions of caste and color," even though it was without constitutional basis.[8] The New York *Sun* found section one of the Fourteenth Amendment "all well enough in a moral sense, but its constitutionality . . . extremely doubtful,"[9] while the *Brooklyn Daily Eagle* thought that section one, standing "alone" was "entirely unobjectionable."[10] Perhaps the most interesting statement of all came from the rabidly anti-Republican *New York Daily News*, in an editorial having no direct reference to the Fourteenth Amendment, which commented on the evils of special legislation. According to the *News*:

> The true end of government is the equal protection of its citizens in "life, liberty, and the pursuit of happiness." . . . But widely have we departed, in practice, from this principle of our

political faith. . . . We have perverted legislation from its high and holy office of equal protection, and debased it into an almoner of special advantages and immunities to a few.

The *News* thought government should be

> restricted to the few plain and necessary purposes contemplated in the Democratic theory, the mere protection of person, life and property. If the guardianship of the equal rights of men were made its sole duty, and its action were directed in all cases, not by the capricious suggestions of temporary expediency, but the eternal and unalterable principles of justice; if it should seek to preserve the harmony and equilibrium of society by general, not by partial laws, by a system founded on the plain principles of universal equity,

an improved tone of public morals and increased individual happiness would ensue.[11] The most radical Republican could not have stated the nation's credo with more eloquence.

The rhetoric of Andrew Johnson, the *Daily News* and others effectively precluded opposition to the principle of equality—a commonplace moral norm on which virtually all Americans, at least in theory, agreed. Opposition thus had to take other forms, and objections to the Fourteenth Amendment did, in fact, take two forms. The most important objections went to the substance of the amendment, but many of the objections did not. Let us consider the nonsubstantive objections first.

▪ Objections to the Process of the Amendment's Passage

One such objection was that the Congress that adopted the amendment and sent it to the states was not duly constituted, since it did not contain representatives from the South. An Oregon legislator, for example, "protested against the whole measure, because it had never received the requisite two-thirds majority in Congress, eleven States being unrepresented,"[12] and a joint committee of the Georgia legislature recommended against ratification since the "Amendments" were not "Constitutionally Proposed."[13] The *Little Rock Daily Gazette* agreed that the amendment was never "acted upon by a Congress of such a character as is provided for by the Constitution, inasmuch as nearly one-third of the States were refused representation in the Congress which acted upon this amendment."[14] Similarly, the

Daily Richmond Enquirer praised the Virginia legislature for refusing to ratify "[a]n amendment proposed by a Congress from whose deliberations we were excluded."[15] The most striking procedural "absurdity" in the amendment's passage was noted by a Pennsylvania legislator, who observed "that the Southern States are competent, at least, to contribute a portion of the three-fourths required . . . for the purpose of ratifying amendments, but [are] out of the Union for the purpose of aiding in proposing amendments."[16]

A second objection to the procedure by which the Fourteenth Amendment was presented to the states sounds somewhat strange in view of our understanding of the amendment process. The objection was that "[t]his proposed amendment was never submitted to the President for his sanction, as it should have been, according to the very letter of th[e] Constitution."[17] The objection seems strange because the Constitution itself does not specifically require the submission of constitutional amendments to the president for his approval, and the practice during the past century has been not to submit them. That practice was less clear, however, in 1866. Although none of the first twelve amendments had been sent to the president prior to their being submitted to the states, the Thirteenth Amendment was sent to President Lincoln, even though many in Congress claimed at the time that his approval was unnecessary. Because the Civil War was a period that saw the reversal of many old governmental practices and the establishment of new precedents, it was not absurd to look to the procedures used in the adoption of the Thirteenth Amendment as a basis for practice in reference to the Fourteenth.[18]

A third objection was to internal procedures in Congress. The objection was stated by Senator Thomas A. Hendricks, Democrat of Indiana, who noted that the second effort of the Joint Committee on Reconstruction to frame a program for Reconstruction

> passed the House, but when it came under discussion in the Senate, and had to bear the test of the independent judgment of Senators, it was found wanting, and its defeat became almost certain. A second defeat of a party programme could not be borne; its effect upon the fall election would be disastrous. A caucus was called, and we witnessed the astounding spectacle of the withdrawal, for the time, of a great legislative measure, touching the Constitution itself, from the Senate, that it might be decided in the secret councils of a party. For three days the Senate Chamber was silent, but the discussions were transferred to

another room of the Capitol, with closed doors and darkened windows, where party leaders might safely contend for a political and party policy.

When the Fourteenth Amendment was brought back to the Senate floor from the caucus, Hendricks continued, "a plausible political platform had been devised."[19]

Hendricks was expressing a quite familiar theme: that the Fourteenth Amendment, as his colleague Garrett Davis of Kentucky put it, was the product of "the law of party necessity" and was designed to secure to the Republicans "the continuance of power, its offices and rich spoils."[20] According to the *Little Rock Daily Gazette*, the Fourteenth Amendment was a scheme "[t]o fix . . . power in the line of perpetuity, so as to make . . . [it] serve the selfish purposes of present possessors" in accordance with "the wishes and sentiments of the temporary majority of a section of the Union."[21] Charles A. Eldridge, a Democratic Congressman from Wisconsin, contended that "the Government is to be revolutionized to secure the ascendency of the Republican party,"[22] and even Republican Senator John B. Henderson argued that a forerunner of section two was "a compromise that the whites may govern the blacks in the State governments of the South . . . provided the northern and eastern States are permitted to control the national Government."[23]

Some more specific arguments were advanced about why the Fourteenth Amendment was, in essence, a political document. It was said, for example, that many Republicans favored suffrage for blacks only because "it is supposed, they can be used for Republican party purposes."[24] A more common argument was that "since it is certain that three-fourths of the States will not ratify the amendment," the "design" of the amendment was "to keep the Southern States permanently unrepresented."[25] The Fourteenth Amendment, according to the *Daily Richmond Enquirer*, "was contrived to exclude, not to admit" the South to the Union[26] and thus to secure victory to the Republicans in the election of 1868.[27]

A fourth objection that was addressed not to the substantive content of the Fourteenth Amendment but to the process of its enactment appeared in newspaper editorials which frequently bore the title "Tinkering the Constitution." In one editorial under that title, the New York *Commercial Advertiser* lamented the "daily attempts at meddling with the Constitution of the United States" as "undignified, uncalled for and injurious and pernicious in their tendency."[28] The Constitution, according to the New York *Evening Post*, "is not a thing to be brought into Congress and tossed from hand to hand in a sort of contempt for its supposed imperfections, and finally mended like an old shoe." In the view of the *Post*, "[w]hatever is of a temporary nature should be provided, if possible, by arrangements independent of the Constitution." The *Post* thought that if "the numerous amendments which have been proposed at the present session of Congress" were adopted, the Constitution would become "more like a mass of statutes, public and private, enacted at some session of Congress than like a plain and well devised system, of wide and permanent application, for the government of a great people."[29] The New York *Sunday Mercury* also objected to "Congressional Solons" who "treat the Constitution with as little ceremony as a tailor would in patching up . . . an old pair of breeches;"[30] it thought the "Constitution ought to be something permanent . . . deal[ing] with general principles."[31] And the *New York Daily News* expressed concern that "[t]he people have so long witnessed one innovation after another upon their form of government, that they have learned to look upon their political system as a mockery, subject to the caprices of experimentalists." It warned that "[t]he mania for amending the Constitution . . . will in time undermine the whole fabric and cause it to crumble of its own weight."[32]

- ## Objections to the Substance of the Amendment

These objections to the process by which the Fourteenth Amendment was adopted have less significance for understanding its meaning, however, than the objections levied against its substantive content. The substantive objections were, in essence, two. One was an argument that the amendment tried to compel equal treatment for blacks when blacks, in fact, were not the equals of whites. The other was that the amendment centralized power and thereby destroyed the essential federal character of the American system of government.

The Inequality of Blacks

Much of the opposition to the Fourteenth Amendment, both Northern and Southern, was deeply racist in tone and character. Although virtually all Americans agreed that people who were equal in fact should stand equally before the law, many white racists claimed that black people were something less than the full equals of whites. The *Oswego Daily Palladium*, for example, said that blacks were "generally as ignorant as the dumb animals about them" and argued "how utterly impossible a free government, or free institutions, are for ignorant and degraded races like the negro and the Indian,"[33] while the *Newark Daily Advertiser* claimed that "careful anatomical studies of his brain . . . show that he [the black] has a much smaller average brain than the white."[34] Equally racist remarks came from Senator Thomas A. Hendricks, who later became vice president in the first Cleveland administration. He asked of blacks:

> What has this race ever produced? What invention has it ever produced of advantage to the world? You need not say it is because of slavery, for we all know it is not. This race has not been carried down into barbarism by slavery. The influence of slavery upon this race—I will not say it is the influence of slavery—but the influence of the contact of this race with the white race has been to give it all the elevation it possesses, and independent and outside of that influence it has not become elevated anywhere in its whole history.[35]

Another Indiana Democrat, Congressman Michael C. Kerr, remarked that whites were the only people "who, in the history of the world, have shown any capacity for self-government."[36] Note should also be taken of the pseudo-scientific remarks of California Senator James A. McDougall that blacks

> can never commingle with us . . . [T]he African race and the Europeans are different, and I here now say it as a fact established by science that the eighth generation of the mixed race formed by the union of the African and European cannot continue their species. Quadroons have few children; with octoroons reproduction is impossible. It establishes as a law of nature that the African has no proper relation to the European, Caucasian blood.[37]

This was Northern racism. Southerners, of course, would make even more outrageous comments. One pseudo-scientific view, held by the *Newbern Daily Times*, was that "inferior races, whether vegetable or animal go before and prepare the way for the advent of the superior races." In this view, having "lost the protection and care of their former masters[,] . . . the negro race in the South is rapidly dying out." "The negro has felled our forest, drained our swamps, cleared our lands, diked our streams, constructed our roads and opened the country," and "having thus performed their part in the development of American civilization," blacks, according to the *Times*, would "gradually die out and finally become extinct, and disappear from the soil, thus leaving the white race the sole occupants and the only proprietors of this vast country."[38]

Accordingly, the *Daily Richmond Examiner* thought it would be "a stupendous folly to remove the blacks from the tutelage of the superior race,"[39] while Kentucky Democrat Garrett Davis compared "the Caucasian race, the highest type of man," with

> negroes, the lowest type, of which race no nation or tribe, from the first dawning of history to the present day, has ever established a polity that could be denominated a Government, or has elaborated for itself any science or literature or arts or even an alphabet, or characters to represent numbers, or been capable of preserving those achievements of intellect when it has received them from a superior race.[40]

The racism of the South was most explicitly summed up, perhaps, by Delaware's Democratic Senator Willard Saulsbury, who commented that God created man with "different hues of skin, different mental and moral organizations . . . different orders of intellect; and I would say different orders of beings."[41] Saulsbury, it should be noted, was in lock step with his constituents, as is evidenced by a resolution of the Delaware legislature that " 'the immutable laws of God have fixed upon the brows of the white races the ineffaceable stamp of superiority, and all attempts to elevate the negro to a social or political equality with the white man are futile.' "[42] As Ohio's Governor J. D. Cox told that state's Senator John Sherman, the white people of America would never accept subordination to or even "equality of political power in the government with a race which is permanently & necessarily alien,"[43] while another correspondent of Sherman agreed "that there cannot be mixed government of the caucasian & negro races."[44]

It would be a mistake, however, to attribute all statements about the inferiority of blacks to such vulgar racism. Many racist statements were made in the context of debates about whether political rights, especially the right to vote, should be granted to the newly freed blacks of the South. Many Americans in the 1860s had different attitudes than we do toward the issues of race and political theory implicated in the voting rights debates, and because these attitudes often sound irrational to us, we are inclined to label them prejudices. But while it might be comforting to label as prejudiced people who opposed suffrage for blacks, the attachment of that label frustrates the central task of history, which is not to condemn the past but to understand and explain why people in the past behaved as they did. Attributing to prejudice the failure of black suffrage to make any headway in 1866 and 1867 makes it especially difficult to account for the ratification by three-fourths of the states of the Fifteenth Amendment less than three years later.

Those who favored extending the right to vote to blacks were not especially saintly, nor were those who opposed the extension unusually evil-minded. On the contrary, the two groups shared a common assumption that in a democracy the quality of government depends on the quality of the electorate. In the words of Senator Waitman T. Willey, Republican of West Virginia, the suffrage ought to be granted only to those with "intelligence, [and] capacity to understand how to exercise this great duty," since there could be "no secure republican institutions unless this foundation of free institutions is securely laid."[45] What separated those who favored extending the right to vote to blacks from those who opposed it was their concept of good government and hence the qualities they wanted in an ideal electorate. To anticipate my argument, those who favored black suffrage admired the moral qualities of potential black voters, while opponents of suffrage extension questioned the capacity of blacks to vote intelligently.

The problem with extending the suffrage to blacks, as Senator Edgar Cowan of Pennsylvania argued, was that "these negroes just emerged from slavery" were not "the fit recipients of the political power of the community." Cowan conceded that no man should be denied the right to vote "simply for the reason that he is black." He would "exclude a black man because black is the evidence that he is an inferior man, of inferior education, of inferior means of knowledge."[46] As Cowan's colleague, George H. Williams, explained, blacks had "been enslaved since the formation of the Government. Degradation and ignorance have been their portion; intelligence has been denied to them."[47] As Senator Waitman T. Willey argued:

> [T]hese freedmen were slaves less than four years ago, the
> descendents of slaves, having all the servile habits and instincts of
> the most inveterate slavery, coming from States whose laws
> forbade their being taught to read, not only the Constitution and
> history of their country, but also the very oracles of salvation;
> debased, degraded, as ignorant as it was possible to make them.
> Are such beings as these the safe depositories of the political
> power of any community?[48]

A New York correspondent of Thaddeus Stevens agreed that "[t]he
mass of the coloured people in the South are unfit for the exercise of
the franchise as they have not the intelligence & information
necessary,"[49] as did a constituent of Senator John Sherman, who
thought "[p]lantation negroes as a class . . . unfit to vote."[50]

Opponents of black suffrage feared that "[b]y pouring into the
ballot-boxes of the country a large mass of ignorant votes, and votes
subjected to pecuniary or social influence, you will corrupt and
degrade your elections and lay the foundation for their ultimate
destruction."[51] As the *Springfield Republican* argued, it was "the
ignorant element in our politics" that put "mercenary place-seekers
and demagogues into Congress—men who do not understand the first
principles of government."[52] Wisconsin Senator James R. Doolittle
found the opposing argument, that "these men just set free are
competent to exercise the right of suffrage and help to shape the laws
of this great Republic . . . abhorrent to my sense of justice, reason, or
propriety."[53] "They would be blind tools in the hands of their late
masters," Thaddeus Stevens was told.[54] Simeon Nash, a constituent
of John Sherman, was even more extreme in his opposition to the
proponents of suffrage for blacks:

> Do these men suppose that an ignorant negro is just as dangerous
> as an ignorant whiteman. We can [word illegible] a certain
> amount of ignorance, when it is largely in the minority, but let it
> once assume the majority, and does not everyone see the Gov is
> gone? Ignorant people never did and never can govern a country.
> Knavery and ignorance will go hand in hand and have done all
> the world over. What made Louis Napoleon Emperor? Did the
> intelligence of France or its ignorance?[55]

There was another related, yet additional reason for denying equal
rights, especially equal political rights, to blacks. "If Universal Negro
suffrage [were] desirable, so [was] Chinese and all other peoples of
any nation who come to our shores."[56] It was impossible to

understand "why we should exclude one race and include another."[57] Thus, the Fourteenth Amendment inevitably raised questions such as:

> Is the child of the Chinese immigrant in California a citizen? Is the child of a Gypsy born in Pennsylvania a citizen? If so, what rights have they? Have they any more rights than a sojourner in the United States? If a traveller comes here. . . , he is entitled, to a certain extent, to the protection of the laws. You cannot murder him with impunity. It is murder to kill him, the same as it is to kill another man. You cannot commit an assault and battery on him, I apprehend. He has a right to the protection of the laws; but he is not a citizen in the ordinary acceptation of the word.[58]

Equality for blacks accordingly was "one of the gravest subjects that ever could be submitted to the people of the United States . . . involv[ing] not only the negro race, but other inferior races that are now settling on our Pacific coast, and perhaps . . . a future immigration to this country of which we have no conception."[59]

Some men in Congress perceived a danger in extending equal rights to people without regard to their race, religion or national origin. For example, Kentucky Democrat Garrett Davis spoke of

> the tide of emigration that might pour in upon the Pacific States from the surcharged populations of eastern Asia . . . a danger that cannot excite too much alarm. Our Christian civilization and our Government of the people by written Constitution and giving limited and delegated powers could not survive a few great waves from that vast hive of an inferior race. . . . Our system of religion and government and of social organization is threatened by this wave of emigration from Eastern Asia. . . . I want no negro Government; I want no Mongolian Government; I want the Government of the white man which our fathers incorporated.[60]

For others in Congress the key issue was not that the Chinese were inferior to whites; many regarded the Chinese as equals. The issue was simply one of who would control California. As Senator Edgar Cowan of Pennsylvania argued:

> [I]s it proposed that the people of California are to remain quiescent while they are overrun by a flood of immigration of the Mongol race? Are they to be immigrated out of house and home by the Chinese? I should think not. It is not supposed that the people of California, in a broad and general sense, have any

higher rights than the people of China; but they are in possession of the country of California, and if another people of a different race, of different religion, of different manners, of different traditions, different tastes and sympathies are to come there and have the free right to locate there and settle among them, and if they have an opportunity of pouring in such an immigration as in a short time will double or treble the population of California, I ask, are the people of California powerless to protect themselves?[61]

Oregon's two Republican Senators expressed similar concerns. According to Henry W. Corbett:

But now the question arises how far we shall extend the suffrage and to what classes of people. With regard to the Chinese, they are a pagan nation. They worship their god "Josh," a god made of wood. . . . With the experience of the past few years on the Pacific coast we have found that this class of people are not beneficial to the advancement of those Christian institutions that lie at the foundation of our Government. The presence of large numbers of them in our midst is not beneficial to the observance of the Sabbath day. . . . Allow Chinese suffrage, and you may soon find established pagan institutions in our midst which may eventually supersede those Christian influences which have so long been the pride of our country. . . . I, for one, must object to granting the right of suffrage to a class of people which embraces a nation composed of perhaps four or six hundred million persons who can come to our shores and supersede us in the establishment of institutions of their own, which may be detrimental to us, and finally overthrow our cherished system.[62]

Oregon's other Republican Senator, George H. Williams, put the matter more succinctly when he expressed his concern that "authorities in China might send over hundreds of thousands of Chinamen to the Pacific coast instructed to become citizens for securing in every possible way the productions of that vast and rich country for the benefit of the Chinese empire," and his belief that "this country has the absolute power to protect itself from Chinamen or any other sort of foreigners" without "violat[ing] the Declaration of Independence."[63]

American Indians constituted another group that some thought might be affected by the Fourteenth Amendment. Whether Indians should be brought within the family of citizens entitled to the rights specified in section one of the amendment was hotly debated. Senator

James R. Doolittle raised the question whether it would be "contended that the Indians of the Territories, and the States . . . are competent to exercise the right of franchise," arguing that it was "impossible that it should be so in the nature of things."[64] Likewise the radical Senator Jacob M. Howard was "not quite so liberal" as "to pass a sweeping act of naturalization by which all the Indian savages, wild or tame, belonging to a tribal relation, are to become my fellow-citizens and go to the polls and vote with me and hold lands and deal in every other way that a citizen of the United States has a right to do."[65] Senator John B. Henderson, on the contrary, expressed anger at the prospect that "[w]e are deciding today" that this Government "was made for the white man and the black man, but that the red man shall have no interest in it,"[66] while an Indiana state legislator urged that the nation could not "take political partnership with the negro, and leave out the noble Indian."[67] The *San Francisco Chronicle* agreed that once blacks were on the road to equality, it was "time to attend to the case of the Indian."[68]

The question of citizenship for Indians was, to say the least, a tricky one in 1866. Most of those who considered the issue agreed that Indians belonging to some of the great Western tribes still enjoying a measure of independence were subjects of independent nations, not citizens of the United States. But what about remnants of some of the Eastern tribes? Or renegades who had left their tribes, roamed as individuals and had various contacts with whites, but did not acknowledge the authority of any American government? Indians in 1866 were in a period of transition from national independence to citizenship in a multiracial America, and the framers of the Fourteenth Amendment tried to deal with this fact by including as citizens only persons "subject to the jurisdiction" of the United States and excluding from the basis of representation "Indians not taxed."[69] Senator George H. Williams, a member of the Joint Committee on Reconstruction that framed the amendment, thought that "any court or . . . any intelligent person" would construe the Fourteenth Amendment to exclude from citizenship "Indians who maintain their tribal relations and who are not in all respects subject to the jurisdiction of the United States."[70] It is sufficient here to note that this formulation did not fully and finally resolve all questions about the relationship of Indians to the American government.

The debates on black, Chinese, and Indian rights thus suggest that some statesmen of the mid-nineteenth century believed that extending equal rights to people not of European descent would destroy the American political system. In part, their beliefs reflected hatred for and lack of understanding of people of other races, but in part they reflected a concern that most people living in America who were not of European descent did not understand or accept the values under- lying the nation's political system and hence could not participate in its maintenance. This concern of opponents of the Fourteenth Amend- ment that the American political system could not survive the addition of non-Europeans to the body politic was exacerbated by the second objection to the amendment—that it centralized power and thereby destroyed the essential federal character of the American system of government.

The Centralization of Power

The objection about centralization was levied not only against the Fourteenth Amendment, but also against the Civil Rights Act of 1866. The two were inextricably linked in the spring of 1866, since section one was added to the amendment at least in part to remove doubts about the constitutionality of the 1866 act. Hence section one increased the power of the federal government at least as much as the Civil Rights Act, and arguments against the act are appropriately understood as arguments against the section as well.

As Senator Garrett Davis of Kentucky argued, the Civil Rights Act threatened to give Congress "power to occupy the whole domain of local and State legislation,"[71] authorizing it "to pass a civil and criminal code for every State in the Union."[72] The act, according to Delaware's Willard Saulsbury, imposed limitations on the "police power" of the states;[73] it required that "State rights and State customs ... yield to the decrees of a central despotism."[74] The Committee on Federal Relations of the Arkansas legislature agreed that the Fourteenth Amendment "would, in effect, take from the States all control over their local and domestic concerns, and virtually abolish the States," and therefore recommended against ratification.[75] Similar views were held by Northerners such as members of the Democratic minority of the New Hampshire legislature's committee on national affairs, who found section one "a dangerous infringement upon the rights and independence of all the States, north as well as south, assuming, as it does, to control their legislation in matter's [sic] purely local in their character."[76] Likewise Congressman Andrew J. Rogers, one of the few Democrats on the Joint Reconstruction Committee, indicated his opposition to section one because it would "take away the power of the States; . . . interfere with the internal police and regulations of the States; . . . [and] centralize a consolidated power in this Federal Government."[77]

Governor R. M. Patton of Alabama outlined the position in great detail in a message to the state legislature recommending against ratification of the Fourteenth Amendment. Patton maintained that section one

> would enlarge the judicial powers of the General Government to such gigantic dimensions as would not only overshadow and weaken the authority and influence of the State courts, but might possibly reduce them to a complete nullity. It would give to the United States courts complete and unlimited jurisdiction over every conceivable case, however important or however trivial, which could arise under State laws. Every individual dissatisfied with the decision of a State court, might apply to a Federal tribunal for redress. It matters not what might be the character of his case. . . . Upon a simple complaint that his rights, either of person or property, had been infringed, it would be the bounden duty of the tribunal to which he made his application to hear and determine his case. The granting of such an immense power as this over the State tribunals would, at the very best, subordinate them to a condition of comparative unimportance and insignificance.[78]

The *Little Rock Daily Gazette* likewise protested against the "attempt to crush out the independence of the State Judiciary, and summarily reform customs of the people that are stronger than the law."[79]

The threat to the judicial and hence the law enforcement and ultimately the lawmaking capacity of the states was enhanced by procedures created under the Civil Rights Act, which appeared in 1866 as the principal legislative vehicle by which section one would be enforced. A key provision of the act made it a crime for a state judge to render a judgment that had the effect of depriving a litigant in his court of any federally protected right of person or property. Unable to foresee in 1866 that the Supreme Court would elaborate a doctrine of judicial immunity that would save state judges from such criminal liability, opponents of the Fourteenth Amendment and of the key legislation for its enforcement argued vehemently. Senator Garrett Davis of Kentucky thought it "preposterous, . . . and absurd and unsound to the last degree" that "the judges and officers who are sworn to uphold the constitution of the State of Kentucky, and to enforce her laws" would be "guilty of a high misdemeanor against the Government of the United States that shall subject them to the pains and penalties of this bill."[80] President Andrew Johnson agreed in what appears to be the strongest section of his message vetoing the 1866 act. The president thought it ought to be possible to protect civil rights

> without invading the immunities of legislators, always important to be preserved in the interest of public liberty; without assailing the independence of the judiciary, always essential to the preservation of individual rights; and without impairing the efficiency of ministerial officers, always necessary for the maintenance of public peace and order. The remedy proposed . . . seems to be in this respect not only anomalous, but unconstitutional; for the Constitution guarantees nothing with certainty if it does not insure to the several States the right of making and executing laws in regard to all matters arising within their jurisdiction, subject only to the restriction that in cases of conflict with the Constitution and constitutional laws of the United States the latter should be held to be the supreme law of the land.

Johnson saved his harshest language for the penalties imposed on

> the State judge who, in the clear exercise of his functions as a judge, not acting ministerially but judicially, shall decide contrary to this Federal law. In other words, when a State judge, acting upon a question involving a conflict between a State law and a Federal law, and bound, according to his own judgment and responsibility, to give an impartial decision between the two, comes to the conclusion that the State law is valid and the Federal law is invalid, he must not follow the dictates of his own judgment, at the peril of fine and imprisonment. The legislative department of the Government of the United States thus takes from the judicial department of the States the sacred and exclusive duty of judicial decision, and converts the State judge into a mere ministerial officer, bound to decide according to the will of Congress.[81]

Even Congressman Henry J. Raymond, a Republican who ultimately voted in favor of the Fourteenth Amendment, was troubled by the prospect of criminal punishment for state judges, asking "is it just, is it right, have we the power to say that a judge of a State court shall be punished by fine and imprisonment for enforcing a State law,"[82] while another key Republican, John A. Bingham, thought such liability could be imposed only by constitutional amendment and not by mere legislation.[83] Senator Trumbull's assurance that state judges would not be punished criminally if they acted innocently but only if they had "a vicious will"[84] assuaged no one's fears and concerns, probably because no one other than Congressman Samuel Shellabarger[85] ever seems to have taken note of Trumbull's propitious idea.

The prospective difficulties of state judges and the threat to their independence were further enhanced by the fact that the provisions of the Civil Rights Bill were "uncertain as to their meaning" and "[i]ts intentions ... expressed in terms which are alike undefined and indefinable."[86] Congressman Benjamin M. Boyer found section one of the Fourteenth Amendment, which "embodie[d] the principles of the civil rights bill, ... objectionable also in its phraseology, being open to ambiguity and admitting of conflicting constructions."[87] The ambiguity of section one and of the Civil Rights Act enabled opponents to assert that they would have extreme effects. For example, Senator Edgar Cowan argued that the Civil Rights Act conferred "upon married women, upon minors, upon idiots, upon lunatics, and upon everybody native born in all the States, the right to make and enforce contracts, because there is no qualification in the bill, and the very object of the bill is to override the qualifications that are upon those rights in the States,"[88] while Senator Reverdy Johnson, one of the leading constitutional lawyers in Congress, believed the Civil Rights Act and hence the Fourteenth Amendment created a right to marry interracially. He conceded that his belief might be in error, but then quickly added that "all the Senate will admit that the error is not so gross a one that the courts may not fall into it."[89]

In the end, the opponents of the Fourteenth Amendment viewed it as simply "in violation of essential principles of the Constitution."[90] As Congressman Andrew J. Rogers explained, "the first section" was "the most dangerous to liberty." He continued:

> It saps the foundation of the Government; it destroys the elementary principles of the States; it consolidates everything into one imperial despotism; it annihilates all the rights which lie at the foundation of the Union of the States, and which have characterized this Government and made it prosperous and great

> during the long period of its existence. . . . It will result in a
> revolution worse than that through which we have just passed.[91]

In order to protect the rights of freedmen, the Republicans, according
to the *Brooklyn Daily Eagle* desired "a change in our government,
which will deprive it of all its distinctive features."[92] As the New
York *Evening Post* saw the issue, "liberty has never been secure
without local and municipal institutions,"[93] and the Republicans
were proposing "a long and fearful step toward the complete
obliteration of State authority and the reserved and original rights of
the States" that would "put . . . the local policy and officers,
executive, ministerial, and judicial, of the States, at the mercy of . . .
petty Federal officers."[94] Congressman Robert S. Hale, a Republican
from New York who ultimately supported the Fourteenth Amendment, took note of "the inevitable tendency of power always to
augment itself,"[95] with the ultimate result that the characteristic
protection which the American system gave to minorities would
disappear.[96] The *New York Daily News* summed up the impact of the
Civil Rights Act and section one of the Fourteenth Amendment as
follows:

> Carry out the doctrines now freely ventilated by the unscrupulous
> Radical leaders . . . and it follows, irresistibly, that, instead of
> being bound by a Constitution, they may claim the omnipotence
> of the British Parliament, and that all the reserved powers of the
> people, or of the States, will be swallowed up at their pleasure, by
> that undefined discretion; in a word, that the Constitution itself,
> so far as respects a limitation of powers, is, by such a doctrine,
> completely annihilated.[97]

In short, the claim of the opponents of the Fourteenth Amendment
was that its adoption would destroy the American constitutional
tradition of local self-rule. As they observed threats to impeach the
president and statutes altering the size of the Supreme Court, the
Democrats also predicted the destruction of related constitutional
traditions, like separation of powers and judicial independence, that
checked the capacity of a national political majority to impose its will
on a recalcitrant minority. As the *San Francisco Daily Examiner* saw
the issue, a "deliberate attempt" was afoot "not only to centralize all
power in the general government, but to prostrate the Judiciary and
Executive at the feet of the Legislative." If successful, it would

"convert the government into a mere party engine, to be wielded, not for the good of the people, but to suit the whims, passions, prejudices, interests and aggrandizement of a successful party."[98] The *Examiner* wished "this conflict brought to a head," so that "the people" may "decide in an unmistakable manner, whether they desire to live under a government in which they are sovereign, or under a central despotism in which a corrupt and unprincipled faction can exercise, through a bogus Congress, unlimited power."[99]

These were strong arguments that could not be ignored or overcome simply by a claim that the libertarian and egalitarian goals of the proponents of the Fourteenth Amendment were sound. Although no American of the mid-nineteenth century would argue that similarly situated people should receive dissimilar treatment at the hands of government, many Americans doubted that blacks and other non-Europeans were in fact the equals of whites. And even those who believed that all people are equal were not always prepared to totally sacrifice other values in pursuit of that equality.

CHAPTER VI

The Republican Rebuttal

The debates examined so far in Congress, in the state legislatures, in the columns of newspapers, and in the correspondence of congressmen contained little analysis of the issues that would come to plague the Supreme Court once section one of the Fourteenth Amendment became part of the Constitution. Instead we have observed Congress and the nation as a whole using the political rhetoric that had been commonplace throughout the first half of the nineteenth century to proclaim hopes for a just society, and to warn of fears that the amendment would destroy local self-rule and thus liberty as Americans had known it.

The content of the debates should not be surprising. When the Fourteenth Amendment came before Congress and the people of the United States in the winter and spring of 1866, and before the individual states in the two years that followed, it was not simply a matter for lawyers. The scope of state power to regulate the economy, to arrest and prosecute criminals, or to control the sexual behavior of its citizens was not the issue at hand. The Fourteenth Amendment was understood less as a legal instrument to be elaborated in the courts than as a peace treaty to be administered by Congress in order to secure the fruits of the North's victory in the Civil War. Since the war had had a greater impact on the American people than any other war in the nation's history,[1] the people were unusually active in discussing the terms of the peace. Of course they could not analyze the terms of peace as legal theoreticians; they could think about the conditions for restoring the Union only in the moral and political language of the mid-century period with which they were familiar. The people's representatives in Congress, in turn, must be understood primarily as participants in this public dialogue about the terms of peace. Thus even though many congressmen had been trained as lawyers, they usually did not address the Fourteenth Amendment in the standard fashion of lawyers seeking to identify the doctrinal issues that would arise when the amendment was placed in operation.

Part of the reason why Republicans could blithely ignore these issues, together with Democratic charges that section one would undermine state lawmaking power, was their assumption that states would conform their laws to the moral precepts incorporated into the amendment so that conflict between state and federal authorities would not arise. Thus in a comment on the 1866 Civil Rights Act, which, as we have already seen, applied to all basic common law rights and thus threatened to draw all lawmaking power to Congress, one radical newspaper article predicted that the act's "practical operation will probably be brief." The act would be "a dead letter in a State if it is guilty of no injustice to any portion of its inhabitants." In these Northern states, the writer continued, the 1866 act would "have no more effect than a law of Congress, enacting, under the severest penalties, that white citizens shall not be denied any civil rights enjoyed by black citizens." "[L]ike all other good laws," it would "form an atmosphere surrounding the good man without his being conscious of it." The inhabitants of "good" states would never sense that the act applied to them because, like other laws, it was " 'not made for the righteous man, but for the lawless and disobedi-ent, the ungodly and sinners.' " Even lawless states, where the act "simply intervene[d] to secure . . . justice," would "hasten to conform their laws and proceedings to it, in order to avoid the constant annoyance to which they would otherwise be subject from the interference of the United States courts and officers in their internal affairs." Once the Southern states conformed to federal law by granting impartial justice, they too would be restored to their plenary lawmaking power, and the new federal law would have no further practical effect.[2]

Even when Republicans recognized that the Fourteenth Amendment might in the future require enforcement by federal authorities, they did not always face up to Democratic charges that federal enforcement would undermine state power. They assumed that Congress, acting pursuant to section five, would possess primary jurisdiction to enforce the amendment, and they could further assume that future Congresses, like themselves, would respect legitimate state rights. Only when the Republican proponents considered the possibility that future Congresses might not respect the states, and especially when they recalled that sections one and five had been recast in separate form in order to render the enforcement power of judges clear, did they find it necessary to respond to Democratic objections and to explain why the Fourteenth Amendment would not have the undesirable effects that its opponents feared. These occasions were infrequent. When they occurred, however, a few Republican lawyers in Congress analyzed the Fourteenth Amendment as something more than a receptacle for moral and political principles and thereby began the task of translating section one into a vehicle for legal doctrine.

The opponents of the Fourteenth Amendment, it will be recalled, had raised several objections to the process by which the amendment came before the states. One of the objections—that the amendment should have been submitted to the president for his approval—was easily answered. No other amendment except the Thirteenth ever had been submitted to the president, and, in the case of the Thirteenth, Congress had declared its understanding that it had no obligation to submit the amendment to him.[3] This first objection to the Fourteenth Amendment was probably worth stating in an effort to transform one recent instance of prior practice into a new line of precedent, but the effort failed and, indeed, was never taken seriously by the proponents of the amendment, who simply did not take the time or trouble to respond to it.

The three other objections to the process by which the Fourteenth Amendment came into being—that the amendment resulted in excessive tinkering with the Constitution, that it was adopted by a Congress from which much of the opposition was excluded, and that it was ultimately political in character—were interrelated. All three objections amounted to a claim that the Republican proponents of the amendment were acting in the service not of broad constitutional principle, but of narrow, partisan goals. The nation did, in fact, divide along party lines in its support of or opposition to the amendment, and, in that sense, the Democratic opponents of the amendment were correct about its partisan quality. To understand the Republicans of Reconstruction simply as radical partisans whose central aim was the retention of political power, however, is to miss the genuinely constitutional thrust of radical Reconstruction.

Republican political leaders and the Republican press did not defend the Fourteenth Amendment against claims of partisanship. They and their supporters among the Northern masses knew that more was at stake in the Republican policies than a simple retention of power. They could ignore claims that they were mere partisans because those claims were, in essence, false. But Republicans could not similarly ignore Democratic claims about the untoward substantive effects the Fourteenth Amendment would have.

One Democratic claim, it will be recalled, was that blacks were fundamentally and inherently inferior to whites; the law, according to the Democrats, could not alter that inferiority, and it was wrong to attempt so to use it. When Democrats made such assertions about black inferiority, Republicans reiterated their belief about the arbitrariness of racial distinctions and classifications and about the essential equality of all people. Republicans understood equality to be the foundation of the American system and further understood that all arbitrary and unequal discriminations in regard to any laws, even laws regulating the right to vote, tended ultimately to corrupt the polity. Thus many Republicans took a stand in favor of "the justice and expediency of impartial suffrage,"[4] perceiving it as "the corner stone of Republican institutions."[5] They contended that political power belonged "not to a portion of the people, not to the learned, not to the ignorant, not to the rich, not to the poor, not to the great, not to the weak, but to all the people," and hence that it was necessary "to give to each individual an equal share of political power."[6] Probably a majority of the Republican party favored a "*Negro franchise* . . . upon the same terms as that of the white people."[7]

One of the more interesting Republican figures was Senator John Conness of California, the state which so many conservatives feared might be overrun by Chinese. Conness, however, would not sacrifice his egalitarian principles to such fears. He was "in favor of . . . declar[ing] that the children of all parentage whatever, born in California, should be regarded and treated as citizens of the United States, entitled to equal civil rights with other citizens of the United States."[8] He urged that the Senate take

> no further trouble on account of the Chinese in California or on the Pacific coast. We are fully aware of the nature of that class of people and their influence among us, and feel entirely able to take care of them and to provide against any evils that may flow from their presence among us. We are entirely ready to accept the provision proposed in this constitutional amendment, that the children born here of Mongolian parents shall be declared by the Constitution of the United States to be entitled to civil rights and to equal protection before the law with others.[9]

Far more troublesome to the Republican proponents of the Fourteenth Amendment was the second Democratic claim about its substance: that it would give Congress power to legislate about matters previously reserved to the states and thereby result in a consolidation of power and the destruction of the federal system as Americans had known it.

This claim was an especially troublesome one because the fear of centralization was not without basis. If the Fourteenth Amendment were understood to give Congress power to hear and act upon essentially political arguments in favor of protecting higher law rights or other citizens' rights—rights of both an economic and a personal nature—then there would be few, if any, areas of life that Congress could not touch. Congress would become a superlegislature and the states, as independent lawmaking entities, would be destroyed.

Proponents of the Fourteenth Amendment made it clear that they did not intend such vast power for Congress. Most Republican supporters of the amendment, like the Democratic opponents, feared centralized power and did not want to see state and local power substantially curtailed. They recognized that the "doctrine of the rights of the States justly construed is as important to the preservation of the republic as any other fundamental political doctrine."[10] They agreed that "concentration of powers in the General Government" was "incompatible with our political organism" and could "not be adopted in this country, for the attainment even of the noblest ends."[11] For most Republicans, there were "other liberties as important as the liberties of the individual citizen, and those [were] the liberties and rights of the States."[12] As holders of such beliefs, the proponents of section one declared vehemently that it would "not destroy the sovereignty of a State" or "even affect its sovereign rights;"[13] in the words of its draftsman, John A. Bingham, the section took "from no State any right that ever pertained to it."[14]

Republicans accordingly set out to explain why the Fourteenth Amendment would not have the devastating effect on the states that its opponents feared. Their explanation, however, demanded considerable creative ingenuity in dealing with some complex theoretical issues. Prior to the drafting of the Fourteenth Amendment, no one doubted that states could legislate to restrict rights granted by God or inherent in the nature of a free society. The amendment, however, appeared to restrict state lawmaking authority and to grant Congress vast power. At the very least, section one was understood to remove all doubts about the constitutionality of the 1866 Civil Rights Act and thus to give Congress legislative power in reference to basic rights of contract, property, and personal security. With such power, it appeared that Congress might be able to reverse state policies concerning the entire common law. The Republican proponents of the Fourteenth Amendment had to explain why it would not have this drastic effect.

The simplest explanation, which was repeated continually during the congressional and state ratification debates, was that the amendment did not protect specific fundamental rights or give Congress and the federal courts power to interfere with state lawmaking that either created or denied rights. The only effect of the amendment was to prevent the states from discriminating arbitrarily between different classes of citizens. As long as a state treated its citizens equally, distinguishing between them only when there was a basis in reason for doing so, the state would remain immune from federal intervention pursuant to the Fourteenth Amendment.

Senator Lyman Trumbull was one of the many Republicans who accepted this analysis of the Fourteenth Amendment not as a charter for federal protection of fundamental rights, but merely as a guarantee of equality. In arguing for passage of the 1866 Civil Rights Act, which he understood to have the same scope as section one, Trumbull explained that the act would "in no manner interfere . . . with the municipal regulations of any State which protects all alike in their rights of person and property. It could have no operation in Massachusetts, New York, Illinois, or most of the States of the Union." The act, according to Trumbull, "neither confers nor abridges the rights of any one" and left every state free to "grant or withhold such civil rights as it pleases." The states, that is, retained plenary lawmaking power; all that the Civil Rights Act and later the Fourteenth Amendment required was that a state provide "an equality among all classes of citizens" and a guarantee that "its laws shall be impartial."[15]

Several months later Senator Lot M. Morrill of Maine made a similar statement:

> The peculiar character, the genius of republicanism is equality, impartiality of rights and remedies among all citizens, not that the citizen shall not be abridged in any of his natural rights. The man yields that right to the nation when he becomes a citizen. The republican guarantee is that all laws shall bear upon all alike in what they enjoin and forbid, grant and enforce. This principle of equality before the law is as old as civilization, but it does not prevent the State from qualifying the rights of the citizen according to the public necessities.[16]

Others took an equivalent position. Thus Congressman James F. Wilson explained that the word "immunities," which was used in the Civil Rights Act and later in section one, "merely secure[d] to citizens of the United States equality in the exemptions of the law," leaving the states plenary power to grant whatever equal exemptions they wanted.[17] Similarly Congressman William Lawrence of Ohio agreed that the 1866 act did "not declare who shall or shall not have the right to sue, give evidence, inherit, purchase, and sell property. These questions are left to the States to determine."[18]

The theme that section one of the Fourteenth Amendment did not direct states either to adopt or not to adopt particular legislation, but merely required that legislation treat all people equally, was reiterated again and again. The substance of section one, according to Thaddeus Stevens, required only that "the same laws must and shall apply to every mortal, American, Irishman, African, German or Turk."[19] It was essential, according to George S. Boutwell, that the lowliest "citizen should enjoy the highest privileges that appertain to citizenship in the State or city of which he is a citizen."[20] Or, as Thaddeus

Stevens explained on another occasion, an early variant of section one barred Congress from "interfer[ing] in any case where the legislation of the State was equal, impartial to all," authorizing federal action only in cases where a state "makes a distinction" in its law between different individuals of the same class.[21] Jacob M. Howard similarly told the Senate that section one abolished "all class legislation in the States and [did] away with the injustice of subjecting one caste of persons to a code not applicable to another."[22] In the language of Representative James F. Wilson, distinctions and limitations in statutes "must always be just and impartial" and required for "the good of the whole,"[23] while in the words of a member of the Pennsylvania legislature that ratified the amendment, section one would "prohibit any judge . . . from looking at the wealth or poverty, the intelligence or ignorance, the condition and surroundings, or even the color of the skin, of any person coming before him" and require the judge "to look solely at the merits of the claim."[24]

This interpretation of section one as a guarantee of equal rather than absolute rights solved the Republican dilemma of wanting to give Congress power to protect rights without giving it power to destroy state legislative freedom. It is also especially helpful in solving a puzzle that has plagued Fourteenth Amendment historiography for a century—the puzzle of incorporation of the Bill of Rights. Throughout the congressional debates on section one, supporters of the provision argued that it would give Congress power to compel states to abide by the first ten amendments. John A. Bingham, the author of section one, argued that the "immortal bill of rights" embodied in the original Constitution rested for its enforcement on the states,[25] eleven of which had failed to enforce it and thereby rendered it "a mere dead letter."[26] Bingham, however, found it "absolutely essential to the safety of the people that it should be enforced" and therefore asked for "the additional grant of power" ultimately contained in section one, noting that those "who oppose[d] this amendment" were simply "oppos[ing] the grant of power to enforce the bill of rights."[27] Jacob Howard, floor manager of the amendment in the Senate, also contended that the privileges and immunities clause of section one comprehended

> the personal rights guarantied and secured by the first eight amendments of the Constitution; such as the freedom of speech and of the press; the right of the people peaceably to assemble

and petition the Government for a redress of grievances, a right appertaining to each and all the people; the right to keep and to bear arms; the right to be exempted from the quartering of soldiers in a house without the consent of the owner; the right to be exempt from unreasonable searches and seizures, and from any search or seizure except by virtue of a warrant issued upon a formal oath or affidavit; the right of an accused person to be informed of the nature of the accusation against him, and his right to be tried by an impartial jury of the vicinage; and also the right to be secure against excessive bail and against cruel and unusual punishments.[28]

Statements such as these have proved puzzling to historians because several Northern states, on which the Fourteenth Amendment, it was said, would have no effect, were not abiding by all the provisions of the first eight amendments, in particular the provision of the Fifth Amendment requiring the institution of criminal proceedings by grand jury indictment. Nonetheless these states undertook ratification of the amendment without objecting to or even discussing the impact that application of the Bill of Rights would have on their criminal process, and after ratification they made no changes in their criminal law. Some historians have therefore concluded that legislators in these states must not have known that section one would require obedience to the Bill of Rights; the historians then argue that the Fourteenth Amendment ought not be given an interpretation of which those who ratified it were unaware.[29] Other scholars, however, give greater weight to the statements of congressional leaders like Bingham and Howard and, despite their puzzlement at the behavior of states that did not abide by all of the first eight amendments, conclude that section one imposes the Bill of Rights on the states.[30]

Understanding section one as an instrument for the equal rather than absolute protection of rights resolves the contradiction in the evidence that has so puzzled historians. American states in the mid-nineteenth century did, in fact, provide their citizens with most of the protections contained in the Bill of Rights, including those mentioned by Jacob Howard in his presentation of the Fourteenth Amendment to the Senate. But the eleven states to which Bingham referred, together with a few other states, had failed to give the rights to their black citizens. By virtue of its guarantee of equality, section one would authorize Congress to rectify that failure and thus enable Bingham to declare that Congress would have power to enforce the

Bill of Rights. But at the same time the amendment would have no impact in a state that allowed the institution of criminal proceedings by information rather than indictment: a state would be free to disregard entirely a provision of the Bill of Rights such as the guarantee of grand jury indictment, and Congress would have no power to intervene. By understanding section one as an equality guarantee, the puzzle of how Congress could simultaneously have power to enforce the Bill of Rights and not have power to impose a specific provision of the Bill on a state is resolved.

Not all the Republican proponents of the Fourteenth Amendment, however, were prepared to interpret section one merely as a grant of equal rights. Consistently with their antislavery backgrounds, some Republicans believed that the Fourteenth Amendment guaranteed protection for specific fundamental rights derived from higher law or from the nature of citizenship in a republic. Other leading Republicans, such as Bingham, spoke on occasion as if section one guaranteed nothing more than equality, but at other times they interpreted it as a guarantor of absolute rights.

Republicans who gave the Fourteenth Amendment an absolute rights reading had an especially difficult time rebutting Democratic claims that the amendment would undermine the states. The economic and personal rights for which they were advocating federal protection were coextensive with rights in the domain of state legislative jurisdiction, and it was difficult to understand how, if Congress had absolute power to legislate with reference to them, any power would remain to the states.

Nonetheless a few Republican thinkers ventured an explanation: even if fundamental rights were derived from higher law or were the entitlement of citizens independent of state law, those rights could be enjoyed only if state legislatures created rules and mechanisms for their enjoyment. Republican supporters of the Fourteenth Amendment maintained that the legislatures would still be empowered to create those rules and mechanisms when the amendment took effect. As James F. Wilson, chairman of the House Judiciary Committee explained, "the rights" which a person "possesse[d] as a citizen of the United States" could "only be secured to him by laws which operate within the State in which he resides."[31] During a debate on an early draft of section one, Congressman Bingham elaborated upon Wilson's point in response to a question whether the proposed amendment would "give to Congress the power to enforce all the rights of married women in the several States."[32] Bingham talked of "rights which are universal," including the "rights of life and liberty." Apparently Bingham regarded "the right of property in married women" as another such right, observing that "this word property has been in your bill of rights from the year 1780 until this hour." But property, he continued, could only be held in accordance with the law of some state:

> [W]ho ever heard it intimated that anybody could have property, protected in any State until he owned or acquired property there according to its local law. . . . I undertake to say no one.
> As to real estate, every one knows that its acquisition and transmission under every interpretation ever given to the word property, as used in the Constitution of the country, are dependent exclusively upon the local law of the States . . . But suppose any person has acquired property not contrary to the laws of the State, but in accordance with its law, are they not to be equally protected in the enjoyment of it, or are they to be denied all protection?[33]

"[T]he whole question"[34] raised by the proposed section one, according to Bingham, was not whether federal constitutional law could create rights of property, for it could not: those rights arose pursuant to some higher law, to some conception of citizens' rights, or to some state law. The proposed section one thus did not threaten state lawmaking power, but merely brought federal power to bear to help enforce the law that states made.

During the course of the debates on the Fifteenth Amendment, Senator George F. Edmunds of Vermont spelled out his understanding of the Fourteenth; it was much the same as Bingham's. Like Bingham, Edmunds drew a distinction between a right itself and the regulation of the right. "Every lawyer," he explained, "knows . . . that it is one thing to have a right which is absolute and inalienable, and it is another thing for the body of the community to regulate . . . the exercise of that right." Edmunds pointed out that, although liberty was clearly a fundamental right that merited constitutional protection,

> yet I may be daily deprived of my liberty under the regulations of the State, which apply to us all alike. If I am deprived of it, rightfully or wrongfully, I can only get restored to it by the

process of the law under the regulations that legislation shall provide. My friend admits that one of the privileges of a citizen of the United States is to hold property. Where is he to hold it? He must hold it in some State or Territory, must he not? Now, then, is he to acquire it in spite of the State law by an instrument unwitnessed, unsealed, unsigned? By no means. He must conform to the regulation of the local law which declares that his deed must be witnessed by two witnesses, must be sealed, must be acknowledged, must be delivered. And yet no man here thought of supposing that a privilege of a citizen was denied, although it is confessedly by my friend agreed to be a privilege, from the fact that the States regulate the exercise of it . . . [E]verybody knows that a right may be perfectly secure and yet be subject to regulation.[35]

In a like vein, the test for Senator Lot M. Morrill of Maine was whether a state regulation could be defended "on the ground of rationality."[36]

With these two arguments, the proponents of the Fourteenth Amendment strove to explain why it gave little new power to the federal government. The first argument, which many in the Republican party accepted, was that the amendment left the states free to grant or deny whatever rights they wanted and gave the federal government power only to make certain that the states distributed the rights they granted equally. Some Republicans, however, appear to have thought that section one protected rights absolutely. A few of these conceded that, even if the amendment would compel states to protect basic rights that Northern states had always protected and that Southern states had protected for whites, the states would be left in possession of the most important of their powers: the power to enact specific, detailed regulations of the conditions under which rights would be enjoyed. The only new power that the Fourteenth Amendment would give to Congress and the federal courts would be to ensure that states regulated rights reasonably, which, as Senator Edmunds explained, meant "equally and fairly."[37]

It is hard to know exactly what to make of this last argument. Perhaps its practical effect was merely to transform an amendment that some of its proponents hoped would "place the fundamental rights of the citizens directly under the safeguard of the General Government"[38] into one that only required the states to apply their regulations equally. Many Republicans were prepared so to interpret section one, and such an interpretation is especially useful in explaining the otherwise inconsistent rhetoric of leading figures such as Bingham, who read section one at times as an equality provision and at other times as an absolute rights provision: it may be that Bingham could switch back and forth randomly between the two interpretations since for him both had the same operative effect. But it is difficult to understand how other Republicans, who apparently favored absolute protection of fundamental rights, could accept a limitation on section one that deprived the section of precisely that effect.

A solution to this puzzle could lie in the fact that the framing generation anticipated that Congress rather than the courts would be the principal enforcer of section one. Unlike courts, which in Fourteenth Amendment cases can only act interstitially to invalidate state legislation shown to be unreasonable or, what is the equivalent, unequal, Congress may have authority pursuant to its section five enforcement power to act in the first instance to protect the rights guaranteed under section one. In the context of this first instance power, there may be a difference between a state's duty to legislate equally and its power to regulate rights reasonably, even when the concept of reasonableness is understood to mean equality. If section one guarantees nothing beyond equality, then Congress's section five enforcement power would have a limited scope analogous to the interstitial power of the courts: Congress could legislate only upon a proper showing that state law discriminated unequally. In contrast, if section one is read as a basic guarantee of absolute rights, then Congress's section five power would support the passage of any legislation designed to protect those rights. Of course states would still retain their power to regulate the rights reasonably or equally, but this state power would not necessarily preclude congressional legislation. State regulation would have to operate in some other fashion as, for example, by incorporating it, under an unconventional approach to federalism, to fill in gaps in Congress's laws.[39]

No evidence exists that the framers or ratifiers of the Fourteenth Amendment ever contemplated an approach of this sort to the matter of reasonable state regulation of constitutionally protected rights. The fact is that no one in 1866 was engaging in precise doctrinal analysis of what the concept of reasonableness might mean. Although the dichotomy between interpretating section one as a guarantee of absolute rights subject to reasonable regulation or understanding it merely as a guarantee of equality would soon become central in litigation in both the federal and the state courts, the distinction was only beginning to emerge in 1866. Most Americans in that year continued to conflate absolute conceptions of higher law and citizens' rights with notions of equality, as they had done throughout the antebellum era. Members of Congress and the state legislatures were more concerned with the articulation of rhetorical principles that might inspire sound civic behavior than with the elaboration of precise doctrine that could be used to control faulty conduct. Only a few congressmen who were closely involved in the drafting and enactment of section one may have begun to appreciate the doctrinal distinction between an equality amendment and a rights amendment, and they do not appear to have seen the difference very clearly.

Only one historical conclusion can therefore be drawn: namely, that Congress and the state legislatures never specified whether section one was intended to be simply an equality provision or a provision protecting absolute rights as well. Historical analysis of the framing and ratification of the Fourteenth Amendment cannot, by itself, resolve the dilemma created by the conflicting commitments of those who participated in the process. Judges and lawyers wishing to be guided only by the original intention cannot know whether to construe the amendment as a guarantor of absolute rights.

History also fails to provide a definitive answer to another question. If an interpreter, by some means other than recourse to original intention, concludes that section one guarantees fundamental rights absolutely, he must next determine what fundamental rights the section protects. Unfortunately the history of the Fourteenth Amendment's adoption will give him little guidance in identifying these rights. Those who framed and ratified it had a set response whenever they were asked to specify the fundamental rights within its umbrella. They refused to answer. Jacob Howard's opening speech during the Senate debate on the Fourteenth Amendment will illustrate. According to Howard, the fundamental rights or privileges and immunities of citizens could not "be fully defined in their entire extent and precise nature," and therefore he declined "to go at length into that question at this time." He added, "It would be a somewhat barren discussion."[40] He did quote extensively from *Corfield v. Coryell*, where Justice Washington had found the enumeration of rights "tedious,"[41] even though he had proceeded to enumerate some of them. But in the end, neither Howard nor any other participant in the congressional and state ratification debates was willing to be pinned down. Howard seemed to think that questions about the specification of fundamental rights would have to be "discussed and adjudicated" on a case-by-case basis "when they should happen practically to arise,"[42] and in view of his failure and the failure of his contemporaries to identify the rights they wanted to protect, he was surely correct.

Of course, the Fourteenth Amendment might be read to protect only equal rather than absolute rights. But then an interpreter seeking guidance from the intentions of the framers must inquire how they distinguished between fair and equal legislation, on the one hand, and arbitrary and irrational discrimination, on the other. In respect to this question, the congressmen and legislators who voted on the amendment engaged in somewhat more useful analysis.

Indeed, there was one point on which nearly all Republicans agreed. No Republican was prepared, as a matter of general principle, to defend as rational a distinction grounded in race.[43] Republicans found "prejudice against race" irrational and "unaccountable," having "its origin in the greed and selfishness of a fallen world" and "belong[ing] to an age of darkness and violence."[44] Iowa's Congressman Wilson thought that "if all our citizens were of one race and one color we would be relieved of most of the difficulties which surround us"; legislation like the Civil Rights Act of 1866 and section one of the Fourteenth Amendment "would be almost, if not entirely, unnecessary."[45] But in the America that existed in 1866 such legislation was needed. As Ohio's Samuel Shellabarger explained to the House:

> Its whole effect is to require that whatever rights . . . the States may confer upon one race or color of the citizens shall be held by all races in equality. Your State may deprive women of the right to sue or contract or testify, and children from doing the same. But if you do so, or do not [do] so as to one race, you shall treat the other likewise. It does not prohibit you from discriminating between citizens of the same race, or of different races, as to what their rights to testify, to inherit, &c., shall be. But if you do discriminate, it must not be "on account of race, color, or former condition of slavery." That is all. If you permit a white man who is an infidel to testify, so you must a colored infidel. . . . It secures—not to all citizens, but to all races as races who are

citizens—equality of protection in those enumerated civil rights which the States may deem proper to confer upon any races.[46]

Even in regard to issues of race, however, there were some disagreements and divisions among Republicans. The most important dispute was whether section one provided a basis for arguing that any blacks were entitled to exercise the right to vote. As the Republicans focused upon this issue, however, it quickly became apparent that it consisted of two distinct subissues: first, whether the Fourteenth Amendment granted anyone the right to vote, and second, whether the amendment spoke at all to the issue of exclusion of blacks from the elective franchise.

The statement most frequently made in debates on the Fourteenth Amendment is that it did not, in and of itself, confer upon blacks or anyone else the right to vote. As William P. Fessenden told the Senate when he presented an early version of the amendment, he personally would have preferred an amendment that did away at once with all distinctions in political rights grounded in race. But, he added, he stood before the Senate as an "organ" of a committee that "did not recommend a provision of that description," and he "approv[ed] what they have done, and [was] not disposed to urge my own peculiar views."[47] Fessenden explained later that "the majority were of a different opinion [from him], not that they differed with me at all in their views with regard to what ought to be done; but they believe[d] it would be impossible at that time to carry it through Congress or to obtain for it the support of the requisite number of States."[48] Iowa's James F. Wilson, chairman of the House Judiciary Committee, reiterated Fessenden's point during the House debates on the Fourteenth Amendment:

> If we will but do our duty as well as we know it . . . , we will leave to posterity little ground to complain of us. We know that impartial suffrage in the insurgent States would leave but little for posterity to quarrel over; but the fall elections lie between us and posterity, and some fear the result of the former more than they consider the welfare of the latter. . . . We will stop short of what most of us know we ought to do.[49]

On the basis of statements such as these, historians have typically concluded that, although many Republican leaders favored granting suffrage to the freedmen, their constituents did not. Historians have pointed out how, during 1866 and 1867, Republicans lost several elections in states where suffrage for blacks was at issue, apparently because of constituents' hostility to black voting. Historians have finally suggested that as a result of this fear of constituents, the Fourteenth Amendment had nothing to do with the right to vote.[50]

Some congressmen did assert that the Fourteenth Amendment affected only civil and not political rights, of which the right to vote was one. For them suffrage was merely "a political right which has been left under the control of the several States, subject to the action of Congress only when it becomes necessary to enforce the guarantee of a republican form of government."[51] As Thaddeus Stevens declared in a succinct campaign statement, section one of the amendment "does not touch . . . political rights,"[52] while Governor Joshua L. Chamberlain of Maine, in presenting the amendment for ratification, noted that it left states free to disfranchise blacks.[53] *The Right Way*, despite its radicalism, similarly stated that only civil and not political rights were comprehended within the term privileges and immunities,[54] and several correspondents of congressmen also thought that the Fourteenth Amendment did not give blacks "the absolute right to vote"[55] or "give the National Legislature discretionary power to enlarge . . . the elective franchise in the States."[56] Indeed, ratification of the amendment was opposed by some Massachusetts radicals precisely for this reason.[57] The point was best made by Aaron H. Cragin, a Republican senator from New Hampshire, when he spoke in 1869 during the debates on the Fifteenth Amendment:

> . . . I remember the struggle that we had here in the passage of the fourteenth amendment; . . . I remember that it was announced upon this floor by more than one gentleman, and contradicted and denied by no one so far as I recollect, that that amendment did not confer the right of voting upon anybody. . . . There is no doubt upon the question. It was the understanding of Congress and of the people of this country that that amendment did not confer and did not seek to confer any right to vote upon any citizen of the United States. . . . [T]hat it conferred the right to vote was distinctly disclaimed on this floor in the caucus which has been alluded to here to-night; and, for one, I am not willing to have it go out from this Senate that we passed that amendment understanding that it conferred any right to vote.[58]

Cragin's point was reiterated constantly in congressional and state legislative proceedings and in the newspapers. Thus Senator Jacob M.

Howard, the floor manager of the Fourteenth Amendment, later recalled that the amendment "[p]lainly and in the clearest possible terms recogniz[ed] the right of each State to regulate the suffrage,"[59] which, he explained, was "not . . . a natural, inalienable right," but merely "a conventional right."[60] Roscoe Conkling of New York likewise said of the amendment that "by the unmistakable force of its language the regulation of suffrage in the States belongs to the States themselves,"[61] while a Republican member of the Massachusetts ratifying legislature called the Fourteenth Amendment "another compromise with slavery" since it gave the South a "tyrannical power" to deny blacks the right to vote.[62] In a like vein, the *Worcester Daily Spy* observed that the amendment left "the political rights of one class of citizens to be abridged or denied at the discretion of another class,"[63] and the *Essex County Mercury* noted that the "republican representatives of New York, Ohio and Indiana, and perhaps one or two other States . . . took strong grounds against the interference by Congress with suffrage in the States."[64]

Some Republicans, however, took a different view. Not every Republican accepted the distinction between civil and political rights; in the words of Senator Richard Yates, "the people" did "not understand that argument which says that Congress may confer upon a man his civil rights and not his political rights. It is the pleading of a lawyer; it is too narrow for statesmanship."[65] In North Carolina the *Newbern Daily Times* also drew no line between civil and political rights when it observed that section one gave blacks "political equality as far as any legislation of Congress can do it," together with the right to "acquire and hold property just as any other citizen." Although the paper objected to other portions of the amendment, including the enforcement power granted to Congress in section five, it urged that the enforcement of section one by the "judiciary" would be "beneficial" since the equal protection of blacks would "stimulate" them to equal "industry, enterprise and economy."[66]

Republicans such as these accepted the conclusion that the Fourteenth Amendment did not confer the right to vote on anyone, but then they further argued that the amendment did require the states to confer that right in a nonarbitrary, equal fashion and that exclusion of all blacks from the franchise constituted an arbitrary, unequal discrimination. It was the same argument made elsewhere: that the

Fourteenth Amendment did not confer any rights but did require that all rights be administered equally.

The argument was expressed with lawyerly precision by J. H. Martindale, the Attorney General of New York:

> [N]early all the precedents in the General & State Govts. up to the time of the late amendment abolishing slavery have recognized the power to classify the inhabitants of African descent, and to deprive them of political & civil rights. As to them, exclusion from the suffrage has not been the result of a want of intelligence to acquire property or education, or any other qualifications, which by the customs of the country, and the Constitution of the U.S. might be imposed by the several States, on the electors of public officers. The disability of the negro penetrated deeper than the rules of *qualification* for the ballot; which rules simply define some conditions that an honest, diligent, & intelligent citizen may usually acquire. His disability was one of caste or class, which made him and his race *liable to be enslaved*. . . . The amendment to the constitution has abolished the liability and all its consequences. . . . There does not remain a logical argument on which to rest the exclusion of the native born black man from all the civil and political rights inherent in citizenship.
>
> No States, North or South, have the constitutional right to classify him & degrade him because he is black, any more than they have the constitutional right to classify and degrade white men. Clearly the States have the power to prescribe equal and impartial qualifications for electors of their legislatures. . . . They may depend on property or intelligence. Universal suffrage is not the constitutional right of white, any more than colored men.[67]

The *Chicago Republican* took a similar view when it noted that the Fourteenth Amendment "recognize[d] the whole body of the people as entitled to political equality" even though it did "not establish negro suffrage" and "concede[d] to each State the exclusive privilege of regulating the elective franchise within its own limits."[68] George Landon, a Republican legislator from Pennsylvania, likewise thought that the amendment "guarantee[d] to all persons born upon American soil the privileges of citizenship, and the immunities of impartial suffrage before the law."[69] Proponents of impartial suffrage reiterated the same position on the floor of Congress when they sought to explain how the Fourteenth Amendment affected state control over suffrage. When he presented the Fourteenth Amendment on the floor of the House, Bingham declared somewhat elliptically that all agreed that "the exercise of the elective franchise, though it be one of the privileges of a citizen of the Republic, is exclusively under the control of the states."[70] Likewise Senator Jacob M. Howard, serving as floor manager of the amendment in the Senate, declared unequivocally that section one did "not give to either of these classes [whites or blacks] the right of voting." It did, however, "establish . . . equality before the law, and . . . give . . . to the humblest, the poorest, the most despised of the race the same rights and the same protection before the law as it gives to the most powerful, the most wealthy, or the most haughty."[71] A far clearer statement was made by Senator Richard Yates when, during debates on the Fifteenth Amendment, Republicans engaged in a bitter wrangle over whether the Fourteenth Amendment already guaranteed equality of voting rights. Yates conceded that "the question of suffrage properly belonged to the States."[72] Nevertheless he maintained that the Fifteenth Amendment, which was also said "not [to] take away the right of the State to control" the franchise but only to bar discrimination on racial grounds,[73] added nothing to the Fourteenth. Yates argued that, although a black had no independent right to vote under the Fourteenth, "he was entitled to vote just as much as though he were white." If nobody denied the vote to whites, Yates asked, "was not the black citizen entitled to vote?" For, as Yates explained, he was "utterly unable to see the difference between the two" except by recourse to what he called "the prejudice of caste."[74]

Bingham also spoke with clarity on some occasions, although not in the debates on the Fourteenth Amendment itself. Thus he declared in 1867 that "[i]t is a guarantied right of every State in this Union to regulate for itself the elective franchise within its limits, subject to no condition whatever except that it shall not . . . transform the State government from one republican in form."[75] This principle of republican government meant "that the majority ought to rule, subject to the equal right of the minority to the same rights with themselves without regard to color."[76] Bingham further suggested that an early draft of section two of the amendment, although it did not give blacks any right to vote, would result in reduction of a state's representation if the state adopted "class legislation which would operate injuriously upon colored people." He went on to add that "if that legislation be general and not class legislation in its character, applying to the white population as well as to the black population, the standard of intelligence for instance, this proposed amendment to the Constitution would not operate." Upon further questioning, he gave the following example:

> [I]f for example, in South Carolina, when that State comes to be recognized, it is generally provided, without regard to race or color, generally provided by law that no citizen of South Carolina shall vote unless such citizen shall be able to read the English language, in that case this provision does not operate to the exclusion of her enfranchised black population who come up to that standard. But if, on the other hand, South Carolina shall by law expressly declare that no colored citizen of the State shall vote unless he can read the English language, leaving the ignorant white man to vote, then this provision declares that South Carolina shall not be entitled to representation upon her black population.[77]

Bingham also spoke clearly in 1868, two months before the Fourteenth Amendment was ratified. At that time he proposed that the Southern states be readmitted to the Union on the condition that "civil and political rights and privileges shall be forever equally secured in said States to all citizens of the United States resident therein." Speaking in support of his proposal, he noted that "if the words 'civil and political rights and privileges of citizens' do not embrace the elective franchise, it is a new discovery to the American people." He also argued that the right to legislate in support of equal voting rights came from "[t]he fourteenth article of the amendments of the Constitution."[78]

Bingham was not the only member of the Thirty-ninth Congress who, after adoption of the Fourteenth Amendment, argued that it guaranteed equality of voting rights even though it did not confer the right to vote on anyone. Charles Sumner, for one, vehemently denied the claim that the Fourteenth Amendment had nothing to do with voting rights. According to Sumner:

> [T]hat was denied at that time, and it would not have passed the Senate had anybody attributed to it that meaning. That I am able to say. It could not have passed the Senate. The Senator knows very well that there was an amendment, as it came from the House of Representatives, that was susceptible of such an interpretation; and I felt it my duty to oppose it, which I did at great length and most elaborately, precisely on the ground that it did abandon to the States the power to discriminate against

colored persons; I refused to support that amendment, and I associated myself with others in that refusal.[79]

Senator Richard Yates confirmed that "[t]he Fourteenth Amendment was worded as it was because of the position assumed by the Senator from Massachusetts and myself and certain other persons in the Senate whom it is not necessary to mention. We maintained that Congress had the power by congressional law to enforce suffrage upon all the States in every section of the Union."[80] Senator George F. Edmunds of Vermont was also

> one of those ... who believe that the fourteenth amendment which we have already adopted has undertaken to secure to citizens of the United States all the privileges and immunities that belong to citizens as such, including, of course, and comprehending all belonging to the class. There is no qualification or limitation, but words the most comprehensive possible in a statute or in a constitution are used. I believe that every citizen of the United States in respect to whom political rights can be asserted at all is entitled now to exercise political privileges, ... that [the] amendment extended to all the citizens similarly situated, without arbitrary and mere fanciful distinctions, such as color, nativity, education, or of religion, an equal right.[81]

Congressman John M. Broomall of Pennsylvania also thought the Fourteenth Amendment gave Congress power to legislate in reference to voting rights. In discussing the proposed Fifteenth Amendment, he argued that the right to vote ought to be placed expressly in the Constitution, even though "we have already the power to effect the same thing by legislation," since "[l]aws may be repealed, and it is not advisable that so important a principle of republican government should be left to the caprices of party."[82] Even the moderate Senator John Sherman believed in 1868 that if legislation setting residency requirements for voting "was aimed against a citizen or a class of citizens it would be unconstitutional; but if it was aimed at all persons who had not resided within the State for a certain length of time it would be clearly constitutional."[83]

Similar ideas emerged in state ratification debates. In the Oregon legislature, for example, one opponent of the Fourteenth Amendment urged that, "if this measure does not in fact carry with it, it will surely bring in [the] future, universal suffrage."[84] When a supporter of the amendment "scouted the idea that this measure proposes to force negro suffrage upon any State," he did not deny the possibility, but only suggested that it was "unwise to trouble ourselves here," since Oregon had few black residents. He then added, "Let the States that have negroes manage that matter for themselves."[85] Governor Oglesby of Illinois, in presenting the amendment to the legislature, praised section one for securing citizenship and "all the political and civil rights citizenship confers."[86] Governor Wells of Louisiana similarly assumed that the Fourteenth Amendment conferred power on Congress "to require of these States ... that they shall ... recognize and establish equal political rights in the privilege of the ballot, to all men,"[87] while the Committee on Federal Relations of the Texas House of Representatives urged that the amendment not be ratified since its privileges and immunities clause would embrace "the exercise of suffrage at the polls, participation in jury duty in all cases, bearing arms in the militia, and other matters which need not be here enumerated."[88] Governor Oliver P. Morton took no position on the Fourteenth Amendment's impact on suffrage when he presented it to the Indiana legislature for ratification, but he did claim that Congress had "vast" power over suffrage pursuant to the guarantee clause.[89]

Competing interpretations, in short, were placed upon the understanding widely shared in 1866 that the Fourteenth Amendment did not confer on blacks the right to vote. Members of Congress had differing views on the many issues about suffrage that arose in the course of the Reconstruction amendments debates. One view was that the amendment concerned only civil rights and not political rights and hence had nothing at all to do with voting.[90] Another was that, although the amendment did not confer the right to vote on anyone, it did require that the States confer the right in a nonarbitrary, equal fashion. Congress, as a collective body, never decided or even addressed the question of whose views and interpretation would be enacted into law by adoption of the Fourteenth Amendment. After considering most of the voting rights questions that have faced the Supreme Court in the century since the Fourteenth Amendment's ratification—including questions as far removed from the issues of Reconstruction as state legislative reapportionment[91]—Congress simply adopted the broad, sweeping and vague language of section one which, in the view of some earlier authorities, applied to voting rights, and, in the view of others, did not.[92] Congress never determined, in its details, what section one meant in reference to the many voting rights issues that it discussed.

Segregation was another issue of periodic concern in the decade after the Civil War. Indeed, even before the war had ended, issues similar to those raised by segregation began to emerge in Congress, as it engaged in debates about school policy and streetcar discrimination in the District of Columbia and heard arguments that white people ought not be compelled to associate with blacks. Some congressmen responded to those arguments, but Congress as an institution acted inconsistently, taking no clear stand on the segregation issue. On the one hand, Congress authorized funding for a segregated public school system in Washington, D.C., albeit without ever considering a desegregated system as an option. On the other hand, Congress required streetcar companies there to accept black passengers in the same accommodations as whites, albeit without ever considering the option of separate seating in the streetcars for the two races.[93]

When the Fourteenth Amendment itself was under consideration, segregation was not an important national issue. Indeed, there was no direct discussion during the ratification debates of any of the issues subsequently raised by *Plessy* v. *Ferguson* or *Brown* v. *Board of Education*. On the one hand, key Republican leaders like Senators William P. Fessenden and Lyman Trumbull gave assurances that the 1866 Civil Rights Act—the forerunner of section one of the amendment—did not render Southern antimiscegenation laws unconstitutional.[94] And Charles Sumner's resolution that no Southern state be readmitted to the Union until it had established "an educational system for the equal benefit of all, without distinction of color or race"[95] made little progress in Congress. On the other hand, occasional arguments that adherence to the principle of equality precluded segregation in the schools appeared in local newspapers. Thus, the *Weekly North-Carolina Standard* reported a debate in the state legislature in which one representative, after observing that "[t]he government was founded upon the fundamental idea that all were equal," added that he "would prefer that the two races should not be educated together, and that they should not intermarry." But, he continued, "the [new state] Constitution, just adopted, had neither the word 'white' nor the word 'black' in it, and therefore class legislation, so far as mere color is concerned, was gone forever." He viewed segregation in the schools as "the same in principle as saying that the whites should sit on the floor of the House, and the blacks in the lobby."[96] In the same spirit a New York editor wrote a series of editorials condemning local voters after they had refused to provide funds for the education of black children except in a separate, overcrowded room.[97] And, as a correspondent of this editor added:

> Either all thus [sic] bluster of words about equality before the law, and before the Source of all justice, means something or nothing, and those who use it and yet refuse to practice it, are trying to cheat the negro and practice a fraud upon white people. . . . [I]f he practices what he preaches, he has no right to exclude any one from such social amenities on *account of race and color*, and all of you negro equality advocates . . . have no right to bar a negro from paying his addresses to your daughters *on account of race and color*. If the negro is the white man's equal before God, before man, and before the law, what other equality of rights can he aspire to? and is it not a transparent piece of jugglery for any one entertaining these views, to deny the effect of their words and affect an indignant nausea at the idea of "eating, drinking and sleeping with negroes."
>
> For myself, I exclude no one from social amenities on account of race, or color. No black man or woman is offensive to me because black. Such people have been to my house, eat at my table, slept in my beds, and will enjoy all these amenities again, long before their oppressors and defamers, and thankers of God that they are better than a negro, will be invited there, or welcome if they come without invitation.[98]

As the correspondent also noted, "[A]ny difference of race or color which is a bar to *intermarriage*, is an equal bar to *education*, suffrage and freedom!"[99] A Connecticut editor also took the view that the grant of equal rights would affect education, when he argued that the Civil Rights Act entitled blacks to "the benefit of the school tax which is now applied to the benefit of white children alone, although levied upon both white and black,"[100] and in Illinois it appears that Republicans were engaged in the spring of 1866 in imposing integration on the school systems of several major towns and cities, including Chicago.[101] Further evidence that at least some members of Congress and the state legislatures may have appreciated the capacity of the Fourteenth Amendment to promote desegregation lies in several widely reported court cases in the spring of 1866, in which blacks urged that the 1866 Civil Rights Act required racial integration.[102]

It bears remembering, though, that nearly two decades earlier the highest court of the most radical state in the Union—the Supreme

Judicial Court of Massachusetts—had in *Roberts* v. *City of Boston*[103] rejected the claim that the equality clause of the Massachusetts constitution mandated integrated schools. Historians who conclude that most Americans in 1866 favored segregated schools are probably correct in their assessment.[104] Nonetheless, it is also important to focus on the fact that Congress never institutionalized this judgment in its debates on the Fourteenth Amendment; the segregation issue simply was not an important one in those debates.

The issue was important, however, in the debates of the 1870s culminating in the adoption of the Civil Rights Act of 1875,[105] the constitutional foundation of which was section one of the Fourteenth Amendment. But here again Congress took an ambiguous position about what the Fourteenth Amendment authorized and what it, Congress, should legislate. As originally proposed, the 1875 act guaranteed blacks equal access not only to public accommodations and conveyances, but to public schools as well. Did those schools have to be integrated in order to be equal? A Republican senator from California, Aaron A. Sargent, sought to clarify the issue with the following amendment:

> *Provided*, That nothing herein contained shall be construed to prohibit any State or school district from providing separate schools for persons of different sex or color, where such separate schools are equal in all respects to others of the same grade established by such authority, and supported by an equal *pro rata* expenditure of school funds.[106]

Sargent's amendment was defeated, however, by a close 21–26 vote, with 26 senators absent.[107]

In the House John Roy Lynch, a black congressman from Mississippi, assured his colleagues that adoption of the bill would not require states to maintain racially mixed schools,[108] and a proviso authorizing separate but equal schools was attached to the bill in committee. The response of the full House, by an overwhelming 128–48 vote, was to delete the proviso together with the original bill's reference to public schools. When a motion was made to substitute the language of the Senate bill, with its ambiguous language of equal access to public schools, the House defeated the motion on a 114–148 vote.[109] As finally passed by both Houses, the 1875 act followed the language of the House bill and said nothing either about public schools or about whether integration was an essential element of equality.

Several conclusions follow from the legislative history of the 1875 act. The Senate appears to have taken one of two positions when it rejected language explicitly authorizing school segregation: either the Senate wanted federal law to require integration or it wanted federal law to remain ambiguous. The House in 1875 wished to do nothing in reference to civil rights in schools, and the Senate ultimately concurred. At no point in the lengthy debates on the Civil Rights Act of 1875, however, did either the House or the Senate express in unambiguous, institutional form its views on the meaning of the Fourteenth Amendment in reference to school or other forms of segregation.

Another issue, on which there was near unanimity at least as to result, was raised by women's claims for equality. Women objected to "backward legislation" that secured "suffrage but to another shade of *man*hood, while we disfranchise fifteen million tax-payers" and "come not one line nearer the republican idea." They urged that "[t]o build a true republic" women had to "come forth with new strength and dignity" from "the baptism of this second revolution."[110] Even their opponents had little doubt that women would "succeed sooner or later, for ideas do not go backwards."[111]

Many of the demands of the women's movement had a quite modern ring. Consider, for example, an 1867 newspaper article on "The Wages of Women," which spoke not only about women "born to poverty," but also about "carefully reared, well educated, accomplished" women who "by the death of fathers or husbands, or by those vicissitudes of fortune" found it necessary to labor. These women were "naturally bewildered and dismayed," as they found "the market . . . over-stocked" and discovered that men "have the preference." Worst of all was *"that, even in cases where the ability is equal, the man gets twice the remuneration of the woman,"* even though "[n]o one charges a woman less than a man when she is the purchaser." The article concluded that "[e]mployers of women take advantage of . . . their necessities to beat them down to starvation rates"—something it found "radically and indefensibly wrong."[112] Similarly, an article on "The Employment of Women" argued that it was "too late in the day to deny the capacity of woman for any pursuit in life that does not, by reason of exposure, hardship, and privation, interdict her engagement in it." Not only should a woman "be welcomed to any profession or avocation in life that her inclination or interest prompts her to adopt," but "she should be educated to one or the other of them" as well.[113]

Congress, however, was quite uniform in refusing to address questions of women's rights in Reconstruction legislation. Even supporters of women's rights concurred. Consider, for example, Senator Henry Wilson, who was prepared to "vote now or at any time for woman suffrage, if . . . offer[ed] . . . as a distinct, separate measure." But Wilson was "unalterably opposed to connecting that question with the pending question of negro suffrage. The question of negro suffrage is now an imperative necessity; a necessity that the negro should possess it for his own protection; a necessity that he should possess it that the nation may preserve its power, its strength, and its unity."[114] Richard Yates of Illinois was also "for suffrage by females as well as males; but that is not the point before us."[115] Likewise Ohio's Benjamin F. Wade agreed "that there is not the same pressing necessity for allowing females as there is for allowing the colored people to vote; because the ladies of the land are not under the ban of a hostile race grinding them to powder."[116] In any event, Wade would not "have agitated it now, although it is as clear to me as the sun at noonday that the time is approaching when females will be admitted to this franchise."[117] Even the great reformer Charles Sumner wanted to leave the question "whether women shall be invested with the elective franchise . . . untouched, contenting myself with saying, that it is obviously the great question of the future, which will be easily settled, whenever the women in any considerable proportion insist that it shall be settled."[118] For nearly all Republicans, "the enfranchisement of women and the enfranchisement of the blacks" had to remain separate and distinct since 1866 was " 'the negro's hour'—an hour which, as it is improved or wasted, may crown with complete victory thirty years toil in his behalf, or once more commit him to the vindictive ferocity of the system from which he seems about to escape."[119]

Republican Senator John B. Henderson was one of a very few who found it difficult to understand why, under section two of the amendment, states should be deprived of representation if blacks were not allowed to vote but would suffer no similar penalty if women were denied the franchise. He suspected that the distinction was "a mere matter of temporary expediency," but added that he would "never give my sanction to a constitutional provision on any such considerations. If there be no principle involved, then the amendment should not be made."[120] Other Republicans, however, were able to articulate principled, even if sexist, reasons why women did not need the vote. One reason was advanced by Senator Jacob Howard, who noted that "there was such a thing as the law of nature which has a certain influence even in political affairs, and . . . by that law women and children were not regarded as the equals of men."[121] Another approach looked to the eighteenth-century principle of virtual representation. Taking this approach, Senator Timothy Howe was "willing to deprive those who are not males of the right of suffrage because they exercise it by proxy, as we all know. Females send their votes to the ballot box by their husbands or other male friends."[122] Similarly, Ben Wade agreed that women were "in high fellowship with those that do govern, who, to a great extent, act as their agents, their friends, promoting their interests in every vote they give, and therefore communities get along very well without conferring this right upon the female."[123]

This final reason why suffrage needed to be granted to blacks but not women was grounded in the most basic concepts of equality—concepts with which we must come to grips in the remainder of this book. The very essence of all law is to discriminate—to separate out the occasions on which one legal consequence rather than an opposite one will obtain. A theory that the state should treat all people equally cannot mean that the state may never treat two people differently, for such a theory would mean the end of all law. In order to sustain a principle of equality under law—the principle for which the framers of the Fourteenth Amendment were striving, it is necessary to have some theory about when discrimination is appropriate and when it is not.

In their efforts to elaborate a theory of equality,[124] statesmen of the generation which framed and ratified the Fourteenth Amendment faced two difficult issues that continue to plague Fourteenth Amendment analysis today. The first one, once they moved beyond obviously defective racial criteria, was to distinguish classifications that would be reasonable under the amendment from those that would be arbitrary. The second one was whether legislation which classified people on both reasonable and arbitrary grounds should be declared unconstitutional.

In dealing with the first issue, the congressional proponents of the

Fourteenth Amendment were always able to specify whether a particular classification was reasonable or arbitrary. But they were persistently unable to elaborate how their conclusions were derived from or compelled by their more general theory; they simply knew an arbitrary exercise of power when they saw one. Thaddeus Stevens faced this difficulty when he was asked whether an early draft of section one would restrict state freedom to distinguish between the rights of married women and the rights of *femmes sole* and men. For Stevens it was obvious that such legislation did not implicate anyone's right to equality. But the best explanation he could give was that, "[w]hen a distinction is made between two married people or two *femmes sole*, then it is unequal legislation; but where all of the same class are dealt with in the same way then there is no pretense of inequality."[125] What Stevens failed to explain was what constituted a class: why, that is, two married women—one black and one white — were members of the same class entitled to equal treatment, whereas two black women—one married and one single—were members of different classes who could be treated differently.

Senator John Sherman had similar difficulty responding to Roscoe Conkling's question about how the Fourteenth Amendment impacted upon a provision of the Arkansas constitution specifying a lengthy residency requirement for voters. Sherman's answer was that if the provision "was aimed against a citizen or a class of citizens it would be unconstitutional; but if it was aimed at all persons who had not resided within the State for a certain length of time it would be clearly constitutional." This was, Sherman added, a "distinction which I know my ingenious friend from New York will perceive at once."[126]

Other limitations upon the right to vote caused additional confusion within the Republican ranks. Three specific limitations were at issue: (1) a property qualification based on ownership of extensive quantities of land, (2) a limitation, like that in effect in the late 1860s in Massachusetts, of voting rights to those capable of reading English, and (3) a religious qualification for voting, like the religious qualification for officeholding in effect in New Hampshire. Each of these limitations proved objectionable to some Republicans, although each limitation also enjoyed more or less support from segments of the party.

The objection to a property qualification was stated by Representative Thomas A. Jenckes of Rhode Island. He argued that, if a

Southern state established a property qualification, the prospect of equal suffrage would be destroyed, "the same oligarchy" that had governed the South prior to the war "would be enthroned," and power would be given "more firmly to that very aristocracy we have sought to overthrow."[127] Although Thaddeus Stevens himself did not support property qualifications and there was little support for them within the Republican party, Stevens maintained that the Fourteenth Amendment, in one of its early forms, would not bar such a limitation; in his own words, "All I can say is that if the law applies impartially to all, then no matter whether it cuts out white or black."[128]

There was widespread support within the Republican party and the nation at large for conditioning suffrage on passage of a literacy test. The *Hartford Daily Courant* thought "[i]t would be worse than folly to extend the suffrage to all classes without the qualification of intelligence,"[129] while the *Springfield Republican* "advocated . . . intelligence" as "the basis for suffrage," adding that "the more we reflect upon the present peculiar aspect of public affairs, the more we are confirmed in our judgment."[130] The *Republican* explained:

> While the ignorant male citizens were but one or two in a hundred, there was no occasion for adding such a test as is now proposed; the element of ignorance in the suffrage was too small to be dangerous; but now, by the immigration of millions of ignorant foreigners, and the freeing of millions of black slaves, we find a very large proportion of our voters . . . unlettered to the last degree; and this addition of a test of intelligence, a simple one, that can be readily met whenever the motive is strong enough, becomes not only quite natural, but we believe absolutely necessary to the maintenance of our institutions in purity and safety.[131]

However, when Maine's Senator Lot M. Morrill offered a literacy amendment to a bill for suffrage in the District of Columbia, he ran into difficulty. Morrill's amendment, which took the obvious form that an 1866 literacy requirement would take, directed that prospective voters had to read the Constitution and write their names in English. This led Senator Samuel C. Pomeroy to object that "a great many well-educated men . . . cannot read in the English language, or write their names in English." He had in mind, in particular, the "many Germans who are educated, loyal, patriotic, and radical."[132] Pomeroy continued:

> The Senator from Maine and myself were born here; but we could not help it. There is no great merit in that. But the man who becomes an American from choice, who looking over the ocean and seeing America, learning of our institutions, breathing somewhat of our freedom, longing to identify himself with us in this great struggle for self-government, comes here and voluntarily assumes the duties of a citizen, enters our Army, and carries our flag to victory; I say such a man, if he cannot write a word in English, is an American; he is a patriot; he is loyal; and he should be entitled to vote.[133]

Pomeroy was followed on the floor by Henry Wilson of Massachusetts, who thought the "whole thing . . . trifling" and opposed "putting in any of this matter about reading." As he added, "[W]hy tell a German, a man of intelligence and character, that he must read the Constitution in the English Language? . . . I think it is all wrong."[134] Morrill's response was that "for the sake of unity, unity in our civilization, unity in our language, unity in our sentiments and opinions," public affairs ought to be conducted only in English. But he did not think his view "of importance enough to divide our friends upon that subject" and was prepared to accept whatever the party as a whole desired.[135]

The Republicans were also divided on whether the Fourteenth Amendment permitted religious classifications, like the one in New Hampshire which permitted only Protestant Christians to hold office. When a constitutional convention in North Carolina proposed that office be restricted to those who " 'believe[d] in the divine authority of the Old and the New Testament,' " M. S. Isaacs wrote to Senator Lyman Trumbull for "counsel and assistance in procuring the rejection of this obnoxious provision . . . that liberal men unhesitatingly condemn."[136] Congressman John A. Bingham was similarly opposed to a draft of the Fifteenth Amendment which, in his view, would "commit . . . this House to the monstrous proposition that every State in the Union may establish a religious test as a qualification of the elective franchise."[137] The House agreed with him in rejecting, 45–95, the language he feared would authorize a religious test,[138] but it also refused, 24–160, to accept the clear language that Bingham proposed to outlaw such tests.[139] It should be noted that no one in the course of the debates explained how issues of religious limitations on voting and officeholding were related to the more general issue of the meaning and content of equality.

There were times, of course, when the Republican proponents of the Fourteenth Amendment saw little ambiguity and were clear as to whether and why a particular classification was reasonable or arbitrary. Republicans were thus in agreement that most classifications on the basis of race, except perhaps those involving political rights, were illegitimate. They were troubled, however, by questions putting hypothetical cases involving legislation that simultaneously classified on both reasonable and arbitrary grounds. We have already seen that Thaddeus Stevens, the chairman of the Joint Committee on Reconstruction, took the view that, if a statute on its face distinguished one group from another in a reasonable fashion, it did not matter that the practical effect of the statute was to treat blacks differently than whites. He took this position in response to an argument made by Congressman Thomas A. Jenckes that Southern legislation establishing a property qualification for voting would have the practical effect of excluding nearly all blacks from the exercise of the franchise. Stevens' response was that, if the property qualification "applie[d] impartially to all," it did not matter that its effect was primarily to exclude blacks from voting.[140]

Another member of the Joint Committee, Roscoe Conkling, took the opposite position before the House on two occasions—one day before and one day after Stevens made his statement. Conkling maintained that a body judging the constitutionality of a state's legislation would look beyond the form of the statute to its substance. He first took this position in response to a query from Congressman Andrew J. Rogers, who asked whether a state could "exclude the colored people from the right of voting" if it declared "that such exclusion was not on account of race or color, but was on account of the want of intelligence or education among the colored people."[141] After remarking that Rogers' question "has nothing but casuistry to recommend it, if it has that," Conkling responded that such an exclusion should be deemed one "on account of race merely, whether it is honestly avowed or cunningly covered up" and hence void. He was confident that there would "never be difficulty in seeing whether . . . [an] exclusion [on racial grounds] is in fact made or not."[142] Two days later Representative Frederick A. Pike, a radical Republican from Maine, asked Conkling whether a state would be permitted, under the then pending draft of the Fourteenth Amendment, to deny the vote not on racial grounds to blacks, but to anyone descended from a slave, whatever his race or color. Conkling's response was that the proposed Fourteenth Amendment was "not to take effect in Greece or Rome," but "in this country, where one race and only one has been held in servitude." When "read, in light of the surrounding circumstances," the amendment would clearly prohibit a statute such as the one proposed. At least Conkling so thought.[143] Representative William Lawrence of Ohio was similarly prepared to look to the impact rather than the form of legislation when he indicated that he would treat a statute which gave a right to a native-born citizen and simply made no provision for a naturalized citizen to enjoy that right the same as he would a statute explicitly denying the naturalized citizen the right.[144]

The Republican proponents of the Fourteenth Amendment made these conflicting statements in reference to section one because the section, as its opponents had so effectively pointed out, was itself uncertain and ambiguous. Charles Sumner, for one, noted that it was like a sign on a highway with different inscriptions on each side, so that people approaching the sign from opposite directions necessarily read it differently.[145]

Section one was indeed uncertain and ambiguous. One reason was that the people who framed the section, who voted for it in Congress, and who later ratified it in the states were acting primarily as statesmen and political leaders, not as legal draftsmen. The Republicans themselves labeled the Fourteenth Amendment as their platform for the congressional elections of 1866: it was their program for resolving the key issue then confronting the nation, the issue of Reconstruction. Like all American party platforms, the Republican platform for 1866 had to be sufficiently ambiguous and broad to attract quite divergent segments of the nation's electorate. As the Republican state chairman of Ohio explained to Chief Justice Salmon P. Chase in October 1866, it was "very difficult, as you well know, in Ohio, with her great variety of people, to tell with any degree of certainty what a majority of them want, or to arrive at the general average of their political condition." It was necessary in the 1866 elections "[i]n the Reserve Counties . . . [to] openly advocate . . . impartial suffrage, while in other places it was thought necessary, not only to repudiate it, but to oppose it."[146] Senator Henry Wilson of Massachusetts made a similar admission to Delaware's Willard Saulsbury when he conceded that he disguised his views on the suffrage question while campaigning in 1866 for Republican candidates in Delaware.[147] Section one of the Fourteenth Amendment was thus a product of compromise. As Thaddeus Stevens told the House when he presented it with the final version of the amendment, he found it an "imperfect . . . proposition." He was prepared to accept it, however, because "men as intelligent, as determined, and as independent as myself" did "not choose to yield their opinions to mine. Mutual concession, therefore," was the "only resort;" it was necessary to "take what we can get now, and hope for better things in further legislation; in enabling acts or other provisions."[148]

The debates on the Fourteenth Amendment also possessed a political quality in a deeper sense. Far more was involved in the political crisis of Reconstruction than a mere search by the Republican party for mechanisms for retention of power. The postwar situation raised fundamental issues of principle and presented Republican leaders with an opportunity to inspire the American public to perform its civic duty toward blacks. The Fourteenth Amendment and the statesmen who debated, framed, and ratified it addressed those issues. Those statesmen were remarkably effective, far more effective than political leaders usually are, in addressing the issues of the day with inspirational oratory. They talked incessantly about basic principles of government—about liberty and equality and about the importance of decentralized government—and, as letters from their constituents indicate, they roused the public's attention. The statesmen who dealt with the Fourteenth Amendment were ineffective not at elaborating or connecting it to general principles, but only in applying those general principles to the specific cases that were occasionally discussed during the Fourteenth Amendment debates. The application of principles to specific cases was not, however, an important part of the historical experience of the legislators. Nor was it their institutional duty. Few people cared in 1866 about the very narrow issues of Fourteenth Amendment jurisprudence that the Supreme Court would face over the course of the next century or about how particular cases would be decided under the new amendment. This lack of concern on the part of the public is not surprising, given the great issues at stake in the late 1860s and the moralistic manner in which Americans had grown accustomed to thinking about those issues during the preceding three decades. Nor is it surprising that congressmen and state legislators understood their job to be "to occupy a high vantage ground, from which ... [their] voice [could] reverberate far out, moving and stirring the hearts of multitudes." They strove to have "the truth ... go out from every deliberative body in the land, as the rays of light radiate from the sun"[149] and paid attention mainly to the substance of the great issues of principle to which they hoped to convert the nation, rather than to how their legal handiwork would be enforced in the future.

But they did not pay attention only to the broad issues of principle. Many of the framers and ratifiers of the Fourteenth Amendment were lawyers, and a few of them took seriously the task of legal drafts-manship, which would determine the future impact of their efforts. One such individual was William P. Fessenden, the ranking Repub-lican senator on the Joint Committee of Reconstruction. He was concerned with matters of precise draftsmanship, but he discovered, as has everyone who has dealt seriously and at length with the Fourteenth Amendment, that it dealt with issues and principles for which legal language is often inadequate. In response to a question whether section two applied to municipal elections, Fessenden noted: "I do not think that this proposition could be held to apply to such elections at all. I do not believe it will be attended with any difficulty. At any rate, to meet the object, we could not devise a better form of words than we have. I know I worked on that second proposition until my head got so thoroughly muddled with it that I would not attempt to make another."[150] Similarly, a Pennsylvania legislator "admit[ted] there are tangled questions in this matter of recon-struction."[151] Thus one reason why Congressman Bingham's initial draft of section one providing that "Congress shall have power to make all laws" to secure the privileges and immunities of citizens and equal protection of rights[152] was rejected was because it seemed not in itself to protect fundamental rights but to leave such protection "to the caprice of Congress"; some Republicans thought it better to "provide by an amendment to the Constitution that no State shall discriminate against any class of its citizens" and in a separate clause give Congress power to enforce that prohibition, thereby insuring that the judiciary would enforce the amendment in case Congress failed to legislate.[153]

In reference to another issue Senator Waitman T. Willey, who was not a member of the committee, conceded that he appreciated "how hard it is to provide any rule that shall operate equally."[154] All sorts of difficulties arose out of the efforts of the amendment's framers to find language that would extend citizenship to some but not all Indians,[155] while similar conceptual difficulty arose in response to the provision of the civil rights bill and thus ultimately the amendment making state judges criminally liable for violating federally protected rights. The chairman of the House Judiciary Committee, James F. Wilson, indicated both his own confusion and the difficulty of dealing with the problem when he was asked "[w]hy not abrogate" state laws depriving people of their rights "instead of inflicting penalties upon the officers who execute writs under them?" Wilson answered, "That is what we are trying to do,"[156] although the committee was trying not merely to abrogate offending state laws but also to deter their adoption and enforcement. The difficulties that existed with language emerge most clearly, perhaps, in a colloquy between Senator Lyman Trumbull of Illinois, chairman of the Judiciary Committee, and Senator Charles Sumner of Massachusetts in regard to the language of the Thirteenth Amendment. The committee had rejected language proposed by Sumner, as Trumbull explained:

> The committee had both these propositions before them. They considered them. There was some difference of opinion in the committee as to the language to be used; and it was upon discussion and an examination of both these propositions . . . that the committee came to the conclusion to adopt the form which is reported here. I do not know that I should have adopted these precise words, but a majority of the committee thought they were the best words; they accomplish the object; and I cannot see why the Senator from Massachusetts should be so pertinacious about particular words. The words that we have adopted will accomplish the object. If every member of the Senate is to select the precise words in which a law shall be clothed, and will be satisfied with none other, we shall have very little legislation.[157]

In short, the statesmen who debated, drafted, and ratified the Fourteenth Amendment faced "great difficulty" when they tried to frame rules that would "enforce justice and give fair play" but could not "be perverted in the hands of bad men to uses not designed by the framers."[158] While they could take pride in their success in elaborating and incorporating important moral principles such as equality and rationality into the Constitution, they made only slight headway in the task of applying those principles to specific cases in accordance with some consistent scheme. But that task was not primarily theirs. Rather, it would belong to the Supreme Court of the United States in the decades that followed the adoption of the amendment.

CHAPTER VII

The Judicial
Elaboration
of Doctrine

The ratification of the Fourteenth Amendment in 1868 did not, of course, bring to an end debate and discussion about its meaning and scope. Between 1868 and the mid-1870s, individual congressmen remained important interpreters of the Fourteenth as Congress debated and passed the Fifteenth Amendment in 1869 and important Civil Rights laws in 1870, 1871, and 1875.[1] Not surprisingly, Congress was no more able to attain a consensus on key issues about the Fourteenth Amendment's meaning during the post facto debates than it had been during the original debates.[2] The problem in Congress was always the same. A few Republicans would speak in support of the amendment or the pending enforcement legislation and in so doing would typically present different interpretations of the amendment's meaning; then the party as a whole would vote overwhelmingly in support of the matter at hand without the individual members identifying the interpretation they preferred. The dynamic of Congress was such that a multiplicity of views about section one would persist.

During these same years, however, the judiciary also began to assume jurisdiction over the Fourteenth Amendment's meaning.

Between 1868 and 1873, judges in the state and lower federal courts heard a number of cases dealing with evidentiary questions, voting rights, segregation, and other matters. In these cases they rehearsed all the familiar arguments that had been advanced in the Thirty-ninth Congress, the state legislatures, statesmen's private correspondence, and the press, and, like everyone else who had tried to interpret section one, they failed to reach a consensus about its application and scope. The structural problem was that each court acted independently of the others, and, as any lawyer knows, the independent views of judges are almost never identical.

In 1873 and 1874 two important events transformed the processes of interpreting the amendment. The first was the Republicans' defeat in the elections of 1874, which deprived the party of control of the House of Representatives once the Forty-third Congress passed out of existence in March of 1875 and made the Civil Rights Act of that year the last such piece of legislation for eight decades. After 1875 Congress, contrary to the expectations of those who had framed and ratified the Fourteenth Amendment, ceased to be an important interpreter of it. The second event was the Supreme Court's decision of its first Fourteenth Amendment case in 1873—a case followed by many others. Soon the Court—a small, cohesive institution whose function is to respond to precise questions with a single answer that a majority of its members support—had become the amendment's main interpreter. The structural conditions that had produced a multiplicity of voices between 1866 and the mid-1870s had suddenly ended, and the possibility of elaborating coherent doctrine had emerged.

It is important, however, to emphasize the continuity that persisted as Congress lost control over the Fourteenth Amendment and section one was taken over by the courts. In the early state and federal cases, for example, the judges who passed on specific issues about section one's meaning were quite faithful to the many divergent viewpoints Americans had held in the 1866–1868 debates. Judges in the first five years of Fourteenth Amendment adjudication in large part simply restated the arguments that others had made earlier, and, like the amendment's earlier discussants, they could not agree that any one approach was best. The Supreme Court, in turn, continued with the work of Fourteenth Amendment adjudication where the state and lower federal courts left off.

The courts were also faithful at a more general level of theory to the twofold purpose of virtually all Republicans who expressed their views about section one. This faithfulness was, again, not surprising given the unanimity of views on the part of the committee that framed the Fourteenth Amendment, the congressmen who adopted it, the state legislators who ratified it, and the people who discussed it. They all understood that the amendment strove to compel the states to abide by principles of higher law, citizens' rights, and equality that had been elaborated in the decades before the Civil War without, however, significantly undermining the lawmaking capacity of the states. At all levels of American government and society in 1866–1868, Republicans agreed that the antebellum principles constitutionalized by section one were not absolute ones overriding state lawmaking power. In speech after speech, the proponents of the amendment took note of its limited scope as frequently as they mentioned the principles which it embodied.

What the proponents did not do effectively was to explain how federal enforcement of principles designed to affect nearly every aspect of human endeavor could be limited so as not to undermine the plenary lawmaking power of the states. The most cogent explanation was that the Fourteenth Amendment would not, in and of itself, create rights, but would leave that task to state law; the amendment's sole restriction on state legislative freedom would lie in its requirement that the states confer equal rights on all.

But not all of the amendment's proponents accepted this view. Consistently with their antislavery heritage, some Republicans claimed that the amendment did more than protect rights equally; it protected absolutely certain fundamental rights such as those specified in the Bill of Rights and those given by common law to enter contracts and to own property. This absolute rights interpretation involved the Republican proponents of the amendment in a serious difficulty, however, because congressional assumption of plenary legislative jurisdiction over basic rights threatened to deprive state legislatures of their authority over the rights. Republicans protested, of course, that they did not intend the Fourteenth Amendment to have this effect, and a few tried to explain why it would not. They urged that, although section one would prohibit states from impairing the enjoyment of fundamental rights, states would remain free to regulate those rights for the public good in a reasonable fashion. Although there was some thought that reasonable regulations were the same as equal regulations, this point was unclear.

The Fourteenth Amendment thus had at least two possible meanings as it emerged from the congressional and state ratification debates. It could be read as guaranteeing either equal rights or absolute rights. Although there was an interpretation of the second approach that, in effect, conflated it with the first, that interpretation had not been advanced by the amendment's proponents with enough frequency for the courts to be confident of its soundness. As a result, the amendment first came into the courts with more than one possible meaning.

■ Early Litigation in the State and Lower Federal Courts

The state and lower federal courts that initially considered section one gave it both meanings and added a few others as well. A common theme in the early cases was that the Fourteenth Amendment made "no pretence . . . of granting rights to anybody."[3] On the contrary, its "fundamental idea and principle" was "an impartial equality of rights."[4] Its "plain and manifest intention was to make all the citizens of the United States equal before the law"[5]—to insure that "[s]pecial privileges can be conferred upon none, nor can exceptional burdens or restrictions be put upon any."[6] Thus the amendment's main effect was "to extend the protection and blessings of the constitution and laws to a new class of persons."[7] As the Supreme Court of Georgia explained, blacks were "not and could not be citizens" prior to the adoption of the Fourteenth Amendment; "they were persons of color, and in the denial to them of the right to be citizens was included the denial of every right not specifically . . . by law conferred upon them." However, when the Fourteenth Amendment removed the barrier of race and made blacks citizens, "they became entitled to the exercise of every right" that white citizens of the state already enjoyed.[8]

The equal protection jurisprudence that developed in the state and lower federal courts immediately grew quite complex. One issue on which a good deal of division and complexity emerged concerned the effect of the Fourteenth Amendment on the practice of racial segregation. On one side, the Supreme Court of Iowa held in a line of cases that the amendment barred segregation in public schools[9] and on public accommodations.[10] The Iowa court reasoned that blacks were denied access to white schools and accommodations "because of prejudice entertained against [their] race, growing out of its former condition of servitude" and argued that the object of the Fourteenth Amendment was "to relieve citizens of the black race from the effects of this prejudice."[11] Iowa received some support from the Deep South, where the highest courts of both Louisiana and Mississippi invalidated segregation pursuant to the command of local legislation.[12]

But other courts disagreed. Judges in California,[13] Indiana,[14] Kentucky,[15] New York,[16] Ohio,[17] and Pennsylvania[18] all upheld the constitutionality of segregation. As the Ohio court reasoned, segregation did "not attempt to deprive colored persons of any rights," but "only regulate[d] the mode and manner" of their enjoyment.[19] And as the California court added, quoting *Roberts* v. *City of Boston*,[20] the power to regulate schools was a legislative one, and when it was " 'reasonably exercised, without being abused or perverted by colorable pretences,' " the legislative decision, made with " 'great deliberation' " and for " 'the good of both classes,' " was " 'conclusive.' "[21]

The courts also divided initially over whether the amendment sanctioned interracial marriage. In the early years of Reconstruction, two Southern states—Alabama and Louisiana—upheld the validity of interracial marriages,[22] with the Alabama court noting that it could "not be supposed" that the prohibition was aimed "otherwise than against the negro."[23] Most early cases, however, held that the Fourteenth Amendment had no effect on state miscegenation legislation,[24] reasoning that state law operated on both races alike by prohibiting both from marrying outside their own race.

A third subject on which courts divided was whether the Fourteenth Amendment conferred equality in respect to political rights, such as the rights to vote and hold office. *White* v. *Clements*,[25] a leading case from Georgia, held that a provision of the Georgia constitution which copied verbatim the privileges and immunities and equal protection clauses of section one guaranteed blacks the right to hold office, while the highest courts of Alabama and Indiana declared in dictum that section one conferred "political" rights.[26] On the other hand, two courts held that the Fourteenth Amendment did not confer equal voting rights on women,[27] while the Indiana Supreme Court explained in dictum that a grant of citizenship, of necessity, confers equal civil but not equal political rights.[28]

Perhaps the most curious cases to analyze the impact of the Fourteenth Amendment's equality requirements on state law arose out of a California statute that prohibited Chinese from testifying against whites. The first case involved a black named George Washington, who was convicted of robbery solely on the testimony of Chinese witnesses; in setting aside the conviction, the California Supreme Court reasoned that the Civil Rights Act of 1866 placed black citizens on a plane of equality with white citizens, so if Chinese could not testify against whites, they could not testify against blacks either.[29]

No one in the *Washington* case seemed concerned that Chinese residents of California did not receive treatment equal to that of white and black residents. But in the next year the state's attorney general did evince concern. Relying on the Fourteenth Amendment, he argued that all persons were entitled to protection from the law and that, if people were not permitted to testify, they could not establish their legal rights and hence could not enjoy the law's protection. He urged that his argument had special force in respect to victims of crime who were not permitted to testify against criminals.[30] The court, however, responded to the attorney general's argument with what had been a familiar line of reasoning during the debates on the amendment and would become even more familiar in the years to come. It observed:

> Now, in passing these laws, the Legislature does not act arbitrarily. It does not exclude a person because of his unbelief in popular theological dogmas, nor the Mongolian for being a Mongolian only. The theory of the law and the idea upon which these laws are based is, that everyone shall be permitted to testify who can aid the Court in coming to a correct conclusion as to the facts upon which it is to adjudicate. The reason why the testimony of such persons would be valueless in judicial investigations may be that they are incapable of testifying intelligently; that they are too unreliable to be of any service; that their admission would probably defeat justice by producing false testimony, or that they have particular prejudices against certain classes which would cause their evidence likely to do harm where the rights of such persons are concerned . . . I am not called upon to say what should be the ruling if it were to appear that, under the pretense of regulating the production of evidence, the State has really deprived any person within its jurisdiction of any substantial means of protection afforded to others by its laws. There is no reason to suppose that the law in question was not passed in good faith, and with the honest purpose of promoting

> the cause of justice, even if that could be called in question here. The relation between the States and the Federal Government would forbid any such suspicion upon the motives of a State Legislature on the part of the Federal Government, and certainly this Court, a co-ordinate branch of the Government, cannot impugn their motives.[31]

The early cases interpreting section one as a guarantee of equality thus picked up all the ideas prevalent in the debates on the section as well as the idea of deference to legislative judgments—an idea familiar to mid-nineteenth century judges.[32] Meanwhile, other early cases turned to a different set of ideas that had also been prevalent in the congressional and ratification debates.

As one federal judge observed, section one sought "not only to guaranty, in the largest sense, . . . the sacred right of equality before the law throughout the whole land; but also, to protect from invasion and abridgement all the privileges and immunities—essential rights— that belong to the citizen."[33] A California attorney agreed that the "office of the Fourteenth Amendment [was] not to simply secure to all persons equal capacities before the law, but it grants to all persons who are citizens the broadest rights which attach themselves to every citizen of the Republic."[34] Another judge ruled that the amendment protected "fundamental rights" even from private infringement, and declared that these rights included all those "expressly secured to the people, either as against the action of the federal or state governments."[35]

But this construction of section one as a guarantor of absolute rights "open[ed] into a field of conjectures limitless as the range of speculative theories, and might work such limitations of the power of the States to manage and regulate their local institutions and affairs as were never contemplated by the amendment."[36] Thus judges who believed that the Fourteenth Amendment protected absolute rights, not simply a right to equality, had to explain why the amendment would not have this devastating effect. Several judges devised an ingenious argument that no one had advanced in the framing and ratification debates. Observing that section one protected the "privileges or immunities of citizens of the United States" and not the privileges and immunities of citizens of particular states, they proceeded to distinguish between rights derived from national citizenship and those stemming from state citizenship. Only the former, the judges argued, were protected by the Fourteenth Amendment. Then they proceeded to define narrowly the rights of national citizenship, holding that the rights to attend school,[37] to marry across racial lines,[38] and to vote[39] were not among those adhering to citizens of the United States by virtue of their national citizenship.

Thus within a few brief years of the Fourteenth Amendment's ratification, all the issues that had plagued the framers had surfaced in the state and lower federal courts. Judges had begun to debate whether the amendment gave the right to vote, prohibited racial segregation, and affected state miscegenation laws. They had also begun to face the intractable problem of construing the amendment so as to protect rights while at the same time preserving state legislative freedom. Finally, they had isolated what would become the main issue in Fourteenth Amendment jurisprudence—the issue whether section one secured fundamental rights absolutely or guaranteed only equality in rights.

- The Emergence of Uniform Doctrine:
  From *Slaughter-House* to *Munn*

The question whether the Fourteenth Amendment protected absolute or only equal rights came to a head in *Live-Stock Dealers' & Butchers' Ass'n* v. *Crescent City Live-Stock Landing & Slaughter-House Co.*[40] At issue in the case was the constitutionality of a Louisiana statute creating a corporation authorized to build a slaughterhouse for the butchering of all animals to be sold in the city of New Orleans. Existing butchers were prohibited from carrying on their trade on their own premises, but instead were directed to rent quarters in the corporation's slaughterhouse. The butchers brought suit, claiming that the statute deprived them of the right to practice their trade guaranteed in section one.

Justice Bradley, riding circuit, ruled in favor of the absolute rights interpretation of section one. More important, he refused to interpret the privileges and immunities clause narrowly, and he included within the list of privileges and immunities protected by the Fourteenth Amendment a citizen's right "to adopt and follow such lawful industrial pursuit ... as he may see fit" and "his privilege to be protected in the possession and enjoyment of his property."[41] Bradley strove to limit the potentially excessive reach of the amendment, as had earlier inquirers into the meaning of section one, by conceding to the state legislatures "an undoubted right to make all police regulations which they may deem necessary" for preservation of "the public health, the public order, and the general well being." However, state regulations had to be "reasonable restrictions" which left the enjoyment of fundamental rights "open to all alike."[42] He found, in contrast, that the Louisiana scheme created "a monopoly of a very odious character" and accordingly held it unconstitutional.[43]

When the Supreme Court finally decided the *Slaughter-House Cases*[44] three years later, Justice Bradley's decision was reversed by a 5–4 vote. In what remains a landmark case—the Supreme Court's first foray into Fourteenth Amendment jurisprudence—four opinions were published: the opinion of the Court authored by Justice Miller and dissenting opinions authored by Justices Bradley, Field, and Swayne. The opinions, especially that of Justice Miller, are not without ambiguity. Indeed, Miller's opinion is susceptible to at least three different readings, with the result that several different interpretations of the Fourteenth Amendment can be found in *Slaughter-House*. Each of these readings can be connected closely to, and was in its essentials derived from, some aspect of the legislative history of the amendment or the early interpretive work of the state and lower federal courts. The Supreme Court, that is, did not create new doctrine out of whole cloth in *Slaughter-House*, but rather began a process of elaborating doctrine in response to the principles and concerns that had induced Congress, the state legislatures, and the lower courts to understand the Fourteenth Amendment as they did. The Court, that is, began its process of elaboration where others had left off, using the same ideas that the others had proclaimed during a brief seven-year period in the course of which the justices, like other politically astute Americans, were close observers of the amendment's unfolding.

Justice Stephen J. Field in dissent wrote the only opinion in the case that stands on its own and can be comprehended fully as an effort to transform into doctrine the antebellum rhetoric underlying section one. The other dissents are supplements to Field's opinion. Even Miller's opinion for the Court is best understood as a response to Field and the other dissenters. Hence it seems appropriate to begin analysis of the case with the Field dissent.

Field's opinion echoed and wove together the basic themes of the proponents of the Fourteenth Amendment and of their predecessors in the antislavery movement. One of those themes was equality. Field argued that the privileges and immunities clause contained in Article IV of the original Constitution protected "citizens of one State against hostile and discriminating legislation of other States."[45] "[U]nder the fourth article of the Constitution," he continued, "equality of privileges and immunities is secured between citizens of different States." It followed that "under the fourteenth amendment the same equality is secured between citizens of the United States."[46] The amendment "inhibit[ed] any legislation which confers special and exclusive privileges like those under consideration."[47] As Field concluded, "[t]his equality of right, with exemption from all disparaging and partial enactments . . . is the distinguishing privilege of citizens of the United States."[48]

Justice Field also repeated the higher law and citizens' rights rhetoric that had been heard in Congress and in the nation during the 1860s and even before. He spoke, for example, of "inalienable rights, rights which are the gift of the Creator, which the law does not confer, but only recognizes."[49] God was not, however, the only source of the rights which the Fourteenth Amendment protected. "The privileges and immunities designated" by section one, according to Field, were "those *which of right belong to the citizens of all free governments.*"[50] These "fundamental rights, privileges, and immunities" belonged to every individual "as a free man and a free citizen" and also "as a citizen of the United States."[51]

How did Justice Field interweave this rhetoric of higher law, citizens' rights, and equality into a holding by which to resolve the pending case? In view of all the varied rhetoric which the opinion contains, this question cannot be answered simply. But the place to begin seems to be with Field's statement that the privileges and immunities of a citizen protected by section one "are always more or less affected by the condition and the local institutions of the State, or city, or town where he resides."[52] Although the rights under section one did "not derive their existence from . . . legislation, and cannot be destroyed" by it,[53] they were subject to reasonable legislative regulation. What, then, constituted a reasonable regulation of a section one right, especially of "the right to pursue a lawful employment in a lawful manner?"[54] In two places in his opinion, Field gave the answer, that every right was held "subject only to such restraints as equally affected all others"[55] and "without other restraint than such as equally affects all persons."[56] Field summed up his holding in the concluding sentence of his opinion where, paraphrasing Blackstone, he observed: "That only is a free government, in the American sense of the term, under which the inalienable right of every citizen to pursue his happiness is unrestrained, except by just, equal, and impartial laws."[57]

Field's dissent effectively combined the higher law, citizens' rights, and equality principles underlying the Fourteenth Amendment into a narrow reading of section one. His opinion is narrow because it held that not all rights, but only fundamental rights, such as the right to engage in the common occupations, are within the ambit of section one and thus subject to federal judicial control. Field's opinion was even narrower in that it did not accord absolute protection to those fundamental rights. On the contrary, Field conceded that the states could regulate those federally protected rights. Like many of those who had participated in the enactment of the Fourteenth Amendment, he required only that state regulations be reasonable, and he defined a reasonable regulation as one that applies generally and equally to all. He indicated that he would have invalidated the Louisiana legislation at issue in the case only because it regulated the right of butchers to engage in their occupation in an unreasonable way by granting monopoly privileges and profits to a favored few. But he also indicated that the states were free to adopt regulations without federal judicial interference if the regulations impinged on fundamental rights equally or perhaps even if they impinged on rights of trivial significance unequally.

One reading of Justice Miller's majority opinion is that it accepted most, if not all, of Justice Field's statement of the law and disagreed only with his interpretation of the facts. More than a third of Miller's opinion is devoted to an analysis of the facts and a rebuttal of the claim, endorsed by Field's dissent, that the Louisiana legislation "creat[ed] a monopoly and conferr[ed] odious and exclusive privileges upon a small number of persons at the expense of the great body of the community of New Orleans."[58] Miller reasoned that, pursuant to what "is called the police power,"[59] "it is both the right and duty of the legislative body . . . to prescribe and determine the localities where the business of slaughtering for a great city may be conducted."[60] The power to zone to eliminate nuisances could not be controverted. Miller further reasoned that the Louisiana legislature, if it had wanted, could have charged the corporation of the City of New Orleans with the administration and enforcement of its zoning determination, but that, since the legislature could choose any means appropriate to its ends, it could also create a separate corporation for the purpose.[61] He found that "[t]he wisdom of the monopoly granted by the legislature may be open to question, but it is difficult to see a justification for the assertion that the butchers are deprived of the right to labor in their occupation." Miller, indeed, noted:

> On the contrary, the Slaughter-House Company is required, under a heavy penalty, to permit any person who wishes to do so, to slaughter in their houses; and they are bound to make ample provision for the convenience of all the slaughtering for the entire city. The butcher then is still permitted to slaughter, to prepare, and to sell his own meats; but he is required to slaughter at a specified place and to pay a reasonable compensation for the use of the accommodations furnished him at that place.[62]

Hence the only right within the scope of section one—the right to engage in the common trade of butchering—was subjected to a reasonable regulation, in that all who sought to exercise the right had to exercise it in the same place and pay the same compensation to do so.

If Justice Miller had said no more, it would have been plain that he and Justice Field disagreed only about the reasonableness of the charge imposed on butchers using the slaughterhouse. They would both have agreed that, if the charge was calculated merely to impose on users a fair and equal share of the costs of operation, then the legislative scheme was an appropriate one for centralizing the slaughter of animals in one district. They would also have agreed that, if the fee was a high one that imposed more of the operating costs on butchers who were not members of the corporation than on butchers who were, then the members of the corporation would have received a special and exclusive privilege that was not justified by the zoning power and was unconstitutional.

At least one contemporary commentator—James Bradley Thayer, a professor at the Harvard Law School—read the *Slaughter-House Cases* in a similar fashion. His own teaching notes indicate that, after he had completed parsing both the Field and Miller opinions, he told his classes "that so far as it relates to the construction of the 14th amend . . . the minority . . . seem to be the sounder."[63] In a set of notes taken in the class one student reports Thayer asking, "Do the privileges and immunities of a citizen of the U.S. include the fundamental privileges of citizenship," and then responding that "[a] very strong argument in favor of the view of the minority on this point could be made."[64] Thayer then continued that "in first considering the nature of the legislation in question," Miller strengthened his opinion "that the St. was not contra to the Amendments." For, as Thayer then explained, "You may admit everything the minority says and still decide the case as it was decided. No privilege or immunity was denied by the Statute in question. It was ordinary and proper legislation."[65]

Despite the plausibility of such an approach and the clarity that Miller could have given his opinion if he had so limited it, Miller's opinion did not stop with his analysis of the Louisiana statute. It went on to address arguments advanced in the opinions of Justices Bradley and Swayne, opinions to which it is next necessary to turn.

Justice Bradley's dissent is so similar to that of Justice Field that one wonders why both of them were published. He agreed that "[t]he right of a State to regulate the conduct of its citizens is undoubtedly a very broad and extensive one" limited only by the "rights" possessed by the "citizens of any free government." He agreed that the state could "prescribe the manner of their exercise, but it cannot subvert the rights themselves."[66] He also agreed that "[e]quality before the law is undoubtedly one of the privileges and immunities of every citizen."[67] Finally, he condemned the Louisiana legislation as "one of those arbitrary and unjust laws made in the interest of a few scheming individuals."[68] These statements appear to suggest that Bradley thought, as Field did, that any equal and general regulation of a federally protected right was constitutional.

But Bradley's opinion can also be read to limit the regulatory power of the states more than did Field. In Bradley's view, the language of the privileges and immunities clause was "fairly susceptible of a broader interpretation than that which makes it a guarantee of mere equality of privileges with other citizens."[69] Some Fourteenth Amendment rights, according to this view, were absolute and thus immune from any legislative regulation. In Bradley's judgment, "it was the intention of the people of this country in adopting . . . [the] amendment to provide National security against violation by the States of the fundamental rights of the citizen."[70]

This interpretation of section one, if Bradley in fact adhered to it, has greater potential than does Field's to intrude upon and limit state lawmaking power. Field would have granted people only one right against governmental infringement—the right to equality—and would have granted even that right only as to matters of fundamental importance. Bradley agreed that "[e]quality before the law is undoubtedly one of the privileges and immunities of every citizen,"[71] but he may also have been prepared to protect other unspecified rights.[72] At the end of his opinion, he recognized the "great fears" that were "expressed" that this

> construction of the amendment will lead to enactments by Congress interfering with the internal affairs of the States, and establishing therein civil and criminal codes of law for the government of the citizens, and thus abolishing the State governments in everything but name; or else, that it will lead the Federal courts to draw to their cognizance the supervision of State tribunals on every subject of judicial inquiry, on the plea of ascertaining whether the privileges and immunities of citizens have not been abridged.[73]

In Bradley's "judgment no such practical inconveniences would arise,"[74] but if they did and

> if the business of the National courts should be increased, Congress could easily supply the remedy by increasing their number and efficiency. The great question is, What is the true construction of the amendment? When once we find that, we shall find the means of giving it effect. The argument from inconvenience ought not to have a very controlling influence in questions of this sort. The National will and National interest are of far greater importance.[75]

Justice Bradley was thus prepared to construe the Fourteenth Amendment in ways that might increase federal power substantially. So was Justice Swayne, whose brief dissent addressed not the question of the meaning of section one but the issue of increased federal power. After taking note of the objection that "the power conferred" by section one was "novel and large," Swayne argued not that the section was not as broad as asserted but rather that "the novelty was known and the measure deliberately adopted."[76] In his opinion, "[t]he prejudices and apprehension as to the central government which prevailed when the Constitution was adopted . . . [had been] dispelled by the light of experience," a vast increase in national power was called for, and the Court should not decline to grant what was needed.[77]

It was in response to the calls of Bradley and Swayne for an increase in national power that Justice Miller wrote the bulk of his opinion for the Court. Unlike Bradley and Swayne, Miller was "convinced"— quite soundly in view of the debates on the Fourteenth Amendment— that "the Congress which proposed the ... amendment" and "the legislatures of the States which ratified" it did not intend "to transfer the security and protection of all ... civil rights ... from the States to the Federal Government" and thereby "to fetter and degrade the State governments by subjecting them to the control of Congress, in the exercise of powers heretofore universally conceded to them of the most ordinary and fundamental character."[78] On the contrary, Miller concluded that there was not in the Fourteenth Amendment

> any purpose to destroy the main features of the general system [of American government]. Under the pressure of all the excited feeling growing out of the war, our statesmen have still believed that the existence of the States with powers for domestic and local government, including the regulation of civil rights—the rights of person and of property—was essential to the perfect working of our complex form of government, though they have thought proper to impose additional limitations on the States, and to confer additional power on that of the Nation.[79]

Accordingly Justice Miller searched for ways to transform the Fourteenth Amendment from a potentially broad charter for federal supervention of state control over routine protection of common law rights into a narrower mechanism that would authorize only limited federal involvement in what had been the traditional domain of state law. His opinion announced two ways to limit sections one's reach. One was to hold that the section applied only in cases of racial discrimination. Thus Miller expressed his "doubt ... whether any action of a State not directed by way of discrimination against the negroes as a class, or on account of their race, will ever be held to come within the purview of this provision. It is so clearly a provision for that race and that emergency, that a strong case would be necessary for its application to any other."[80] Miller's second approach was to read the privileges and immunities clause of section one narrowly. Following the analysis of several state judges, Miller held that the clause did not apply to ordinary civil rights such as the right to property and the right to enter into contracts—rights which were theretofore protected only by state law. Miller concluded that the privileges and immunities clause applied only to rights that "owe their existence to the Federal government, its National character, its Constitution, or its laws"— rights such as the right " 'to come to the seat of government,' " to transact business with or petition the government and to claim the protection of the government when traveling overseas.[81]

Both of Justice Miller's approaches for narrowing the reach of section one were flatly inconsistent with the history of its framing in Congress and its ratification by the state legislatures. Hence they constituted clear instances of judicial lawmaking of which Justice Miller must have been quite aware. While equality for blacks was surely the central concern of the amendment's framers and ratifiers, it was never their sole and exclusive concern. Those who discussed the amendment were aware of its implications for other groups, such as Chinese, Indians, women, and religious minorities. Moreover, there is no doubt that the proponents of the amendment meant to protect yet another group—namely, Northern whites who were migrating to the South after the Civil War and were threatened with potentially discriminatory legislation at the hands of Southern states and localities. It was simply wrong for Justice Miller to suggest that the Fourteenth Amendment could be limited only to cases of discrimination against blacks.

Miller was equally wrong in limiting the privileges and immunities clause only to rights which owed their existence to the federal government or to national law. No one who sat in Congress or in the state legislatures that dealt with the Fourteenth Amendment doubted that section one was designed to put to rest any doubt about the power of the federal government to protect basic common law rights of property and contract. Both the proponents and the opponents of the amendment so understood the section. While there were doubts about the extent to which the section protected basic rights, there was no doubt that it extended some protection to them. Moreover, as James Bradley Thayer suggested to his students, the privileges and immunities "clause seems to be unnecessary" if one construes it as did Justice Miller,[82] for Thayer thought that the rights specified by Miller were already subjects of constitutional protection before the Four-

teenth Amendment was adopted. Unless one attributes to the draftsmen of the amendment an intention that the due process and equal
protection language of section one carry all its weight and that the
privileges and immunities language be superfluous, Justice Miller's
reading of the section must be rejected.

Justice Miller was not, however, the only member of the Court
who ignored the recent history of the framing and ratification of the
Fourteenth Amendment in drafting his *Slaughter-House* opinion.
The same must be said of Justice Swayne's suggestion that the
framers and ratifiers of the amendment adopted it deliberately with
full knowledge that it would enhance vastly the central government's
power, and of Justice Bradley's advice that, if federal jurisdiction did
expand, the easy remedy would be to appoint more judges and other
officials to carry out the government's responsibilities. The fact is
that the proponents of the Fourteenth Amendment did not want the
jurisdiction and power of the federal government or the size of the
federal bureaucracy to increase significantly as a result of the
amendment's adoption; when they were warned that the amendment
might have such effects, they protested that it would not. Just as
Justice Miller's opinion in the *Slaughter-House Cases* must be
criticized for ignoring the design of section one to provide federal
protection for the basic rights of all citizens, so too the opinions of
Justices Bradley and Swayne must be faulted for ignoring the
concern that the amendment should not substantially change the
balance of federal-state power.

Only the dissenting opinion of Justice Field read the historical
background of the Fourteenth Amendment with any degree of
accuracy. His stated concern with providing equal protection for the
fundamental rights of all citizens was consistent with the concerns of
the amendment's proponents, while his limitation of section one only
to cases involving unequal state action in reference to those fundamental rights minimized federal intrusion into state affairs, as the
proponents of the amendment had striven to do. Indeed, Field's
emphasis both upon protection of individual rights and upon retention of local self-rule was consistent with the basic values of most
mid- and late nineteenth-century Americans. It is thus not surprising
that his moderate reading of the amendment, which did violence to
neither of these values, quickly became the basic doctrine of American
constitutional law.

It took only four years after the decision of the *Slaughter-House Cases* for Justice Field to command a majority on the Court in support of his views. In the first case decided after *Slaughter-House*, *Bradwell* v. *Illinois*,[83] the various justices simply reiterated what they had earlier said. The issue in this now famous case was whether Illinois could refuse to admit Myra Bradwell to the practice of law in that state solely because she was a woman. Eight justices voted to affirm the judgment of the Illinois Supreme Court denying admission to Bradwell; only Chief Justice Salmon P. Chase, who had been a member of the four-man minority in *Slaughter-House*, dissented in *Bradwell*, and he did so without writing any opinion. The eight justices were sharply divided, however, in the reasoning underlying the affirmance. Writing for himself and the four other members of the Court who had joined his opinion in *Slaughter-House*, Justice Miller planted himself firmly on that case, rejecting Bradwell's claim that she was denied a privilege and immunity of a citizen of the United States when she was denied admission to the bar. Miller agreed that the Fourteenth Amendment protected some privileges and immunities, "[b]ut the right to admission to practice in the courts of a State is not one of them. This right," he continued, "in no sense depends on citizenship of the United States." He then concluded:

> The opinion just delivered in the *Slaughter-House Cases* renders elaborate argument in the present case unnecessary; for, unless we are wholly and radically mistaken in the principles on which those cases are decided, the right to control and regulate the granting of license to practice law in the courts of a State is one of those powers which are not transferred for its protection to the Federal government, and its exercise is in no manner governed or controlled by citizenship of the United States in the party seeking such license.
> It is unnecessary to repeat the argument on which the judgment in those cases is founded. It is sufficient to say they are conclusive of the present case.[84]

Justice Bradley, writing for himself and Justices Field and Swayne, did not question Bradwell's general claim that the new Fourteenth Amendment protected the right "to engage in any lawful employment for a livelihood,"[85] but simply viewed the Illinois regulation as a reasonable exercise of the police power. It treated all similar people equally and distinguished between men and women for purposes of admission to the bar only because that distinction lay in the nature of things. In a sexist opinion that tracked what had been said in the Fourteenth Amendment debates, Bradley explained why:

> [T]he civil law, as well as nature herself, has always recognized a wide difference in the respective spheres and destinies of man and woman. Man is, or should be, woman's protector and defender. The natural and proper timidity and delicacy which belongs to the female sex evidently unfits it for many of the occupations of civil life. The constitution of the family organization, which is founded in the divine ordinance, as well as in the nature of things, indicates the domestic sphere as that which properly belongs to the domain and functions of womanhood. The harmony, not to say identity, of interests and views which belong, or should belong, to the family institution is repugnant to the idea of a woman adopting a distinct and independent career from that of her husband. . . . The paramount destiny and mission of woman are to fulfill the noble and benign offices of wife and mother. This is the law of the Creator. And the rules of civil society must be adapted to the general condition of things, and cannot be based upon exceptional cases. . . . In the nature of things it is not every citizen of every age, sex, and condition that is qualified for every calling and position. It is the prerogative of the legislator to prescribe regulations founded on nature, reason, and experience for the due admission of qualified persons to professions and callings demanding special skill and confidence. This fairly belongs to the police power of the State; and, in my opinion, in view of the peculiar characteristics, destiny, and mission of woman, it is within the province of the legislature to ordain what offices, positions, and callings shall be filled and discharged by men, and shall receive the benefit of those energies and responsibilities, and that decision and firmness which are presumed to predominate in the sterner sex.[86]

The next case handed down by the Court involving construction of section one was *Bartemeyer v. Iowa*.[87] The appellant in *Bartemeyer* had been convicted of selling one glass of whiskey in violation of Iowa's temperance act. He claimed that the act violated his Fourteenth Amendment privileges and immunities. Since he had owned the whiskey prior to passage of the act, he also claimed that the act deprived him of property without due process of law.

The Supreme Court was unanimous in rejecting Bartemeyer's claims. Writing for himself and Justices Field and Swayne, Justice Bradley reiterated their common view in *Slaughter-House* that by virtue of section one it had "now become the fundamental law of this country that life, liberty, and property (which include 'the pursuit of happiness') are sacred rights, which the Constitution of the United States guarantees to its humblest citizen against oppressive legislation, whether national or local." Bradley then continued:

> But police regulations, intended for the preservation of the public health and the public order, are of an entirely different character. So much of the Louisiana law as partook of this character was never objected to. It was the unconscionable monopoly, of which the police regulation was a mere pretext, that was deemed by the dissenting members of the court an invasion of the right of the citizen to pursue his lawful calling. A claim of right to pursue an unlawful calling stands on very different grounds, occupying the same platform as does a claim of right to disregard license laws and to usurp public franchises.[88]

To which Justice Field in a separate opinion added: "No one has ever pretended . . . that the fourteenth amendment interferes in any respect with the police power of the State. . . . It was because the act of Louisiana transcended the limits of police regulation, and asserted a power in the State to farm out the ordinary avocations of life, that dissent was made."[89]

The continued willingness of Justices Bradley, Field, and Swayne to restate their *Slaughter-House* dissent suggests that they did not regard the majority opinion in that case as resolving definitively the meaning of section one. Justice Miller's opinion for the Court in *Bartemeyer* suggests that he too recognized that the section's meaning had not been finally determined. Indeed, it may be that all the justices were taking the same approach as Justice Bradley, who the year after the *Bartemeyer* case described himself as "rather in the condition of *seeking for truth*, than that of dogmatically laying down opinions" about the Fourteenth Amendment's meaning.[90]

For whatever reason, while Miller held that Bartemeyer should be denied relief since his case fell "within the principles laid down by this court in the *Slaughter-House Cases*,"[91] he also offered an alternative ground. After observing that Bartemeyer had no legal right to engage in the sale of liquor prior to the passage of the Fourteenth Amendment and that the right he claimed must therefore be derived from the amendment, Miller observed that "the most liberal advocate[s] of the rights conferred by that amendment"—that is, the dissenters in the *Slaughter-House Cases*—"have contended for nothing more than that the rights of the citizen previously existing, and dependent wholly on state laws for their recognition, are now placed under the protection of the Federal government, and are secured by the Federal Constitution."[92] It is difficult to see why Miller made mention of this dissenting view unless he thought it still possessed some attractiveness or even validity for those who might read his opinion.

The majority of the Court moved a step closer to Justice Field's *Slaughter-House* position a year later in a unanimous opinion by the new Chief Justice, Morrison Waite. The opinion was written in *Minor* v. *Happersett*,[93] which held that the Fourteenth Amendment did not confer the right of suffrage on women. Waite did not simply declare in *Happersett*, as other lower court judges had done in analogous cases and as he might have done if he had wished to adopt Justice Miller's *Slaughter-House* views, that the right to vote was not one of those special privileges that arose solely out of national citizenship. Instead, he wrote a delphic paragraph which suggests, when some of its unexpressed assumptions are articulated, that he was prepared to adopt the position of Justice Field.

Waite began by observing that the Fourteenth Amendment "did not add to the privileges and immunities of a citizen," but "simply furnished an additional guaranty for the protection of such as he already had."[94] Waite seems to be suggesting here that the privileges and immunities of citizens are created other than by the federal constitution: either by state law or by some concept of higher law or citizens' rights. The fact that he believes them to be created by state law is established later in the opinion when he turns to state law prior to the adoption of the Fourteenth Amendment to determine what was then the precise scope of voting rights.[95]

Waite next observes that "[n]o new voters were necessarily made by" the amendment. Then comes a key sentence:

> Indirectly it may have had that effect, because it may have increased the number of citizens entitled to suffrage under the constitution and laws of the States, but it operates for this purpose, if at all, through the States and the State laws, and not directly upon the citizen.[96]

The sentence makes little sense except by reference to the point made frequently in the Fourteenth Amendment debates: the amendment did not create rights but instead left their creation to state law; all it did was require the states to give to their least favored citizens the same rights they gave to those who were most favored. Thus the amendment itself would not give anyone the right to vote, but it might extend voting rights already existing under state law to people not previously enjoying them.

This was, of course, the essence of Justice Field's position in his *Slaughter-House* dissent: that a state could not permit some butchers to enjoy exclusive rights not granted to all other butchers, at least when the rights at stake were of such a fundamental nature as the right to engage in a common calling. Within two years of that dissent, the Court seemed to be moving in his direction. It was, however, only tentative movement in a delphic piece of dictum written by a new Chief Justice, whose opinion the justices in the *Slaughter-House* majority may have joined only to promote harmonious relations.

But the Court had begun its march. It took a giant step forward in *Loan Association v. Topeka*,[97] a unanimous opinion written, para-doxically, by Justice Miller. The issue in the case was whether the city of Topeka could refuse to make payments on municipal bonds, for whose payment the power of taxation had been pledged, issued in aid of a privately owned manufacturing corporation. The Court held that it could refuse since the bonds were void from the moment of their issue; the bonds were void, the Court reasoned, because the people had a right to be taxed only for public purposes, not in aid of private interests. Four paragraphs of Justice Miller's opinion require extensive citation:

> [W]here the purpose for which the tax was to be issued could no longer be justly claimed to have this public character, but was purely in aid of private or personal objects, the law authorizing it was beyond the legislative power, and was an unauthorized invasion of private right.
>
> It must be conceded that there are such rights in every free government beyond the control of the State. A government which recognized no such rights, which held the lives, the liberty, and the property of its citizens subject at all times to the absolute disposition and unlimited control of even the most democratic depository of power, is after all but a despotism. It is true it is a despotism of the many, of the majority, if you choose to call it so, but it is none the less a despotism. It may well be doubted if a man is to hold all that he is accustomed to call his own, all in which he has placed his happiness, and the security of which is essential to his happiness, under the unlimited dominion of others, whether it is not wiser that this power should be exercised by one man than by many.
>
> The theory of our governments, State and National, is opposed to the deposit of unlimited power anywhere. The executive, the

legislative, and the judicial branches of these governments are all of limited and defined powers.

There are limitations on such power which grow out of the essential nature of all free governments. Implied reservations of individual rights, without which the social compact could not exist, and which are respected by all governments entitled to the name. No court, for instance, would hesitate to declare void a statute which enacted that A. and B. who were husband and wife to each other should be so no longer, but that A. should thereafter be the husband of C., and B. the wife of D. Or which should enact that the homestead now owned by A. should no longer be his, but should henceforth be the property of B.[98]

How can Justice Miller's opinion in *Loan Association* be squared with *Slaughter-House*? Why would the justice strike down a state legislative act on such broad grounds after refusing, merely two years earlier, to read any significant content into section one of the Fourteenth Amendment? Miller gave his answer in the 1878 case of *Davidson* v. *New Orleans*,[99] where he complained about the "strange misconception" held by many lawyers about "the scope" of section one. "[I]t would seem," he continued, "from the character of many of the cases before us, and the arguments made in them, that the clause under consideration is looked upon as a means of bringing to the test of the decision of this court the abstract opinions of every unsuccessful litigant in a State court." Litigants, according to Miller, were urging the Supreme Court to apply "principles of general constitutional law." According to Miller, the Court "could take jurisdiction" of those general principles only when "sitting in review of a Circuit Court of the United States, as we were in *Loan Association* v. *Topeka*," but not when it was sitting in review of a state court judgment.[100] In the latter sort of case, the Court was limited to what he believed to be the narrow grounds of review spelled out in the Fourteenth Amendment.

It is not clear whether a majority of the Court agreed with Miller's distinction in *Davidson* between diversity cases, where under the rule of *Swift* v. *Tyson*[101] the Court could apply expansive constitutional rules, and federal question cases, where it was bound to read the Fourteenth Amendment narrowly. Nor is it clear that such a distinction makes sense. It is by no means a prescription for minimizing federal intervention in state affairs: the diversity clause has been and can be productive of extensive litigation and, if a rule like *Swift* is applied, of extensive lawmaking on the part of the federal courts. The question raised by the *Davidson* distinction is on whose behalf federal lawmaking will take place. If the Fourteenth Amendment is read broadly and the diversity power construed narrowly, citizens within a state who lack power to influence legislative proceedings will be able to turn to the federal courts and to federal law for relief. If, on the other hand, the diversity power is read broadly and the amendment narrowly, those residing outside the state will be able to obtain federal relief. While Miller's approach was quite consistent with antebellum patterns of federalism, it diverged sharply from the values of Reconstruction political leaders. Miller's approach was also not what the future would find attractive: in the century since *Slaughter-House*, *Loan Association*, and *Davidson*, the federal courts have placed increased emphasis on protection of rights derived from federal law, especially from the Fourteenth Amendment, and have deemphasized the diversity jurisdiction. Although Miller's colleagues were, on the whole, prepared to concur in his broad reading of federal lawmaking authority in diversity cases, they would soon prove unwilling to read the Fourteenth Amendment as narrowly as he would have done.

Two years after it had decided *Loan Association v. Topeka*, the Court adopted the essence of Justice Field's *Slaughter-House* dissent in *Munn v. Illinois*,[102] which upheld the constitutionality of Illinois legislation fixing maximum rates for storage of grain. In an opinion for a seven-man majority, the Chief Justice began with the obvious point, one frequently made during the Reconstruction debates, that when a person "becomes a member of society, he necessarily parts with some rights or privileges." In particular, an individual entering society surrendered to government power to regulate "the conduct of its citizens one towards another, and the manner in which each shall use his own property, when such regulation becomes necessary for the public good." When a person devoted his property to a use that "affect[ed] the community at large," he had to "submit to be controlled by the public for the common good, to the extent of the interest he has thus created."[103] Chief Justice Waite reasoned that the price charged for storage of grain in Chicago's grain elevators affected the community and could therefore be regulated for the common good.

The central assumption of the Chief Justice, which he derived from Justice Field's *Slaughter-House* opinion rather than from Justice

Miller's, was that the Court had jurisdiction under the Fourteenth Amendment to protect property rights. The Chief Justice also agreed with Field that the right to property was limited by the police power— the power, as Justice Bradley had defined it, to preserve "the public health" and "the public order."[104] The thrust of the Chief Justice's opinion in *Munn* was that property could not be regulated in the interest of a few individuals, but only in the interest of the general public. Although Waite did not explicitly so state, his view appeared to agree with the one Justice Field had taken in *Slaughter-House*: that unequal legislation granting special privileges to a few was unconstitutional; on the other hand, legislation which drew distinctions between people in order to accomplish some vision of the common good would be constitutional.

The Chief Justice's opinion in *Munn*, adopting the reasoning of the *Slaughter-House* dissent, was joined by four members of the *Slaughter-House* majority, including the author of the majority opinion, Justice Samuel Miller. Although Miller retained his view that "[t]he Fourteenth Amendment did not radically change the whole theory of the relations of the State and Federal Governments to each other"[105] and "was not designed to interfere with the power of a State to protect the lives, liberty, and property of its citizens,"[106] he abandoned his *Slaughter-House* dicta that the amendment protected only rights created by federal law or was of benefit only to blacks. Miller ultimately accepted the position of the *Slaughter-House* dissenters that section one requires that state "laws operate on all alike, and . . . not subject the individual to an arbitrary exercise of the powers of government."[107] While Miller claimed that " [t]he duty of protecting all its citizens in the enjoyment of an equality of rights" remained with the states, he came around to the dissenters' view that the Fourteenth Amendment created an "obligation resting upon the United States . . . to see that the States do not deny the right."[108] This was precisely what the Court had declared the term before *Munn* in *United States* v. *Cruikshank*.[109]

Two dissenters in *Slaughter-House*—Justices Bradley and Swayne —also joined the *Munn* majority, which had accepted their core views about the scope and meaning of section one. But Justice Field did not. Although the Court in *Munn* had accepted his basic analysis of the Fourteenth Amendment's first section, it was applying the analysis differently, and he refused to join in the application.

Field dissented particularly from the portion of the Chief Justice's opinion that permitted regulation of any property devoted to a use that affected the public interest. Field observed:

> If this be sound law. . . , all property and all business in the State are held at the mercy of a majority of its legislature. The public has no greater interest in the use of buildings for the storage of grain than it has in the use of buildings for the residences of families, nor, indeed, anything like so great an interest; and, according to the doctrine announced, the legislature may fix the rent of all tenements used for residences. . . . The public is interested in the manufacture of cotton, woollen, and silken fabrics, in the construction of machinery, in the printing and publication of books and periodicals, and in the making of utensils of every variety, useful and ornamental; indeed, there is hardly an enterprise or business engaging the attention and labor of any considerable portion of the community, in which the public has not an interest in the sense in which that term is used by the court in its opinion. . . .
>
> [T]he doctrine of this court, that, whenever one's property is used in such a manner as to affect the community at large, it becomes by that fact clothed with a public interest, and ceases to be *juris privati* only, appear[s] to me to destroy, for all useful purposes, the efficacy of the constitutional guaranty. . . .
>
> No reason can be assigned to justify legislation interfering with the legitimate profits of that business (i.e., storage of grain), that would not equally justify an intermeddling with the business of every man in the community, so soon, at least, as his business became generally useful.[110]

Field was not as far apart from the majority of the Court, however, as his language may to some suggest. The only issue that divided Field from Waite was whether grain elevators constituted a special industry that could be subjected to burdensome regulations to which other industries were not subjected. Field's point, which seems well taken, was that the majority's test was insufficient to differentiate the grain elevator business from any other business. But, like the majority, Field was prepared to recognize that states possessed a broad police power to "control the use and possession of . . . property, so far as may be necessary for the protection of the rights of others, and to secure them the equal use and enjoyment of their property." As he further explained:

> It is true that the legislation which secures to all protection in their rights, and the equal use and enjoyment of their property, embraces an almost infinite variety of subjects. Whatever affects

> the peace, good order, morals, and health of the community comes
> within its scope . . . If one construct a building in a city, the State
> . . . may well require its walls to be of sufficient thickness for the
> uses intended; it may forbid the employment of inflammable
> materials in its construction, so as not to endanger the safety of his
> neighbors; if designed as a theatre, church, or public hall, it may
> prescribe ample means of egress, so as to afford facility for escape
> in case of accident; it may forbid the storage in it of powder,
> nitro-glycerine, or other explosive material; it may require its
> occupants daily to remove decayed vegetable and animal matter,
> which would otherwise accumulate and engender disease; it may
> exclude from it all occupations and business calculated to disturb
> the neighborhood or infect the air. Indeed, there is no end of
> regulations with respect to the use of property which may not be
> legitimately prescribed, having for their object the peace, good
> order, safety, and health of the community, thus securing to all the
> equal enjoyment of their property.[111]

But the police power, according to Field, did not give government
power to single out one particular form of property and control the
price which its owners received for its use.[112]

Thus within a four-year period beginnning with the *Slaughter-
House Cases* in 1873 and ending with *Munn* v. *Illinois* in 1877, the
justices, whatever the vagaries of their opinions in individual cases,
had manifested their agreement on some basic doctrinal issues. First,
they had agreed that section one of the Fourteenth Amendment
protected property and by implication other rights against infringement by the states. Second, they had recognized that the states could
regulate protected rights as long as their regulations were reasonable.
Third, they had defined reasonable regulations as those that furthered
the public good and were equal in their impact. None of these
doctrinal conclusions was surprising, since the Court was compelled
to reach all three either by the original meaning of the Fourteenth
Amendment or by the logic of the doctrinal milieu within which the
mid-nineteenth century legal profession functioned.

The conclusion that section one protected property and other rights
flowed from the original understanding of the Fourteenth Amendment; no one can read the history of its enactment without concluding
that the Republican party genuinely intended to guarantee the rights
for which its leaders had struggled for three decades and for which the
Northern people had sacrificed over 300,000 lives. Likewise, the
constant refrain in the legislative history that section one would not

undermine state lawmaking power dictated the further conclusion that the section would override only arbitrary or unreasonable state laws; the contrary conclusion—that section one would override reasonable laws—would have given Congress and the federal courts plenary power to supplant the states.

The history of the Fourteenth Amendment's enactment did not, however, compel the Court to define reasonable regulations as those that were equal. That definition had been expressed in the debates, but not with enough frequency to generate confidence that Republicans in general accepted it. But the concept of reasonableness could have no other meaning for the Supreme Court as it was deciding its first Fourteenth Amendment cases in the years from 1873 to 1876.

Perhaps some Republicans in the 1860s had understood an unreasonable regulation to be one inconsistent with God-given precepts of morality and truth. Many antislavery advocates, after all, had been moral absolutists. But the events of Reconstruction undercut the old morality, and by the 1870s moral absolutism had become a weak foundation on which to rest constitutional doctrine. Evangelical religion was in sharp decline, while scientific Darwinism, though on the rise, did not command universal acquiescence. At a more mundane level, corruption had appeared in the Grant administration. Even more important was the old morality's failure to provide compelling answers to the political issues of Reconstruction, as former moral comrades like Salmon P. Chase, William H. Seward, and Charles Sumner found themselves at odds in regard to the novel political issues they faced. Antislavery moral principles also collapsed in the *Legal Tender Cases*, as justices on both sides of the controversy put the principles to use in their opinions. The *Legal Tender Cases* even witnessed the inconsistency of a Chief Justice holding invalid currency over whose issuance he had presided as Secretary of the Treasury. Even more troublesome was the behavior of the Court as a whole: in 1870, in the 5–3 case of *Hepburn v. Griswold*,[113] it declared the paper currency at issue a less than full substitute for specie, but in 1871, with two new justices on the bench, it reversed itself and held, 5–4, in the *Legal Tender Cases*[114] that creditors were bound to accept the paper as the equivalent of specie.[115]

These and other events between the end of the Civil War and the decision of *Slaughter-House* transformed politics. Those who had hoped in the 1860s to make government conform to transcendent moral values could not be as confident in the early 1870s as they once had been about their capacity to translate morality into law. If the moralists of 1866 had faced a "grand and blessed . . . opportunity,"[116] those same moralists several years later confronted "a kind of moral anarchy,"[117] in which it appeared that "the moral law had expired." "[T]ruths *a priori* held their own against truths purely relative," and "no one could surely say where the real authority, or the real law, lay."[118] With moral truth no longer obvious, the Court could not persuasively define as reasonable legal doctrines which reflected that truth and as unreasonable those which failed. It had to turn instead to other definitions.

One alternative, used occasionally by the Court toward the end of the nineteenth century, defined reasonable as that which was customary and traditional.[119] Such a definition was not commonplace in the middle of the century, however, and to my knowledge no one either in the congressional or state ratification debates on the Fourteenth Amendment or in the early cases construing the amendment defined reasonableness in this fashion. This is not surprising. After all, the principal purpose of the Reconstruction Amendments was to give blacks, at least in the South, rights and protections they had not customarily possessed, and a rule permitting custom to legitimate distinctions between the rights of blacks and whites would have thwarted that purpose.

Since neither morality nor tradition could provide adequate definitions for the concepts of reasonableness and public good, they had to be defined otherwise. This task turned out, in fact, not to be difficult, because the material for an alternative definition was readily at hand in the distinction drawn by nineteenth-century courts between class legislation and legislation enacted for the purpose of benefiting the polity as a whole.

This approach had been elaborated most fully by Lemuel Shaw in *Commonwealth* v. *Alger.*[120] At issue in *Alger* was whether the state could limit the length to which docks extended into Boston harbor in order to insure the free passage of vessels in shipping channels. The court held that "all real estate . . . is subject to some restraint for the general good" and that the legislature had "power, by a general law affecting all . . . equally and alike, to make reasonable regulations, declaring the public right."[121] Earlier in the opinion Shaw had seemed to define regulations for the public good as ones that would prevent property from being "injurious to the equal enjoyment of others having an equal right to the enjoyment of their property."[122] In sum, Shaw defined reasonable legislation enacted for the public good as those laws that protected equally the rights and interests of all members of the community and impinged equally on all who threatened those equal rights. Laws that benefited and affected all equally were to be distinguished, in turn, from class legislation— laws that, in common nineteenth-century jargon, took property or rights away only from A merely for the purpose of giving the same property or rights to B.[123] Such class legislation was, of course, arbitrary and unreasonable.[124]

While this distinction between laws enacted for all members of the community equally and laws enacted for the benefit of special interests may not seem useful to modern political theorists who view all law as a product of interest-group conflict, it did make sense to nineteenth-century Americans possessing a different conception of politics. But most important for present purposes is the overlap between such a conception and notions of equality before the law. A law enacted for the benefit of the public that will achieve its aims by imposing the same burdens on all members of the public is an equal as well as a reasonable law, while class legislation—a law that benefits class A at the expense of class B—is arbitrary and unequal. In this sense, a law can be reasonable only if it treats all people equally, and will be unreasonable whenever it treats people unequally.

Although the conceptions of reasonableness and equality before the law may not be identical, the Supreme Court did equate them with each other in the cases culminating in *Munn*, and the equation served the justices well. Of course, the concept of equality by itself resolved few, if any, issues: it merely told the justices that like people must receive the same treatment and that people could be treated differently only if they were, in fact, different. It thereby directed the justices to decide whether people were in fact alike or different. Nonetheless the concept was useful because it enabled the Supreme Court to interpret the Fourteenth Amendment without foundering on the difficulty that had split the Republican party into factions between 1865 and 1872.

The difficulty was that an ideology of fundamental rights could attract support in a pluralistic culture only as long as the ideology remained vague. The majority of the Northern electorate could readily unite against slavery in the late 1850s, when the ideology required no more than vigilance against the extension of an evil slave system. But when Reconstruction raised issues such as federal protection of civil rights and military support of black governments, Republican leaders like William H. Seward and Salmon P. Chase split off from their former compatriots in Congress. Unfortunately for the Court, the nature of the common law adjudicatory process is such that its acceptance of the invitation of cases like *Slaughter-House* and *Bradwell* to specify the rights of individuals in detail would have invited litigants to bring every claim of right to the Court's attention. And, as it passed judgment on each claim, the Court would have faced a constant erosion and fragmentation of its support.

Instead, the Court had recourse to equality, an ideology whose very vagueness and emptiness[125] had helped to keep it acceptable to diverse groups in pluralistic, late nineteenth-century America. The Court was able thereby to avoid divisive declarations of principle and to focus instead on questions of a more empirical nature about whether groups classified differently by legislation were, in fact, similar and hence entitled to equal treatment. At times, the Court was also able to take advantage of widespread agreement on specific factual assumptions about whether differences between people would justify legislation treating them differently. Thus in *Bradwell* it could rest on the widely shared perception that women should have a different social role than men, while in *Bartemeyer* it could rely on the shared understanding that prohibition laws were not enacted so that the class of nondrinkers would improve their welfare at the expense of drinkers, but in order to enhance the well-being of all. Of course, in some key areas, especially those involving race relations and business regulation, the Court often could not rely on any significant public agreement about the facts that must underlie its decisions. But even in these cases, recourse to the rhetoric of equality enabled the Court to avoid divisive statements of principle, to decide cases on factual grounds that did not loudly proclaim unpopular doctrine or greatly limit the Court's capacity to approach future cases on their own merits, and thus to avoid the sort of public outcry generated by decisions creating inflexible constitutional rights, such as *Scott* v. *Sandford*,[126] *Lochner* v. *New York*,[127] and *Roe* v. *Wade*.[128] And, as we shall see, the Court was also able to decide the cases it faced in the troublesome areas of race and business regulation without depriving section one of the impact it was designed to have as a protector of personal rights, or transforming it into an engine for the destruction of the police power of the states. The justices, on the contrary, "temperately construed and applied the amendment" in a manner marked by "ability and moderation"[129] that was consistent with the history of the amendment's framing and ratification.

One extreme position the justices had rejected by 1876 was the one Justice Miller put forward in *Slaughter-House*—that the Fourteenth Amendment applied only to cases involving blacks and did not protect fundamental rights, such as rights of property and contract. That position, as we have already seen, would have narrowed the scope of section one far beyond the intentions of those who put it into the Constitution.[130] The Court also rejected a position at the opposite extreme suggested by Justice Bradley in dissent. This position would have precluded any state lawmaking in reference to certain fundamental rights, such as the right to engage in a trade or to use one's property to generate income; as we have also seen, few of the framers and ratifiers of the Fourteenth Amendment meant to limit so radically the lawmaking power of the states.

The Court was left with the principle " 'that every citizen shall hold his life, liberty, property, and immunities, under the protection of the general rules which govern society.' "[131] "Those who make the laws," according to Thomas M. Cooley, were " 'to govern by promulgated, established law, not to be varied in particular cases;' "[132] "[e]quality of rights, privileges, and capacities unquestionably should be the aim of the law."[133] Distinctions in the law had to "rest upon some reason upon which they can be defended,—like the want of capacity in infants and insane persons"[134] or the fact that it was "from the nature of the case . . . impossible" that some privilege could be "possessed and enjoyed by all."[135] Cooley continued:

> [I]f the legislature should undertake to provide that persons following some specified lawful trade or employment should not have capacity to make contracts, or to receive conveyances, or to build such houses as others were allowed to erect, or in any other way to make such use of their property as was permissible to others, it can scarcely be doubted that the act would transcend the due bounds of legislative power.[136]

Other late nineteenth-century commentators repeated like themes. William D. Guthrie noted that in considering the validity of a state enactment under section one,

> the inquiry is whether the regulation or classification has been designed to subserve some reasonable public purpose, or is a mere device or excuse for an unjust discrimination, or for the oppression or spoliation of a particular class. Any regulation of the internal affairs of the State, fairly subserving a valid police purpose and reasonably exercised for the benefit of the community at large, will be upheld; but if it be arbitrary and have no substantial relation to the health, morals, peace, or welfare of the community, it will be nullified.[137]

Christopher G. Tiedeman likewise concluded that the Supreme Court would invalidate "[a]ny law . . . which undertakes to abolish rights, the exercise of which does not involve an infringement of the rights of others, or to limit the exercise of rights beyond what is necessary to provide for the public welfare and the general security."[138] James Bradley Thayer agreed that "[w]hat may be called the *regulative* power of the leg[islature] . . . adjusts the rights of each by refer[ence] to the rights of all others."[139] Students report Thayer stating in his constitutional law class that the Fourteenth Amendment "operate[d] to check *police power* . . . [o]nly by securing equal *protection* of *laws*."[140] "An exercise of the police power," he continued, "must not be an arbitrary deprivation of life, liberty or property."[141] "The first question is whether there is a *rational public reason* for it. A class cannot be selected because they have red hair, but . . . [only] on the ground of some rational public reason."[142] A state statute would be constitutional only if it was enacted "for a public purpose and the equal benefit."[143]

Thayer emphasized that "[e]*qual* protection & security is the important point" of the Fourteenth Amendment's section one. The "[a]mendment doesn't *secure* every thing to every body but simply equality." Indeed, the Fourteenth Amendment did not give "an individual any rights," according to Thayer;[144] rights were derived from state law, and all that the Fourteenth Amendment did was ensure that less favored citizens received the same rights as those who were more favored. Thomas M. Cooley also told his students that rights could not be antecedent to state law; one of his students recorded him as saying that " [t]here can be no liberty until there are governmental protections for it."[145] For Cooley, as we have seen, the Fourteenth Amendment merely guaranteed equality.

Even the most ardent scholarly proponent of natural rights in the late nineteenth century agreed. Christopher G. Tiedeman recognized that, strictly speaking, no such thing as a natural right could exist, "for there can be no legal right which is not recognized or created by the sovereign power of the state."[146] Tiedeman claimed only that ideas about natural rights were important since they influenced popular views about the law.[147] But he did not argue that the Supreme Court should enforce rights unsanctified by a sovereign lawmaking body. On the contrary, Tiedeman joined in the prevailing consensus that state legislators were the primary creators of rights and that the task of the Supreme Court in enforcing the Fourteenth Amendment was only to police how the states distributed the rights.

▪ The Application of Uniform Doctrine, 1877–1900

It may have been inevitable that legal thinkers in the last quarter of the nineteenth century would develop a consensus that section one of the Fourteenth Amendment left states free to determine the rights their citizens would enjoy and gave federal courts power only to ensure that the states distributed rights equally in a fashion designed to promote the public good. The consensus of treatise writers, after all, mirrored a more general consensus to which nearly all political leaders and most of the American people, Democrats as well as Republicans, adhered. As we saw in previous chapters, Republicans agreed with Democrats about the importance to liberty of preserving state governments as viable lawmaking entities. Similarly, Democrats agreed with Republicans that states should not draw arbitrary lines between their residents but should govern them equally. A principle of law that left the states free to determine the rights of their people as long as they conferred rights equally and nonarbitrarily was fully consistent with this more general political consensus.

Moreover, insofar as judges respected an obligation to act consistently with the intentions of the amendment's framers, no other approach seemed available. Federal judges could not have determined on a case-by-case basis the personal and economic rights that individuals possessed since that would have made the judges rather than the legislatures the governors of the states, contrary to the contemplation of the framers. It was equally clear that judges could not read all substantive content out of the amendment, as Justice Miller tried to do in *Slaughter-House*, since the amendment had been designed to provide remedies not only for blacks but also for others who were victims of arbitrary state laws. Judges and legal thinkers had only two choices consistent with the framers' intentions: they could interpret the Fourteenth Amendment as a guarantee merely of equal rights, or they could read it as an absolute protection of fundamental rights, subject, however, to power on the part of the states to regulate those rights equally. Perhaps there were marginal variations in these two approaches that would become important if a state attempted to deprive all its citizens of a fundamental right. But in the closing decades of the nineteenth century, no one argued that states were totally depriving citizens of fundamental rights; the only allegations presented to the Court were claims that states were unreasonably regulating rights or distributing rights unequally. In the face of such claims, the two approaches were not materially different and, as a result, they were conflated by the Court into a single line of doctrine prohibiting unequal and unreasonable regulations. During the last two decades of the nineteenth century, the Supreme Court enforced this line of doctrine in a series of cases that transformed American "constitutional history . . . [into] little more than a commentary on the Fourteenth Amendment"[148] and made that amendment "the most important of all the additions" to the Constitution.[149]

Some of the cases applied the amendment in obvious ways designed to protect the rights of blacks. One such case was *Strauder* v. *West Virgina*,[150] which reversed a conviction of a black man because he had been indicted by a grand jury and found guilty by a petit jury from which blacks were excluded by statute. The Court recognized that the Fourteenth Amendment left states free to "prescribe the qualifications of its jurors, and in doing so [to] make discriminations." A state could "confine the selection to males, to freeholders, to citizens, to persons within certain ages, or to persons having educational qualifications."[151] Section one did not prevent state lawmaking and state regulation of citizens' rights, but it did provide protection for certain "rights and immunities, prominent among which is an immunity from inequality of legal protection."[152] "It was designed to assure to the colored race the enjoyment of all the civil rights that under the law are enjoyed by white persons." The Fourteenth Amendment "not only gave citizenship and the privileges of citizenship to persons of color, but it denied to any State the power to withhold from them the equal protection of the laws."[153] It granted "the right to exemption from unfriendly legislation against them distinctively as colored,—exemption from legal discriminations, implying inferiority in civil society, lessening the security of their enjoyment of the rights which others enjoy, and discriminations which are steps toward reducing them to the condition of a subject race." As the Court observed:

> The very fact that colored people are singled out and expressly denied by a statute all right to participate in the administration of the law, as jurors, because of their color, though they are citizens, and may be in other respects fully qualified, is practically a brand upon them, affixed by the law, an assertion of their inferiority, and a stimulant to that race prejudice which is an impediment to securing to individuals of the race that equal justice which the law aims to secure to all others.[154]

The Court was prepared to enforce the Fourteenth Amendment's core principle of equality even when a state judge, without statutory direction, acted in a racially discriminatory fashion. *Ex parte Virginia*[155] arose when a judge of a Virginia state court was indicted for violating a federal statute prohibiting blacks from being disqualified from serving on juries on racial grounds. The Commonwealth of Virginia did not by statute bar blacks from serving on juries, but the judge who was indicted nonetheless had taken it upon himself to exclude all blacks from juries he was charged with selecting. Upon his indictment, the judge sought a writ of habeas corpus from the Supreme Court. It denied the writ.

Ex parte Virginia constituted an important extension of previous Fourteenth Amendment cases because it involved a discriminatory practice that was being carried on under a statute that was racially neutral on its face. It thus raised the question whether the Fourteenth Amendment barred only discriminatory legislation or reached any discrimination carried out by any state official. According to the Court, the amendment

> must mean that no agency of the State, or of the officers or agents by whom its powers are exerted, shall deny to any person within its jurisdiction the equal protection of the laws. Whoever, by virtue of public position under a State government, deprives another of property, life, or liberty, without due process of law, or denies or takes away the equal protection of the laws, violates the constitutional inhibition; and as he acts in the name and for the State, and is clothed with the State's power, his act is that of

the State. This must be so, or the constitutional prohibition has no meaning.[156]

The Court was also prepared to permit use of the amendment in a way that opponents had feared it might be used: as a basis for a criminal proceeding against a state judge. What the Court actually did in *Ex parte Virginia* was to affirm the power of the federal government to indict and prosecute the Virginia judge; as the Court explained, the federal government had to be able to proceed against officials of the state because otherwise the state would be able to "clothe . . . one of its agents with power to annul or to evade [the constitutional provision]."[157] But despite its decision holding the judge for trial, the Court acted in a fashion that pointed toward creation of a doctrine of judicial immunity and hence toward a weakening of the Fourteenth Amendment. It held the judge subject to prosecution because it found that the activity of selecting jurors was a ministerial rather than a judicial act that "often is given to county commissioners, or supervisors, or assessors" and "[i]n former times . . . was made by the sheriff."[158] The fact that Virginia gave the task to a judge did not make the task a judicial one and thereby immunize it from federal regulation. But the plain implication of the opinion was that genuine judicial tasks, even if performed in a patently racist manner by a patently racist judge, were beyond the reach of federal control.[159]

In so deciding *Ex parte Virginia*, the Court acted in the commonplace way of all nineteenth-century American institutions in dealing with Fourteenth Amendment issues in the context of racial discrimination. In race cases, the amendment invariably generated a tension between enforcement of its promise of equality for blacks and some other value basic to the American system of government as understood by Americans of the time. Invariably the institutions of the time strove to avoid resolution of that basic value conflict, searching instead for some way to balance the competing values so as to accommodate both to the greatest extent possible. During the course of the Fourteenth Amendment debates in 1866–1868, the fundamental tension of which the framers and ratifiers were aware was between the need for federal protection of rights and the tradition of local lawmaking power over the details of citizens' lives. Those who supported the amendment argued that both values could be served if the amendment were understood to leave lawmaking power to the states and to give the federal government jurisdiction only to require that states legislate on behalf of all citizens equally. As we have already seen, all the justices of the Supreme Court accepted this balanced position sometime between 1873 and 1877, in the line of cases from *Slaughter-House* to *Munn*.

Ex parte Virginia placed the need for federal protection of rights in tension with judicial independence—the institutional practice which has served as a foundation for protection of individual rights through most of Anglo-American legal history. Not surprisingly, the Court strove to balance the competing values. It tried to leave intact the doctrine of judicial immunity and hence the independence of the bench, while at the same time protecting the right of the minority to sit on juries. The Court behaved similarly in another of the leading race cases of the late nineteenth century, *Plessy v. Ferguson*.[160] Although *Plessy* appears as the quintessentially racist case to those of us raised on the progressivism of *Brown v. Board of Education*,[161] it will take on a more balanced, moderate appearance when examined in its own context.

Plessy upheld the constitutionality of a Louisiana statute requiring railroads to furnish separate facilities for the transportation of white and black passengers. The opinion of the Court, by Justice Henry B. Brown, was not racist in tone; rather, it was legalistic in style,[162] relying chiefly on precedent and analogy to sustain its result. Until the analogy and the precedents on which the Court's opinion are based are examined, the values that were in tension in the case and the manner in which the tension was resolved cannot be appreciated.

The analogy to which the Court turned in *Plessy* was public education. One value at stake in public school cases in the late nineteenth century was, of course, the right of black children to equal educational opportunity. The competing value was best articulated in two of the many state cases which, prior to *Plessy*, had already authorized racial segregation in the public schools. Thus in *Lehew v. Brummell*,[163] after the Supreme Court of Missouri had conceded that school segregation involved a "classification . . . based on color," it went on to explain, consistently with widely held Darwinian concepts of social science,[164] that

> color carries with it natural race peculiarities which furnish the
> reason for the classification. There are differences in races, and
> between individuals of the same race, not created by human laws,
> some of which can never be eradicated. These differences create

different social relations recognized by all well-organized governments. If we are to cast aside chimerical theories and look to practical results, it seems to us it must be conceded that separate schools for colored children is a regulation to their great advantage.[165]

Likewise, in *Roberts* v. *City of Boston*,[166] the Supreme Judicial Court of Massachusetts had explained the basis for segregated schools as follows:

> It is urged, that this maintenance of separate schools tends to deepen and perpetuate the odious distinction of caste, founded in a deep-rooted prejudice in public opinion. This prejudice, if it exists, is not created by law, and proabably cannot be changed by law. Whether this distinction and prejudice, existing in the opinion and feelings of the community, would not be as effectually fostered by compelling colored and white children to associate together in the same schools, may well be doubted; at all events, it is a fair and proper question for the committee to consider and decide upon, having in view the best interests of both classes of children placed under their superintendence.[167]

Nineteenth-century courts recognized the legitimacy of white parents' claims that they should have some autonomy in determining the people with whom their children associated in school, and were not prepared to subordinate that claim entirely to the interest of blacks in equal educational opportunity for their children.

But the courts were not racist. Although they accepted white claims of freedom of association, they nonetheless demanded that black children receive an equal education. Three years after *Plessy* the Supreme Court indicated that, if a local school board refused to provide a school for blacks while providing one for whites, and its refusal was motivated by a "hostility to the colored population because of their race," it would set aside the board's action as arbitrary.[168] Moreover, in permitting segregated education, the courts were clear that "[u]nder it, the colored children . . . have made a rapid stride in the way of education."[169] From the perspective of *Brown* v. *Board of Education*, the argument that separate schools could provide adequate and equal educational opportunities for blacks seems absurd, if not dishonest. But to deferential judges, who understood their obligation to accept legislative fact-findings that were not clearly erroneous, the argument that segregated schools are capable of providing equal educational opportunity might not have seemed outrageous in the context of the 1890s—when three decades of schooling, albeit separate, had done much to narrow the gap between white and black educational attainments.[170] Even if a judge thought this argument wrong, his practice of deference might lead him to accept it.

The point, however, is not to provide justification for *Plessy* or to cast doubt on the holding of *Brown*: it is that the *Plessy* court acted in much the same fashion as had the framers of the Fourteenth Amendment. When confronted with competing claims of principle, each having strong support among different segments of society, the men of both institutions compromised, made concessions to both points of view, and left ultimate issues unresolved. The Reconstruction Congress did not resolve the question whether the Fourteenth Amendment permits or prohibits segregation, nor should *Plessy* be understood to have legitimated the practice except in a context where it held out some promise of ultimate racial equality. Indeed, not even *Brown* should be understood to have spoken the final word about race relations in America: the Supreme Court during the past three decades has permitted nearly all white parents to keep their children out of schools containing large numbers of black children[171] even while it has proclaimed the importance of racial equality and integration. The nation values the right of blacks to equality, but it also values the competing right of freedom of association. Americans in 1866, in 1896, and today have persistently refused to determine which right they value more. All that has occurred over the course of 120 years is doctrinal oscillation between the competing values as the courts have striven to preserve both.

The Court adopted a similar balanced posture in a trilogy of cases arising out of the efforts of the San Francisco Board of Supervisors to regulate the city's laundry industry and its principal group of workers —the Chinese. The first case to come before the Court was *Barbier* v. *Connolly*,[172] which upheld a provision of a city ordinance prohibiting the washing and ironing of clothes in a public laundry between the hours of 10 P.M. and 6 A.M. In an opinion for a unanimous Court, Justice Field emphasized the broad reach of the Fourteenth Amendment. He wrote that the first section

> undoubtedly intended not only that there should be no arbitrary deprivation of life or liberty, or arbitrary spoliation of property, but that equal protection and security should be given to all

under like circumstances in the enjoyment of their personal and civil rights; that all persons should be equally entitled to pursue their happiness and acquire and enjoy property; that they should have like access to the courts of the country for the protection of their persons and property, the prevention and redress of wrongs, and the enforcement of contracts; that no impediment should be interposed to the pursuits of any one except as applied to the same pursuits by others under like circumstances; that no greater burdens should be laid upon one than are laid upon others in the same calling and condition, and that in the administration of criminal justice no different or higher punishment should be imposed upon one than such as is prescribed to all for like offences.[173]

But Field followed his statement about the breadth of the amendment with a statement about the broad scope which the amendment left for the lawmaking power of the states. According to Field,

the amendment—broad and comprehensive as it is . . . was [not] designed to interfere with the power of the State, sometimes termed its police power, to prescribe regulations to promote the health, peace, morals, education, and good order of the people, and to legislate so as to increase the industries of the State, develop its resources, and add to its wealth and prosperity. From the very necessities of society, legislation of a special character, having these objects in view, must often be had in certain districts, such as for draining marshes and irrigating arid plains. Special burdens are often necessary for general benefits—for supplying water, preventing fires, lighting districts, cleaning streets, opening parks, and many other objects. Regulations for these purposes may press with more or less weight upon one than upon another, but they are designed, not to impose unequal or unnecessary restrictions upon any one, but to promote, with as little individual inconvenience as possible, the general good. Though, in many respects, necessarily special in their character, they do not furnish just ground of complaint if they operate alike upon all persons and property under the same circumstances and conditions. Class legislation, discriminating against some and favoring others, is prohibited, but legislation which, in carrying out a public purpose, is limited in its application, if within the sphere of its operation it affects alike all persons similarly situated, is not within the amendment.[174]

Field elaborated further upon the broad power of the legislature in *Soon Hing* v. *Crowley*,[175] decided later in the same term. *Soon Hing* upheld legislation almost identical to that upheld in *Barbier*. The importance of the case lies in Field's statement of bases, additional to those listed in *Barbier*, for exercise of the police power. He focused in *Soon Hing* on regulation of "the hours of labor," observing:

> On few subjects has there been more regulation. How many hours shall constitute a day's work in the absence of contract, at what time shops in our cities shall close at night, are constant subjects of legislation. Laws setting aside Sunday as a day of rest are upheld, not from any right of the government to legislate for the promotion of religious observances, but from its right to protect all persons from the physical and moral debasement which comes from uninterrupted labor. Such laws have always been deemed beneficent and merciful laws, especially to the poor and dependent, to the laborers in our factories and workshops and in the heated rooms of our cities.[176]

Even if the motive of the legislation was not to regulate hours of labor in general, but to protect white laborers from competition by hard-working Chinese, Field said the legislation would be valid since courts could not "inquire into the motives of the legislators in passing" laws.[177]

Thus, after describing with broad strokes the power conferred on the federal courts by the Fourteenth Amendment to protect individual rights, Justice Field had gone on in *Barbier* and *Soon Hing* to uphold the legislation at issue on the basis of an equally broad description of the police power. In the next term, however, the balance redressed itself when the Court, in *Yick Wo v. Hopkins*,[178] overturned a conviction for violating another San Francisco ordinance regulating the laundry industry. In essence, the ordinance prohibited the operation of laundries in wooden buildings without first obtaining a permit from city authorities. On its face, the ordinance was plainly within the police power, since laundries could not function in the nineteenth century without fires, and fires were a special hazard in a windy city like San Francisco. The evidence, however, showed that permission to operate laundries in wooden buildings was denied to every Chinese applying for it, but granted to all but one non-Chinese applicant. On the basis of this evidence the Court found that San Francisco authorities were acting

> with a mind so unequal and oppressive as to amount to a practical denial by the State of that equal protection of the laws which is secured to the petitioners. . . . Though the law itself be fair on its face and impartial in appearance, yet, if it is applied and administered by public authority with an evil eye and an

unequal hand, so as practically to make unjust and illegal discriminations between persons in similar circumstances, material to their rights, the denial of equal justice is still within the prohibition of the Constitution.[179]

As the Court had earlier declared in dictum,

[T]he fundamental rights to life, liberty, and the pursuit of happiness, considered as individual possessions, are secured by those maxims of constitutional law which are the monuments showing the victorious progress of the race in securing to men the blessings of civilization under the reign of just and equal laws. . . . [T]he very idea that one man may be compelled to hold his life, or the means of living, or any material right essential to the enjoyment of life, at the mere will of another, seems to be intolerable in any country where freedom prevails, as being the essence of slavery itself.[180]

Despite the broad language of *Yick Wo*, the Court continued to pursue a balance between protecting rights and preserving legislative power. It recognized that a fundamental right should "not [be] regarded strictly as a natural right, but as a privilege merely conceded by society according to its will."[181] The Court was prepared to grant legislatures broad discretion in regulating private rights and would not intervene lightly upon a claim that those rights were violated. But it would intervene when, as in *Yick Wo*, it was confronted with egregiously unequal or arbitrary state action.

The Court strove for similar balance in the many business regulation cases that crowded its docket in the last two decades of the century. *Crowley* v. *Christensen*,[182] authored by Justice Field in 1890, set the tone. The case came to the Court because Christensen, a retail liquor dealer, and the court below had misread *Yick Wo*. San Francisco had an ordinance, analogous to that struck down in *Yick Wo*, prohibiting retail sale of liquor without a license, and Christensen, like Yick Wo, had been denied a license. Arguing that his case fit within *Yick Wo*, Christensen applied to the federal circuit court in San Francisco for a writ of habeas corpus that would bar state prosecution of him for selling liquor without a license, and the court granted the writ.

The Supreme Court reversed. Justice Field explained that *Christensen* was "essentially different" from *Yick Wo*, where the ordinance held invalid had "vest[ed] uncontrolled discretion in the board of supervisors with reference to a business harmless in itself and useful to the community" and the discretion had "been exercised for the express purpose of depriving the petitioner of a privilege that was extended to others."[183] Field took pains to explain why the use of liquor was potentially harmful to the community and also took note of evidence—namely of thefts committed on Christensen's premises by his wife—suggesting that good reason existed for denying him his license. He then repeated what he and the Court had said so often about the scope of individual rights and the police power of the state:

> It is undoubtedly true that it is the right of every citizen of the United States to pursue any lawful trade or business, under such restrictions as are imposed upon all persons of the same age, sex and condition. But the possession and enjoyment of all rights are subject to such reasonable conditions as may be deemed by the governing authority of the country essential to the safety, health, peace, good order, and morals of the community. Even liberty itself, the greatest of all rights, is not unrestricted license to act according to one's own will. It is only freedom from restraint under conditions essential to the equal enjoyment of the same right by others. It is then liberty regulated by law. The right to acquire, enjoy, and dispose of property is declared in the constitutions of several States to be one of the inalienable rights of man. But this declaration is not held to preclude the legislature of any State from passing laws respecting the acquisition, enjoyment and disposition of property . . . And as to the enjoyment of property, the rule is general that it must be accompanied with such limitations as will not impair the equal enjoyment by others of their property. *Sic utere tuo ut alienum non laedas* is a maxim of universal application.
>
> For the pursuit of any lawful trade or business, the law imposes similar conditions. Regulations respecting them are almost infinite, varying with the nature of the business. Some occupations by the noise made in their pursuit, some by the odors they engender, and some by the dangers accompanying them, require regulations as to the locality in which they shall be conducted. Some by the dangerous character of the articles used, manufactured or sold require, also, special qualifications in the parties permitted to use, manufacture or sell them. All this is but common knowledge.[184]

Indeed, as the business of selling liquor was "attended with danger to the community," it could be "entirely prohibited,"[185] as it had been under legislation upheld in *Mugler* v. *Kansas*,[186] where the Court had taken note of "[t]he power which the States have of prohibiting such use by individuals of their property as will be prejudicial to the health, the morals, or the safety of the public."[187]

The Court likewise sustained the police power of the state in *Powell v. Pennsylvania*,[188] when it upheld legislation prohibiting the manufacture or sale of oleomargarine as a substitute for butter. The Court took note of the danger that oleomargarine could be sold fraudulently as butter, and declared that the decision whether to prevent such fraud by prohibition or merely by regulation of the industry involved "questions of fact and of public policy which belong to the legislative department to determine."[189] In *Missouri Pacific Railway* v. *Mackey*,[190] the Court also upheld legislation making railroads but not other industries responsible to their employees for the negligence of fellow servants, with Justice Field declaring:

> But the hazardous character of operating a railway would seem to call for special legislation with respect to railroad corporations, having for its object the protection of its employe[e]s as well as the safety of the public. The business of other corporations is not subject to similar dangers to their employe[e]s, and no objections, therefore, can be made to the legislation on the ground of its making an unjust discrimination.[191]

The Court also sustained state regulation of intrastate railroad rates in *Stone* v. *Farmer's Loan & Trust Co.*[192] and *Wabash, St. Louis and Pacific Ry.* v. *Illinois*[193] on the same ground that it had sustained regulation of grain elevator rates in *Munn* v. *Illinois*[194]— that railroads were of specially public character and concern. The Court was careful to state, however, that it should "not ... be inferred that this power of ... regulation is ... without limit,"[195] and when the Court was confronted with a case in which a railroad claimed that it was denied an opportunity to present evidence in court that a rate setting commission had treated it arbitrarily, the Court applied *Yick Wo*, gave the railroad its day in court, and invalidated the statute which set rates without any judicial review whatever.[196]

Hundreds of state cases reaffirmed the approach taken by the nation's highest court. State judges regularly declared unconstitutional regulatory legislation that contained unequal classifications or worked for the benefit of a narrow class rather than the community as a whole. But at the same time state governments continued to engage vigorously in activities promoting and regulating the economy, and the courts sustained their activities when there were plausible arguments that they were carried on for the benefit of the people as a whole.[197]

Criminal procedure was a final area where the Supreme Court deferred to state lawmaking as long as state law was not clearly arbitrary. Thus in *Hurtado* v. *California*[198] the Court declined to hold that section one of the Fourteenth Amendment incorporated the Bill of Rights and required a state to abide by the Fifth Amendment's requirement that no person be held to a criminal charge except upon indictment by a grand jury. As Chief Justice Melville W. Fuller declared in *Caldwell* v. *Texas*,[199] "[b]y the Fourteenth Amendment the powers of the States in dealing with crime within their borders are not limited." "But," as the Court said in *Hurtado*,

> it is not to be supposed that these legislative powers are absolute and despotic, and that the amendment prescribing due process of law is too vague and indefinite to operate as a practical restraint. It is not every act, legislative in form, that is law. Law is something more than mere will exerted as an act of power. It must not be a special rule for a particular person or a particular case . . . Arbitrary power, enforcing its edicts to the injury of the persons and property of its subjects, is not law, whether manifested as the decree of a personal monarch or of an impersonal multitude. And the limitations imposed by our constitutional law upon the action of the governments, both State and national, are essential to the preservation of public and private rights, notwithstanding the representative character of our political institutions. The enforcement of these limitations by judicial process is the device of self-governing communities to protect the rights of individuals and minorities, as well against the power of numbers, as against the violence of public agents transcending the limits of lawful authority, even when acting in the name and wielding the force of the government.[200]

As the Court added in *Caldwell*, no state could use the criminal process to "deprive particular persons or classes of persons of equal and impartial justice under law." Every state had to grant criminal defendants "due process," as "secured by laws operating on all alike."[201]

The moderate course pursued by the Court during the last quarter of the nineteenth century in cases dealing with race relations, business regulation, and criminal procedure preordained the outcome of the most important Fourteenth Amendment case decided by the Court between *Slaughter-House* and the end of the century—the *Civil Rights Cases*,[202] in which the Supreme Court declared unconstitutional an act of Congress prohibiting discrimination in the furnishing of transportation and public accommodations to blacks. The Court reasoned that the act sought to prevent discrimination by private individuals and that the Fourteenth Amendment did not reach that far, prohibiting only discrimination by state governments and state officials.

The issue at the root of the *Civil Rights Cases* was whether section one should be construed to guarantee fundamental civil rights absolutely or only to protect equality in the enjoyment of those rights. If the amendment protected fundamental rights absolutely, and if access to transportation facilities and public accommodations was a fundamental right, then it could be argued that a violation of the Fourteenth Amendment occurred whenever anyone, either a private individual or a public official, deprived another of such a right. If, on the other hand, the amendment only provided equal protection for rights created by state law, then it gave neither Congress nor the federal courts any jurisdiction over matters as to which the states decided not to create rights.

This basic issue had already been resolved, however, in the *Slaughter-House Cases* and in *Munn* v. *Illinois*, and Justice Bradley's opinion in the *Civil Rights Cases* merely reaffirmed that resolution. Bradley wrote that the Fourteenth Amendment did "not invest Congress with power to legislate upon subjects which are within the domain of State legislation . . . [or] to create a code of municipal law for the regulation of private rights."[203] It did not "cover the whole domain of rights appertaining to life, liberty and property, defining them and providing for their vindication. That would be to establish a code of municipal law regulative of all private rights between man and man in society. It would be to make Congress take the place of the State legislatures and to supersede them."[204] The amendment did not give Congress power to enact "general legislation upon the rights of the citizen, but corrective legislation . . . for counteracting such laws as the States may adopt or enforce" denying some person or class rights granted to others.[205] Although the Court was prepared to assume that the right of blacks to "equal accommodation and privileges in all inns, public conveyances, and places of public amusement, [was] one of the essential rights of citizens [created by state law] which no State can [arbitrarily] abridge,"[206] it was not prepared to treat mere inaction on the part of a state in failing to protect the right as a warrant for Congressional legislation.

The main premise of the *Civil Rights Cases* was thus the main premise of American constitutionalism in the last third of the nineteenth century. That premise was that individual rights did not preexist law and were not created by federal law; individual civil rights were the creations of state law. The federal government could have no power to determine the content of civil rights if it was to remain the government of limited power that all Americans wanted. The only power that the Fourteenth Amendment granted to Congress and the federal courts was power to hold the states to the rule of law: the power to insure that the states extended the same rights to all individuals equally except on those occasions when the good of the public at large demanded that distinctions between individuals be drawn.

Not even Justice Harlan, who dissented in the *Civil Rights Cases*,[207] questioned these basic assumptions of late nineteenth-century constitutionalism. Harlan did not claim that blacks had any right of access to public conveyances and accommodations or any right to equal treatment from white individuals, for such rights would have obliterated the freedom of association of white individuals as well as state power. Harlan argued only that the common law and hence existing state law already required hotels, common carriers, and the like to furnish services to all who sought them and that the congressional legislation at issue in the *Civil Rights Cases* thus insured, as the Fourteenth Amendment required, only that state law be applied equally to blacks and whites.

In taking this position Harlan was merely pursuing an early dictum in *United States* v. *Cruikshank*,[208] and an even earlier suggestion made by Justice Bradley, the author of the majority opinion in the *Civil Rights Cases*. Like the *Civil Rights Cases*, *Cruikshank* had held that Congress has no power under the Fourteenth Amendment to protect one person from being deprived of his rights by another. This holding, as we have seen, followed from the Court's conclusion in the 1873–1877 era that "equality of the rights of citizens" was the "principle of republicanism" that the Fourteenth "[A]mendment guarantees, but no more."[209] States were free under this interpretation to fail to grant any particular right at all; the only limitation on their power was that they could not grant a right to some citizens and arbitrarily deny it to others. What *Cruikshank* recognized, however, in the even earlier language of Justice Bradley, is that "the XIVth

Amendment not only prohibits the *making* or *enforcing of laws* which shall *abridge* the privileges of the citizen; but prohibits the States from *denying* to all persons within its jurisdiction the equal protection of the laws. *Denying* includes inaction as well as action. And denying the equal protection of the laws includes the omission to protect, as well as the omission to pass laws for protection."[210] And this was, of course, Justice Harlan's point: having granted whites a right of access to public accommodations, states could not deny the same right to blacks, whether the denial took the form of an affirmative legislative act declaring blacks could not use the facilities, or took the form of inaction when the states learned that blacks were being denied access to that which was legally accessible to whites.

The early analysis of Bradley, to which Justice Harlan adhered in his *Civil Rights* dissent, seems preferable in some respects to the later analysis that Bradley wrote into the opinion of the Court.[211] Distinctions between action and inaction are, after all, always somewhat obscure. Still, even the majority opinion in the *Civil Rights Cases* was part of a comprehensive pattern of constitutional jurisprudence elaborated by the federal and state courts in the late 1870s and early 1880s. The jurisprudence did not require state legislatures to provide citizens with any rights whatever, and thus gave Congress and the federal courts no basis for declaring that any one citizen or class of citizens possessed particular rights as against other citizens. All the jurisprudence required was that, once government granted a right to some, it must not, either through affirmative action or, according to Justice Harlan, through inaction, deny the right to others, whether they be black or white, rich or poor, in control of the mechanisms of political power or far removed from the centers of power.

The constitutionalism of the last quarter of the nineteenth century thus rested on a jurisprudence of rationality and equality, and required the courts to determine, with due deference to other branches of government, whether the law treated blacks, Chinese, laborers, or businessmen arbitrarily. From *Slaughter-House*, through the railroad rate cases and the *Civil Rights Cases*, to *Allgeyer* v. *Louisiana*,[212] that was the constitutional activity in which American courts, from the highest to the lowest, engaged.

CHAPTER VIII

Lochner v. *New York* and the Transformation of the Amendment

In deciding the *Civil Rights Cases* and other late nineteenth-century cases arising under the Fourteenth Amendment as they did, the justices of the Supreme Court paid heed both to the legislative history of the framing and ratification of the Fourteenth Amendment and to the basic political and social facts that determined and limited the constitutional capacity of the Court. The two key facts about the framing and ratification of section one were that the victorious Northern public demanded that the postwar South be restrained in the future from discriminating against blacks and Northerners, and that this restraint be imposed without altering radically the structure of the federal system or increasing markedly the powers of the federal government. Perhaps these two Northern wishes were inconsistent, but the political leaders who framed and ratified the Fourteenth Amendment were bound by them and had striven to draft an amendment that accommodated them.

Once the amendment had been adopted, the Supreme Court confronted the same two values, often in tension with each other. On the one hand, late nineteenth-century Americans believed passionately in the principle of equality and expected the Court to enforce it. On the other hand, they wanted their legislatures to make law: that is, to adopt rules drawing distinctions between people and treating those people differently. Faithful to the compromises that had taken place during the framing and ratification of the amendment, the late nineteenth-century Court, like the framers and ratifiers, avoided extreme positions and usually deferred to legislative judgments. Only when the Court found that legislative acts were plainly arbitrary would it declare them unconstitutional, thereby protecting rights.

The Court's Fourteenth Amendment jurisprudence was encapsulated in the 1898 case of *Holden* v. *Hardy*,[1] which upheld the constitutionality of Utah legislation setting a maximum eight-hour workday for miners. On the one hand, the Court declared "that there are certain immutable principles of justice which inhere in the very idea of free government."[2] On the other hand, it recognized that "while the cardinal principles of justice are immutable," they could not be "construed" in a fashion that would "deprive the States of the power to so amend their laws as to make them conform to the wishes of the citizens as they may deem best for the public welfare." Indeed, the Court stated " 'that there is nothing in the Constitution to prevent any State from adopting any system of laws or judicature it sees fit.' "[3] The issue always was "whether the legislature has adopted the statute in exercise of a reasonable discretion, or whether its action be a mere excuse for an unjust discrimination, or the oppression, or spoliation of a particular class."[4] In *Holden*, the legislature had made a judgment prohibiting work in mines from being "too long pursued" because it found such work "detrimental to the health of the employe[e]s." Since the Court thought there were "reasonable grounds for believing that this is so," the legislature's "decision" could "not be reviewed by the Federal courts."[5]

This late nineteenth-century jurisprudence began to undergo change, however, soon after the twentieth century commenced. In *Lochner* v. *New York*,[6] the majority of the Court in an alternative holding started off in uncharted directions authorized neither by a uniformly shared original understanding of the Fourteenth Amendment nor by the three decades of case law following it. *Lochner* involved the constitutionality of New York legislation setting a maximum ten-hour workday for bakery workers. The statute did not apply, however, to workers in other industries, and the Court, finding "no contention that bakers as a class are not equal in intelligence and capacity to men in other trades or manual occupations,"[7] held the act invalid for arbitrarily singling out the bakers. Such an analysis, of course, was entirely consistent with the basic doctrine of American constitutionalism extracted in the preceding three decades of adjudication from the Fourteenth Amendment: that a statute which, without reason, distinguishes between two groups of similarly situated citizens is unreasonable, arbitrary, and therefore void.

But *Lochner* can also be read as resting on an alternative ground. In the words of Justice Peckham writing for the Court, the "general right to make a contract in relation to his business is part of the liberty of the individual protected by the 14th Amendment."[8] Finding "no reasonable ground for interfering with the liberty of the person or the right of free contract,"[9] the Court perceived the New York act as "an illegal interference with the rights of individuals, both employers and employees, to make contracts regarding labor upon such terms as they may think best."[10] The *Lochner* court thus began to give the impression that the right of free contract was of such fundamental stature that no government could infringe it.

Of course, even on this reading *Lochner* can be harmonized with Justice Field's dictum in *Soon Hing* v. *Crowley*[11] giving states broad power to regulate the conditions of labor, and with the mainstream of nineteenth-century constitutional authority. It is only necessary to assume that states may reasonably restrict freedom of contract and further to assume that New York's regulation was arbitrary since it distinguished bakers from other workers without any reason. Such a reading of *Lochner* would render it a coherent whole, authorizing the Supreme Court to overturn legislation pursuant to the Fourteenth Amendment when a legislature drew arbitrary distinctions and to sustain legislation when its distinctions were reasonable.

Although the 1908 case of *Muller* v. *Oregon*[12] read *Lochner* in this fashion, this was not the reading given to it by courts and commentators in the next three decades. They read the case as authority for the federal courts to immunize fundamental rights from all legislative regulation;[13] they thereby transformed the Fourteenth Amendment from a bar to arbitrary and unequal state action into a charter identifying fundamental rights and immunizing them from all legislative regulation. Not surprisingly, the newly transformed Fourteenth Amendment began, in the language of Justice Harlan in dissent, to "involve consequences of a far-reaching and mischievous character."

What came to be understood as the jurisprudence of *Lochner* "seriously cripple[d] the inherent power of the states to care for the lives, health, and well-being of their citizens." It ignored the original understanding of the framers that "[t]he preservation of the just powers of the states is quite as vital as the preservation of the powers of the general government," and thereby "enlarg[ed] the scope of the [Fourteenth] amendment far beyond its original purpose."[14] Indeed, in the Great Depression, this broad reading of *Lochner* threatened to prevent government from acting to rehabilitate the nation's economy.[15] For reasons that the proponents of the Fourteenth Amendment had fully appreciated, the broad reading had to be rejected.

But by the time it rejected the broad reading, the Roosevelt Court appears to have forgotten the line that the proponents of the Fourteenth Amendment and late nineteenth-century judges had drawn in order to prevent the amendment from overwhelming the states.[16] Or perhaps that line seemed inappropriate to the Court in the late 1930s, when government seemed to need unusually broad powers to deal with the economy, and when personal rights of a noneconomic sort appeared gravely threatened throughout the world.[17] For whatever reason, the Court did not cut back on *Lochner* by distinguishing between reasonable and arbitrary state regulations, permitting the former and prohibiting the latter; instead, it distinguished in the *Carolene Products* case[18] between economic and noneconomic rights, giving government plenary power to regulate the former and little power over the latter. A half century after *Carolene Products*, the nineteenth century's approach to limiting the reach of the Fourteenth Amendment had been largely forgotten.

NOTES

INDEX

Notes

I. The Impasse in Scholarship

1. Henry Brannon, *A Treatise on the Rights and Privileges Guaranteed by the Fourteenth Amendment to the Constitution of the United States* (Cincinnati: W. H. Anderson, 1901), iii–iv.
2. William D. Guthrie, *Lectures on the Fourteenth Article of Amendment to the Constitution of the United States* (Boston, 1898), 1–2.
3. Brannon, *Fourteenth Amendment*, iv.
4. 83 U.S. (16 Wall.) 36 (1873).
5. 109 U.S. 3 (1883).
6. 163 U.S. 537 (1896).
7. 165 U.S. 578 (1897).
8. 198 U.S. 45 (1905).
9. 208 U.S. 412 (1908).
10. 236 U.S. 1 (1915).
11. 261 U.S. 525 (1923).
12. 347 U.S. 483 (1954).
13. 410 U.S. 113 (1973).
14. 438 U.S. 265 (1978).
15. 92 L.Ed.2d 140 (1986).
16. *See United States* v. *Carolene Products Co.*, 304 U.S. 144, 152 n.4 (1938); David A. J. Richards, *Sex, Drugs, Death and the Law: An Essay on Human Rights and Overcriminalization* (Totowa, N.J.: Rowman and Littlefield, 1982); Louis Lusky, "Minority Rights and the Public Interest," *Yale Law Journal*, 52 (1942), 1; J. Skelly Wright, "Professor Bickel, The Scholarly Tradition, and the Supreme Court," *Harvard Law Review*, 84 (1971), 769.
17. *See Baker* v. *Carr*, 369 U.S. 186, 266 (1962) (dissenting opinion of Frankfurter, J.); Alexander M. Bickel, *The Supreme Court and the Idea of Progress*, 2d ed. (New Haven: Yale University Press, 1978), 81–100; Learned Hand, *The Bill of Rights* (Cambridge, Mass.: Harvard University Press, 1958); James B. Thayer, "The Origin and Scope of the American Doctrine of Constitutional Law," *Harvard Law Review*, 7 (1893), 129.
18. Horace E. Flack, *The Adoption of the Fourteenth Amendment* (Baltimore: Johns Hopkins University Press, 1908).
19. Jacobus tenBroek, *The Antislavery Origins of the Fourteenth Amendment* (Berkeley: University of California Press, 1951). TenBroek's findings have

been elaborated upon by William M. Wiecek, *The Sources of Antislavery Constitutionalism in America, 1760–1848* (Ithaca, N.Y.: Cornell University Press, 1977).

20. Graham's articles have been collected in Howard Jay Graham, *Everyman's Constitution: Historical Essays on the Fourteenth Amendment, the "Conspiracy Theory," and American Constitutionalism* (Madison: State Historical Society of Wisconsin, 1968).

21. *See* Chester J. Antieau, *The Original Understanding of the Fourteenth Amendment* (Tucson: Mid-America Press, 1981); Judith A. Baer, *Equality under the Constitution: Reclaiming the Fourteenth Amendment* (Ithaca, N.Y.: Cornell University Press, 1983); Michael Kent Curtis, *No State Shall Abridge: The Fourteenth Amendment and the Bill of Rights* (Durham, N.C.: Duke University Press, 1986).

22. *See, e.g.,* Alfred H. Kelly, "The Fourteenth Amendment Reconsidered: The Segregation Decision," *Michigan Law Review*, 54 (1956), 1049.

23. *See* William Van Alstyne, "The Fourteenth Amendment, the 'Right' to Vote, and the Understanding of the Thirty-ninth Congress," in Philip B. Kurland, ed., *1965 Supreme Court Review* (Chicago: University of Chicago Press, 1965), 33.

24. *See* Robert J. Kaczorowski, "Revolutionary Constitutionalism in the Era of the Civil War and Reconstruction," *New York University Law Review*, 61 (1986), 863; Michael P. Zuckert, "Congressional Power under the Fourteenth Amendment—The Original Understanding of Section Five," *Constitutional Commentary*, 3 (1986), 123.

25. *See* Alexander M. Bickel, "The Original Understanding and the Segregation Decision," *Harvard Law Review*, 69 (1955), 1; Charles Fairman, "Does the Fourteenth Amendment Incorporate the Bill of Rights? The Original Understanding," *Stanford Law Review*, 2 (1949), 5.

26. *See* Earl M. Maltz, "The Fourteenth Amendment as Political Compromise—Section One in the Joint Committee on Reconstruction," *Ohio State Law Journal*, 45 (1984), 933, 969–970; Earl M. Maltz, "Fourteenth Amendment Concepts in the Antebellum Era" (forthcoming in *American Journal of Legal History*, October, 1988). *See also* Earl M. Maltz, "The Concept of Equal Protection of the Laws—A Historical Inquiry," *San Diego Law Review*, 22 (1985), 499.

27. Raoul Berger, *Government by Judiciary: The Transformation of the Fourteenth Amendment* (Cambridge, Mass.: Harvard University Press, 1977).

28. *Id.* at 18.

29. *See, e.g.,* William R. Brock, *An American Crisis: Congress and Reconstruction, 1865–1867* (New York: St. Martin's Press, 1963); LaWanda and John H. Cox, *Politics, Principle, and Prejudice, 1865–1866: Dilemma of Reconstruction America* (New York: The Free Press, 1963); James M. McPherson, *The Struggle for Equality: Abolitionists and the Negro in the Civil War and Reconstruction* (Princeton: Princeton University Press, 1964), 308–366.

30. *See* Howard K. Beale, *The Critical Year: A Study of Andrew Johnson and Reconstruction* (New York: Harcourt, Brace, 1930), 1–9, 225–299; Michael Les Benedict, *A Compromise of Principle: Congressional Republicans and Reconstruction 1863–1869* (New York: W. W. Norton, 1974), 49–56,

262–265, 300–308; Eric L. McKitrick, *Andrew Johnson and Reconstruction* (Chicago: University of Chicago Press, 1960), 253–363. Two books on the Fourteenth Amendment itself which take this view are Joseph B. James, *The Framing of the Fourteenth Amendment* (Urbana: University of Illinois Press, 1956), and Joseph B. James, *The Ratification of the Fourteenth Amendment* (Macon, Ga.: Mercer University Press, 1984). Because of the perspective from which they are written, these two books will frustrate any lawyer who is reading them to learn what the framers and ratifiers of section one thought it meant. But the same perspective makes the books exceedingly valuable in explicating the political maneuvering involved in the amendment's passage.

31. *See* Robert J. Kaczorowski, *The Politics of Judicial Interpretation: The Federal Courts, Department of Justice and Civil Rights, 1866–1876* (New York: Oceana Publications, 1985).
32. Maltz, "The Concept of Equal Protection," 540.
33. Baer, *Equality under the Constitution*, 102–103.
34. I include within this category all the books written solely about the adoption, ratification, or original meaning of the Fourteenth Amendment as well as articles published in law reviews. Innumerable historians who have written about Reconstruction or some aspect thereof have also written in passing about the Fourteenth Amendment, sometimes at length. My comments in this paragraph are not addressed to their work.
35. Benjamin B. Kendrick, *The Journal of the Joint Committee of Fifteen on Reconstruction* (New York: Columbia University Press, 1914).
36. This has begun to change with the recent publications of Antieu, *The Original Understanding*, and James, *Ratification*, which both examine new material dealing with the amendment's ratification, and Kaczorowski, "Revolutionary Constitutionalism," which is deeply steeped in newspapers and in the private correspondence of key Fourteenth Amendment actors.
37. *See* Hearings on Abortion Before the Senate Subcommittee on Constitutional Amendments, Pt. IV, 94th Cong., 1st. Sess. (1976), 525–528, 541–543 (remarks of Professor Joseph P. Witherspoon); Hearings on the Human Life Bill Before the Senate Subcommittee on Separation of Powers, 97th Cong., 1st Sess. (1982), 433–468 (remarks of Professors Carl Degler, James C. Mohr, William H. Marshner, and Victor G. Rosenblum).
38. Bickel, "The Original Understanding and the Segregation Decision." I have chosen this article for analysis because I regard it as the most sophisticated and important piece of work that any lawyer has done on the Fourteenth Amendment.
39. *Id.* at 58–59.
40. 347 U.S. 483 (1954).
41. Harold M. Hyman, *A More Perfect Union: The Impact of the Civil War and Reconstruction on the Constitution* (New York: Alfred A. Knopf, 1973), 435–436.
42. *See id.* at 438–440.
43. 83 U.S. (16 Wall.) 36 (1873).
44. 198 U.S. 45 (1905).
45. For an analysis of how judges should use history in constitutional adjudica-

tion, *see* William E. Nelson, "History and Neutrality in Constitutional Adjudication," *Virginia Law Review*, 72 (1986), 1237.

46. For a recent analysis of balancing as a method of constitutional adjudication, *see* T. Alexander Aleinikoff, "Constitutional Law in the Age of Balancing," *Yale Law Journal*, 96 (1987), 943.

47. The position that courts should elaborate general concepts into specific conceptions is developed by Ronald Dworkin, *Law's Empire* (Cambridge, Mass.: Harvard University Press, 1986), 70–72, 90–96.

II. Ideas of Liberty and Equality

1. *See* Edward Pessen, *Jacksonian America: Society, Personality, and Politics*, rev. ed. (Homewood, Ill.: Dorsey Press, 1978), 77–100.

2. *See, e.g.*, Robert M. Cover, *Justice Accused: Antislavery and the Judicial Process* (New Haven: Yale University Press, 1975); Eric Foner, *Free Soil, Free Labor, Free Men: The Ideology of the Republican Party before the Civil War* (New York: Oxford University Press, 1970); William E. Nelson, *The Roots of American Bureaucracy, 1830–1900* (Cambridge, Mass.: Harvard University Press, 1982), 41–61; Jacobus tenBroek, *The Antislavery Origins of the Fourteenth Amendment* (Berkeley: University of California Press, 1951); William M. Wiecek, *The Sources of Antislavery Constitutionalism in America, 1760–1848* (Ithaca, N.Y.: Cornell University Press, 1977).

3. N. H. Carter et al., eds., *Reports of the Proceedings and Debates of the Convention of 1821, Assembled for the Purpose of Amending the Constitution of the State of New York* (Albany, 1821), 221.

4. Arthur M. Schlesinger, Jr., *The Age of Jackson* (Boston: Little, Brown, 1945), 15.

5. Carter, *Convention of 1821*, 225.

6. *Id.* at 224–225. At least two other delegates spoke in favor of universal suffrage. *See id.* at 363–364 (remarks of Mr. Briggs and Col. Young).

7. Cornelius C. Blatchly, *An Essay on Common Wealths* (New York, 1822), 8–10, quoted in Sean Wilentz, *Chants Democratic: New York City and the Rise of the American Working Class, 1788–1850* (New York: Oxford University Press, 1984), 159–160.

8. Frances Wright, *Course of Popular Lectures* (New York, 1829), 45. *See also* Wilentz, *Chants Democratic*, 207; "The Great Nation of Futurity," *Democratic Review*, 6 (1839), 426.

9. Quoted in Harold M. Hyman and William M. Wiecek, *Equal Justice Under Law: Constitutional Development, 1835–1875* (New York: Harper and Row, 1982), 29. For what still remains, despite questions of interpretation, the most useful survey of newspaper and pamphlet rhetoric about equality in the 1830s and 1840s, *see generally* Schlesinger, *Age of Jackson*, 159–200.

10. *Subterranean*, November 8, 1845, quoted in Wilentz, *Chants Democratic*, 332.

11. *New York Tribune*, January 2, 1851, quoted in Wilentz, *Chants Democratic*,

383. *See also* Orestes A. Brownson, "An Address to the Workingmen of Charlestown, Mass.," *Boston Quarterly Review*, 4 (1841), 112, 117; Frederick Robinson, *Oration Delivered before the Trades Union of Boston and Vicinity*, quoted in Schlesinger, *Age of Jackson*, 168; Wilentz, *Chants Democratic*, 336.

12. "Anti-Bank Meeting," *Boston Post*, March 18, 1834, p. 1, col. 1–2 (emphasis in original).

13. James D. Richardson, ed., *A Compilation of the Messages and Papers of the Presidents*, 2 (Washington, 1899), 576, 590.

14. *Register of Debates*, 21st Cong., 2d Sess. 50–75 (1831) (remarks of Sen. Benton), quoted in Schlesinger, *Age of Jackson*, 81.

15. Letter by Thomas H. Benton of November 12, 1835, in Washington *Globe*, November 21, 1835, p. 3, col. 1.

16. Quoted in D. M. Ludlum, *Social Ferment in Vermont, 1791–1850* (New York: Columbia University Press, 1939), 204.

17. Quoted in Carl B. Swisher, *Roger B. Taney* (New York: Macmillan, 1935), 366–367.

18. Martin Van Buren to Isaac Lippincott, September 14, 1840, quoted in Schlesinger, *Age of Jackson*, 316.

19. *Official Report of the Debates and Proceedings in the State Convention . . . to Revise and Amend the Constitution of the Commonwealth of Massachusetts*, 2 (Boston, 1853), 58–62, quoted in Foner, *Free Soil*, 22.

20. *Congressional Globe*, 34th Cong., 1 Sess. 276 app. (1856) (remarks of Sen. Harlan).

21. George E. Baker, ed., *The Works of William H. Seward*, 3 (New York, 1853), 209.

22. *Id.* at 498.

23. George E. Baker, ed., *The Works of William H. Seward*, 4 (New York, 1861), 302.

24. *Bangor Daily Whig and Courier*, September 3, 1839, quoted in David M. Gold, "John Appleton and Responsible Individualism in Nineteenth-Century Law" (Ph.D. diss., Ohio State University, 1982), 64.

25. *Roberts* v. *City of Boston*, 59 Mass. (5 Cush.) 198, 206 (1849). Some historians, the most recent of whom is Daniel Walker Howe, *The Political Culture of the American Whigs* (Chicago: University of Chicago Press, 1979), take the view that equality was not an important concern of the Whigs. *See id.* at 21–22, 38–39, 133–134. Even Howe concedes, though, that younger Whigs like Lincoln and Seward often used egalitarian rhetoric. *See id.* at 202–205, 290–291. My only claim is that many Whigs, especially those who later became Republicans, valued equality and used egalitarian rhetoric; for understanding the Fourteenth Amendment's background it is not necessary to make judgments about how much Whigs valued equality or where it fit within their hierarchy of values.

26. This is the burden of Earl M. Maltz, "Fourteenth Amendment Concepts in the Antebellum Era" (forthcoming in *American Journal of Legal History*, October, 1988).

27. John Taylor, *Inquiry into the Principles and Policy of the Government of the United States* (Fredericksburg, 1814), 274.

28. *Congressional Globe*, 25th Cong., 2d Sess. 55 (1837), reprinted in Wiecek, *Antislavery Constitutionalism*, 292. *See also* tenBroek, *Antislavery Origins*, 42.
29. Quoted in Maltz, "Fourteenth Amendment Concepts."
30. 60 U.S. (19 How.) 393 (1857). For the leading book on the case, see Don E. Fehrenbacher, *The Dred Scott Case: Its Significance in American Law and Politics* (New York: Oxford University Press, 1978).
31. 60 U.S. at 426.
32. Quoted in Nelson, *Bureaucracy*, 50.
33. Call for the Macedon Convention (1847), quoted in tenBroek, *Antislavery Origins*, 138.
34. *Ibid.*
35. Quoted in Nelson, *Bureaucracy*, 51 (emphasis in original). *See also* Foner, *Free Soil*, 290–291.
36. Theodore Dwight Weld, *The Power of Congress over Slavery in the District of Columbia*, reprinted in tenBroek, *Antislavery Origins*, 243, 277.
37. Henry B. Stanton, *Remarks in the Representatives Hall on the 23rd and 24th of February, before the Committee of the House of Representatives of Massachusetts* (Boston, 1837), 35.
38. *Congressional Globe*, 35th Cong., 2d Sess. 346 (1859) (remarks of Sen. Giddings).
39. Quoted in tenBroek, *Antislavery Origins*, 47.
40. Quoted in *id.* at 44.
41. Liberty party platform of 1844, quoted in Wiecek, *Antislavery Constitutionalism*, 217–218.
42. *See* David Donald, *Charles Sumner and the Coming of the Civil War* (New York: Alfred A. Knopf, 1960), 180–181; David Donald, *Charles Sumner and the Rights of Man* (New York: Alfred A. Knopf, 1970), 243–247, 281–287, 579–587.
43. "Extension of the Right of Suffrage," *Wisconsin State Journal*, August 1, 1857, p. 2, col. 1.
44. "Unpalatable Counsel," *New York Tribune*, September 22, 1855, p. 4, col. 3–4.
45. Philadelphia *North American*, quoted in Foner, *Free Soil*, 297.
46. "Negro Intellect—Ellis and Douglass, and Uncle Tom," Washington *National Era*, June 2, 1853, p. 2, col. 2–4.
47. *Congressional Globe*, 35th Cong., 2d Sess. 346 (1859) (remarks of Sen. Giddings).
48. William H. Seward, quoted in Foner, *Free Soil*, 300.
49. "The Republican Administration—Mr. Lincoln's Views on Slavery," *New York Times*, November 8, 1860, p. 4, col. 2.
50. Roy P. Basler, ed., *The Collected Works of Abraham Lincoln*, 2 (New Brunswick, N.J.: Rutgers University Press, 1953), 405.
51. J. W. Schuckers, *The Life and Public Services of Salmon Portland Chase* (New York, 1874), 158.
52. *See* John A. Bingham, *The Constitution of the United States and the Proslavery Provisions of the 1857 Oregon Constitution*, reprinted in tenBroek, *Antislavery Origins*, 320.

53. *Report of the Debates and Proceedings of the Convention for the Revision of the Constitution of the State of Ohio*, 2 (Columbus, 1851), 636.
54. "The Colored People," ms. in Chase Papers, quoted in Foner, *Free Soil*, 293.
55. *Congressional Globe*, 36th Cong., 1st Sess., 232 app. (1860) (remarks of Rep. Duell).
56. *Debates and Proceedings of the Constitutional Convention for the Territory of Minnesota* (St. Paul, 1858), 351.
57. *Proceedings of the Convention of the Colored Freemen of Ohio* (Cincinnati, 1852), 15–20, 24–25, quoted in Foner, *Free Soil*, 298.
58. Basler, *Works of Lincoln*, v. 4, p. 24 (emphasis in original).
59. *Congressional Globe*, 33d Cong., 1st Sess. 1072 (1854) (remarks of Rep. Wade).
60. *Cf.* Peter Westen, "The Empty Idea of Equality," *Harvard Law Review*, 95 (1982), 537.
61. Charles G. Finney, *Sermons on Gospel Themes* (New York, 1876), 252.
62. Theodore Parker, "The Administration of President Polk," in his *The Rights of Man in America*, ed. F. B. Sanborn (Boston: American Unitarian Association, 1911), 48, 88.
63. John Pierpont, *Moral Rule of Political Action: A Discourse Delivered in Hollis Street Church . . . 1839*, quoted in Wiecek, *Antislavery Constitutionalism*, 204.
64. Liberty party platform for 1843, quoted in tenBroek, *Antislavery Origins*, 60 n.5. *See also* Octavius B. Frothingham, *Gerrit Smith* (New York, 1878), 172–173; Theodore Dwight Weld, *Slavery in the District of Columbia*, 244; *Declaration of Sentiments of the American Anti-Slavery Society in December, 1833*, quoted in tenBroek, *Antislavery Origins*, 59.
65. *See* Cover, *Justice Accused*; Nelson, *Bureaucracy*, 41–61; Wiecek, *Antislavery Constitutionalism*, 168–171, 228–234.
66. *See* Liberty party platform for 1843, quoted in tenBroek, *Antislavery Origins*, 60 n.5.
67. Theodore Weld to Elizur Wright, Jr., January 10, 1833, in *Letters of Theodore Dwight Weld, Angelina Grimke Weld and Sara Grimke, 1822–1844*, ed. Gilbert H. Barnes and Dwight L. Dumond, 1 (New York:D. Appleton-Century, 1934), 100 (emphasis in original). *See also* James G. Birney, *Can Congress, under the Constitution, Abolish Slavery in the States* (1847), reprinted in tenBroek, *Antislavery Origins*, 296, 310.
68. Quoted in Foner, *Free Soil*, 110.
69. Quoted in Cover, *Justice Accused*, 172.
70. Call for the Macedon Convention (1847), quoted in tenBroek, *Antislavery Origins*, 138. *See also* Bingham, *Proslavery Provisions of the 1857 Oregon Constitution*, 340.
71. George McDuffie, "Message to Legislature, 1835," reprinted in *Journal of the General Assembly . . . of South Carolina . . . 1835*, quoted in Wiecek, *Antislavery Constitutionalism*, 180.
72. Thomas R. Dew, *Review of the Debate in the Virginia Legislature, 1831–32*, quoted in Wiecek, *Antislavery Constitutionalism*, 148.

73. John L. Wilson, "Message to Legislature of South Carolina," quoted in Wiecek, *Antislavery Constitutionalism*, 138.
74. Quoted in Schlesinger, *Age of Jackson*, 95.
75. 3 U.S. (3 Dall.) 386 (1798).
76. *Id.* at 388 (emphasis in original).
77. 10 U.S. (6 Cranch) 87 (1810).
78. *Id.* at 139.
79. 6 Fed. Cas. 546 (C.C.E.D.Pa. 1823).
80. *Id.* at 551-552.
81. 27 U.S. (2 Pet.) 627 (1829).
82. *Id.* at 657.
83. *Regents of the University of Maryland v. Williams*, 9 G. & J. 365, 408 (Md. 1838). Text writers agreed that for a "government [to] be a republic" (Weld, *Slavery in the District of Columbia*, 244) all its citizens must enjoy "certain inalienable rights"; indeed, "[t]he very pith and essence of a republican form of government is the protection and security of those rights." William Goodell, *Views of American Constitutional Law in Its Bearing upon American Slavery* (Utica, 1844), quoted in tenBroek, *Antislavery Origins*, 75. *See also* Weld, *Slavery in the District of Columbia*, 271; tenBroek, *Antislavery Origins*, 73; Wiecek, *Antislavery Constitutionalism*, 274.
84. Weld, *Slavery in the District of Columbia*, 256.
85. "Declaration of Sentiments of the Honeoye Liberty Mass Meeting," 1846, reprinted in tenBroek, *Antislavery Origins*, 142, 143.
86. 7 Co. Rep. 1a, 77 Eng. Rep. 377 (1608).
87. Birney, *Can Congress Abolish Slavery*, 317.
88. Weld, *Slavery in the District of Columbia*, 278.
89. Platform of Free Democracy party, 1852, quoted in Wiecek, *Antislavery Constitutionalism*, 209.
90. Quoted in William E. Nelson, "The Impact of the Antislavery Movement upon Styles of Judicial Reasoning in Nineteenth Century America," *Harvard Law Review*, 87 (1974), 513, 541.
91. Quoted in *id.* at 534.
92. St. George Tucker, ed., *Blackstone's Commentaries*, 2 (Philadelphia, 1803), app. 41–42 (emphasis in original). *See also* Weld, *Slavery in the District of Columbia*, 255.
93. Ames, ed., *State Documents on Federal Relations*, quoted in Wiecek, *Antislavery Constitutionalism*, 141.
94. Whitemarsh B. Seabrook, *A Concise View of the Critical Situation, and Future Prospects of the Slave-Holding States, in Relation to Their Coloured Population* . . . (Charleston, 1825), quoted in Wiecek, *Antislavery Constitutionalism*, 131.
95. 2 Strob. 41 (S.C. 1846).
96. *Id.* at 43.
97. Kentucky Constitution of 1850, quoted in Wiecek, *Antislavery Constitutionalism*, 279.
98. *Congressional Globe*, 25th Cong., 2d Sess. 620 app. (1838) (remarks of Senator Tallmadge).

99. 27 U.S. (2 Pet.) 627 (1829).
100. *See* Hyman and Wiecek, *Equal Justice under Law*, 20–54; Nelson, *Bureaucracy*, 11–16.
101. The best scholarship on this issue is quite out of date. *See* Edward S. Corwin, "National Power and State Interposition, 1787–1861," *Michigan Law Review*, 10 (1912), 535; Charles Warren, "Federal and State Court Interference," in Association of American Law Schools, ed., *Selected Essays on Constitutional Law*, 3 (Chicago: Foundation Press, 1938), 1089; Charles Warren, "Legislative and Judicial Attacks on the Supreme Court of the United States—A History of the Twenty-Fifth Section of the Judiciary Act," *American Law Review*, 47 (1913), 1, 161.
102. Jacob E. Cooke, ed., *The Federalist* No. 28 (Hamilton) (Middletown, Conn.: Wesleyan University Press, 1961), 179–180.
103. *See Cohens v. Virginia*, 19 U.S. (6 Wheat.) 264 (1821); *Martin v. Hunter's Lessee*, 14 U.S. (1 Wheat.) 304 (1816).
104. *See Dennie v. Harris*, 26 Mass. (9 Pick.) 364, 367 (1830).
105. *See, e.g., Commonwealth v. Cushing*, 11 Mass. 67 (1814); *State v. Dimick*, 12 N.H. 194 (1841); *Matter of Stacy*, 10 Johns. 328 (N.Y. 1813), *Commonwealth v. Murray*, 4 Binney 487 (Pa. 1812); *Bagnall v. Ableman*, 4 Wis. 163 (1855). The power of state courts to issue the writ was not terminated until *Ableman v. Booth*, 62 U.S. (21 How.) 506 (1859).
106. *See* William F. Duker, *A Constitutional History of Habeas Corpus* (Westport, Conn.: Greenwood Press, 1980), 126–35. *See also id.* at 149–50.
107. *See, e.g., Harris v. Dennie*, 28 U.S. (3 Pet.) 292 (1830); *Slocum v. Mayberry*, 15 U.S. (2 Wheat.) 1 (1817). This liability was ended by the Act of March 2, 1833, sec. 3, 4 Stat. 632, 633 (1833), which authorized officials sued in state court to remove the actions pending against them into federal court. The best general survey of early nineteenth-century state judicial interventions against the exercise of federal power remains Warren, "Legislative and Judicial Attacks."
108. *See* Leonard W. Levy, *Emergence of a Free Press* (New York: Oxford University Press, 1985), 279–281, 305–310; Marshall Smelser, *The Democratic Republic, 1801–1815* (New York: Harper and Row, 1968), 53.
109. *See generally* William W. Freehling, *Prelude to Civil War: The Nullification Controversy in South Carolina, 1816–1836* (New York: Harper and Row, 1965). For a discussion of the standoff, *see id.* at 260–297. For the Force Act, *see* Act of March 2, 1833, 4 Stat. 632 (1833).
110. *See* George Dangerfield, *The Awakening of American Nationalism, 1815–1828* (New York: Harper and Row, 1965), 2–4; Smelser, *Democratic Republic*, 310–311.
111. *See* Allan R. Millett and Peter Maslowski, *For the Common Defense: A Military History of the United States of America* (New York: Macmillan, 1984), 133, 142; Russell F. Weigley, *Towards an American Army: Military Thought from Washington to Marshall* (New York: Columbia University Press, 1962), 63.
112. *See* Lawrence Delbert Cress, *Citizens in Arms: The Army and the Militia in American Society to the War of 1812* (Chapel Hill: University of North Carolina Press, 1982), 121–129.

113. 1 Stat. 264 (1792).
114. *See* Lawrence Delbert Cress, "Central Authority and Local Control: The Militia in Anglo-American Constitutional Debate, 1641–1827" (unpublished paper in possession of the author).
115. 25 U.S. (12 Wheat.) 19 (1827).
116. *See* Freehling, *Prelude to Civil War*, 278–284.
117. *See* Millett and Maslowski, *For the Common Defense*, 159; Emory M. Thomas, *The Confederacy as a Revolutionary Experience* (Englewood Cliffs, N.J.: Prentice-Hall, 1971), 1–2, 35, 44–51.
118. *See* Millett and Maslowski, *For the Common Defense*, 114.
119. The classic essay, which made Madison's idea familiar, is Douglass Adair, "The Tenth Federalist Revisited," *William and Mary Quarterly* (3d ser.), 8 (1951), 48.
120. *See* Herbert J. Storing, *What the Antifederalists Were For: The Political Thought of the Opponents of the Constitution* (Chicago: University of Chicago Press, 1981), 19–21.
121. Kentucky Resolutions, November 16, 1798, in Henry Steele Commager, ed., *Documents of American History*, 1, 9th ed. (Englewood Cliffs, N.J.: Prentice Hall, 1973), 178, 179, 181.
122. *See* The State of Rhode Island and Providence Plantations to Virginia, February 1799, in Commager, *Documents of American History*, 184.
123. Kentucky Resolutions, November 16, 1798, in Commager, *Documents of American History*, 178–179.
124. Report and Resolutions of the Hartford Convention, January 4, 1815, in Commager, *Documents of American History*, 209.
125. *See id.* at 211.
126. An Ordinance To Nullify Certain Acts of the Congress of the United States, Statutes at Large of South Carolina, 1 (1836), 329.
127. *Ibid.*
128. Kentucky Resolutions of 1799, February 22, 1799, in Commager, *Documents of American History*, 183, 184.
129. John C. Calhoun, *A Disquisition on Government*, ed. by C. Gordon Post (New York: Liberal Arts Press, 1953), 20, 28, 29, 37–38.
130. On the postwar development of such standards, *see* Nelson, *Bureaucracy*, 82–112.
131. *See generally* Thomas D. Morris, *Free Men All: The Personal Liberty Laws of the North, 1780–1861* (Baltimore: Johns Hopkins University Press, 1974).
132. *See* Paul Finkelman, *An Imperfect Union: Slavery, Federalism, and Comity* (Chapel Hill: University of North Carolina Press, 1981), 101–180.
133. *See id.* at 285.
134. 62 U.S. (21 How.) 506 (1859).
135. *See In re Booth and Rycraft*, 3 Wis. 157 (1854).
136. *Id.* at 190.
137. *Id.* at 204.
138. *Id.* at 198–199 (emphasis in original).
139. *Id.* at 199.
140. *Id.* at 208–209.
141. *Id.* at 209.

142. 62 U.S. (21 How.) 506 (1859).
143. 80 U.S. (13 Wall.) 397 (1872).
144. Salmon P. Chase, *Speech in the Case of the Colored Woman Matilda Who Was Brought before the Court of Common Pleas of Hamilton County, Ohio, by Writ of Habeas Corpus March 11, 1837* (Cincinnati, 1837), quoted in tenBroek, *Antislavery Origins*, 63.
145. "Resolutions of Anti-Slavery Convention at Rochester, N.Y., February 10–11, 1857," New York *National Anti-Slavery Standard*, February 21, 1857, p. 2, col. 3.
146. *Congressional Globe*, 33rd Cong., 1st Sess. 138 app. (1854) (remarks of Sen. Chase).
147. Quoted in Cover, *Justice Accused*, 95–96.
148. Quoted in *id.* at 156.
149. Free Soil Democratic Platform of 1852, quoted in tenBroek, *Antislavery Origins*, 140.
150. Speech of F. W. Pickens, January 1836, quoted in tenBroek, *Antislavery Origins*, 42.
151. Chase, *Case of the Colored Woman Matilda*, quoted in tenBroek, *Antislavery Origins*, 63.
152. Declaration of Sentiments of the Honeoye Liberty Mass Meeting, 1846, quoted in tenBroek, *Antislavery Origins*, 142.
153. John A. Bingham, *Proslavery Provisions of the 1857 Oregon Constitution*, 340.
154. Address, To the People of Massachusetts, Virginia, etc., Statutes at Large of South Carolina, 1 (1836), 346, 349.
155. *Id.* at 347.
156. *Id.* at 348.
157. Calhoun, *Disquisition*, 19–22.
158. *Id.* at 7.
159. *Id.* at 40–44.
160. *Id.* at 43–44.
161. *In re Booth*, 3 Wis. 1, 87, 91 (1854) (concurring opinion) (emphasis in original).
162. *Id.* at 88.
163. *See* Robert Kelley, *The Transatlantic Persuasion: The Liberal-Democratic Mind in the Age of Gladstone* (New York: Alfred A. Knopf, 1969), 403–404, 417–418.

III. The Drafting and Adoption of the Amendment

1. J. W. Sprague to John Sherman, April 4, 1866, John Sherman Papers, Library of Congress, Washington, D.C.
2. S. Cerley to Thaddeus Stevens, February 6, 1866, in Thaddeus Stevens Papers, Library of Congress, Washington, D.C.
3. John Kirkwood to Salmon P. Chase, December 4, 1866, in Salmon P. Chase Papers, Library of Congress, Washington, D.C.
4. William Mithoff to John Sherman, December 17, 1865, in John Sherman

Papers, Library of Congress, Washington, D.C. *See also* "The Unsatisfactory Character of the Southern Elections," *New York Times*, December 2, 1865, p. 4, col. 2–3.

5. Jesse Shortess to John Sherman, December 24, 1865, in Sherman Papers.

6. W. W. Trimble to John Sherman, February 12, 1866, in Sherman Papers. Newspapers repeated the theme. *See* "The Nation's Responsibility," St. Louis *Daily Missouri Democrat*, January 17, 1866, p. 2, col. 1.

7. *Harper's*, 33 (1866), 671 (reporting Butler's speech in Gloucester, Mass., in August 1866).

8. Lyman Trumbull to Mrs. Gary, June 27, 1866, in Lyman Trumbull Papers, Library of Congress, Washington, D.C.

9. *Harper's*, 32 (1866), 808 (reporting testimony of General Alfred H. Terry).

10. *Ibid. See also* "The Reconstructed," *Rochester Democrat*, February 13, 1866, p. 1, col. 2.

11. Lyman Trumbull to Mrs. Gary, June 27, 1866, in Trumbull Papers.

12. A. Stone to John Sherman, April 1, 1866, in Sherman Papers. *Accord,* "Condition of the South," *Portsmouth Journal*, February 10, 1866, p. 2, col. 1.

13. "Northern Men in the South," St. Louis *Daily Missouri Democrat*, February 17, 1866, p. 2, col. 1. *See also* "The State of Feeling Toward Northern People in the South," *Cincinnati Commercial*, February 10, 1866, p. 4, col. 3–4.

14. M. Stone to John Sherman, December 27, 1865, in Sherman Papers (emphasis in original).

15. *Harper's*, 33 (1866), 671 (reporting Butler's speech in Gloucester, Mass., in August 1866). *Accord,* "The Reconstructed," *Rochester Democrat*, February 13, 1866, p. 1, col. 2.

16. Joseph Bailey to Edwin M. Stanton, October 3, 1866, Edwin M. Stanton Papers, Library of Congress, Washington, D.C.

17. *Harper's*, 32 (1866), 808 (reporting testimony of General Alfred H. Terry). *See also* "Plain Reasons Why the Freedmen Will Not Work," *Cincinnati Commercial*, December 18, 1865, p. 4, col. 2–3; "Negro Outrages," *Cincinnati Commercial*, January 13, 1866, p. 4, col. 3–4.

18. *See* Harold M. Hyman and William M. Wiecek, *Equal Justice under Law: Constitutional Development, 1835–1875* (New York: Harper and Row, 1982), 319–322.

19. Simeon Nash to John Sherman, December 7, 1865, in Sherman Papers.

20. William D. Lewis to John Sherman, March 1, 1866, in Sherman Papers.

21. A. S. Packard to James G. Blaine, December 18, 1865, in James G. Blaine Papers, Library of Congress, Washington, D.C.

22. Crafts J. Wright to John Sherman, February 27, 1866, in Sherman Papers. *Accord,* E. B. Sadler to John Sherman, February 16, 1866, in *ibid.*; Willis Merriman to John Sherman, February 28, 1866, in *ibid.*; C. L. Blakeslee to John Sherman, March 3, 1866, in *ibid.*

23. Horace White to Edwin M. Stanton, March 15, 1866, in Edwin M. Stanton Papers, Library of Congress, Washington, D.C. *Accord, Congressional Globe*, 39th Cong., 1st Sess. 2798 (remarks of Senator Stewart); "Public Opinion and the Civil Rights Bill," *Bangor Daily Whig and Courier*, April 2,

1866, p. 2, col. 1; "Senator Sherman on the President's Policy," *New York Times*, March 4, 1866, p. 4, col. 5; J. G. Wilson to Lyman Trumbull, January 21, 1866, in Trumbull Papers.

24. "The Voice of the Freedmen of North Carolina," *Washington Sunday Chronicle*, May 13, 1866, p. 1, col. 2 (reprinting resolves of meeting of freedmen of Newbern, N.C.).

25. John W. Pease to John Sherman, March 14, 1866, in Sherman Papers.

26. "The Source of Mr. Stevens's Power," New York *Evening Post*, April 3, 1866, p. 3, col. 1. *See also* "Senator Trumbull on the Veto," *Hartford Daily Courant*, April 7, 1866, p. 2, col. 2; "The President's Message," *Johnstown Tribune*, December 15, 1865, p. 2, col. 1; "Reconstruction: Important Resolutions Introduced into the State Senate by Harry White," *Johnstown Tribune*, January 19, 1866, p. 1, col. 2–3; "Reconstruction: The Great Meeting at Laing's Hall on Friday Night," *Leavenworth Daily Times*, January 7, 1866, p. 2, col. 3–5; "The Passage of the Civil Rights Bill," *Memphis Daily Post*, April 10, 1866, p. 4, col. 1.

27. W. Bryce to John Sherman, January 21, 1866, in Sherman Papers. *See also* "A Plan of Reconstruction," Nashua *New Hampshire Telegraph*, May 19, 1866, p. 2, col. 1; "The Reconstruction Report," Trenton *Daily State Gazette*, May 2, 1866, p. 2, col. 2.

28. Samuel Craig to Thaddeus Stevens, February 5, 1866, Stevens Papers.

29. "Letter from a North Carolinian," *The Right Way*, November 18, 1865, p. 1, col. 4–5 (emphasis in original). *See also* "Abusing the Radicals," *Chicago Republican*, February 20, 1866, p. 4, col. 2.

30. J. B. Bloss to John Sherman, undated, in Sherman Papers. *See also* "The 'Radicals,'" *Norfolk Post*, February 20, 1866, p. 2, col. 2–4; Thomas Richmond to John Sherman, February 27, 1866, in Sherman Papers.

31. Resolutions of June 19, 1866, Sherman Papers. For another endorsement of the house–divided speech, *see* "Reconstruction: A Lecture by Fred. Douglass," *Daily Illinois State Journal*, April 5, 1866, p. 2, col. 2.

32. "Governor's Message," Des Moines *Iowa State Register*, January 15, 1868, p. 3, col. 7. *See also* "Reconstruction," *Bangor Daily Whig and Courier*, December 25, 1865, p. 2, col. 1; "The Reconstruction Report," *Newark Daily Advertiser*, April 30, 1866, p. 2, col. 1.

33. *Congressional Globe*, 38th Cong., 1st Sess. 1203 (1864).

34. A. Noble to Thaddeus Stevens, February 2, 1866, in Stevens Papers. *Accord*, "Abusing the Radicals," *Chicago Republican*, February 20, 1866, p. 4, col. 2–3.

35. A. M. M'Clure to Thaddeus Stevens, January 13, 1866, in Stevens Papers (emphasis in original).

36. "Wendell Phillips on the Amendment," *Milwaukee Sentinel*, January 31, 1867, p. 2, col. 2.

37. *Congressional Globe*, 39th Congress, 1st Sess. 57 app. (1866). Even the Democratic *Charleston Daily Courier* agreed about the revolutionary character of the times. *See* "The Debates in Congress and the Issues as to the Restoration of the Republic," *Charleston Daily Courier*, January 20, 1866, p. 2, col. 1.

38. "Governor Fenton's Message," New York *Commercial Advertiser*, January

2, 1867, p. 4, col. 1. *See also* [Pennsylvania] *Daily Legislative Record . . . of 1867* (Harrisburg, 1867), 7 app. (remarks of Mr. Landon).

39. *Congressional Globe*, 39th Congress, 1st Sess. 385 (remarks of Representative Baker). *See also* "Ninety-Second Legislature," Trenton *Daily State Gazette*, March 6, 1868, p. 2, col. 3 (reporting speech of Senator Cobb opposing recission of the earlier ratification of the Fourteenth Amendment).

40. *Congressional Globe*, 39th Cong., 1st Sess. 322 (1866) (remarks of Sen. Trumbull).

41. *Congressional Globe*, 39th Cong., 1st Sess. 385 (1866) (remarks of Rep. Baker).

42. Thomas Richmond to John Sherman, February 27, 1866, in Sherman Papers.

43. *Congressional Globe*, 40th Cong., 2nd Sess. 354 app. (1868) (remarks of Sen. Yates). *See also* "Civil Rights Bill," *Leavenworth Daily Times*, April 12, 1866, p. 2, col. 2.

44. C. Hammond to Henry L. Dawes, May 2, 1866, in Henry L. Dawes Papers, Library of Congress, Washington, D.C.

45. J. Ransom to E. B. Washburn, February 7, 1866, in E. B. Washburn Papers, Library of Congress, Washington, D.C.

46. For an example of an effort to organize a petition campaign on behalf of equal rights, *see The Right Way*, January 20, 1866, p. 1, col. 2, and p. 3, col. 1–2.

47. For an example of a signed petition that found its way to a Congressman, *see*, "Memorial to His Excellency Andrew Johnson, President of the United States," attached to letter from Abner C. Twining to Lyman Trumbull, June 1, 1866, in Trumbull Papers.

48. *See* Hyman and Wiecek, *Equal Justice under Law*, 387–395.

49. "Mr. Conkling's Amendment," New York *Evening Post*, January 23, 1866, p. 2, col. 1. *Accord*, "Constitutional Amendment," *Cazenovia Republican*, January 31, 1866, p. 2, col. 1.

50. *See Congressional Globe*, 39th Cong., 1st Sess. 357 (1866), for a chart placed on record by Roscoe Conkling to illustrate the effect that adding the freedmen to the South's representation would have.

51. *See Historical Statistics of the United States, Colonial Times to 1970*, 2 (Washington: Government Printing Office, bicentennial ed. 1975), 1140.

52. A. L. Brewer to John Sherman, December 28, 1965, in Sherman Papers.

53. "The Congressional Plan," *Springfield Republican*, May 12, 1866, p. 4, col. 1.

54. William A. Howard to John Sherman, February 27, 1866, in Sherman Papers.

55. *Congressional Globe*, 39th Cong., 1st Sess. 385 (1866) (remarks of Rep. Baker).

56. *Congressional Globe*, 40th Cong., 2nd Sess. 40 (1867) (remarks of Sen. Wilson).

57. *See* Hyman and Wiecek, *Equal Justice under Law*, 386–404; Robert J. Kaczorowski, "To Begin the Nation Anew: Congress, Citizenship, and Civil Rights after the Civil War," *American Historical Review*, 92 (1987), 45, 47–49.

58. Two Republican congressmen, John A. Bingham and Henry J. Raymond, expressed explicit doubts about the constitutionality of the Civil Rights Act,

see Congressional Globe, 39th Cong., 1st Sess. 1291–1292, 2502 (1866), while one Republican senator, John B. Henderson, seemed to understand that the Thirteenth Amendment went no farther than to abolish the master-slave relationship. *See id.* at 122 app. Several Republicans made reference during the debates on the Fourteenth Amendment to the doubts that others had about the constitutionality of the 1866 act. *See id.* at 2498 (remarks of Rep. Broomall), 2511 (remarks of Rep. Eliot), 2896 (remarks of Sen. Doolittle).

59. *See* Benjamin B. Kendrick, *The Journal of the Joint Committee of Fifteen on Reconstruction* (New York: Columbia University Press, 1914), 142–146.
60. *See id.* at 155–197.
61. *Id.* at 46. As the draftsman of section one, Bingham might be thought to enjoy special importance in the history of the Fourteenth Amendment. For this reason, I was keenly interested in obtaining access to a collection of Bingham papers privately held by Professor James A. McPherson of the University of Iowa and regret not having had access to it. However, since I understand section one to be a manifestation of ideas widely held by large segments of the American public over a period of decades rather than a product peculiarly of Bingham's intellect, I doubt that the papers held by Professor McPherson would have significantly altered the conclusions of this book.
62. *Id.* at 51.
63. *Id.* at 50–51.
64. *See Congressional Globe*, 39th Cong., 1st Sess. 351 (remarks of Rep. Stevens).
65. *See id.* at 538.
66. The amendment was taken up in the Senate on February 5, *see id.* at 644, and debated until March 9, when further debate was postponed until March 15. *See id.* at 1289 (remarks of Sen. Fessenden). On March 15, the Senate agreed to a further postponement without date in order to consider the Civil Rights Bill. *See id.* at 1413 (remarks of Sen. Trumbull).
67. *See id.* at 806.
68. *See id.* at 1033–1034 (remarks of Rep. Bingham).
69. *See id.* at 1095.
70. Kendrick, *Journal of the Joint Committee*, 61.
71. *Springfield Republican*, January 23, 1866, p. 2, col. 1.
72. *See Congressional Globe*, 39th Cong., 1st Sess. 358, 405 (remarks of Rep. Shellabarger), 383 (remarks of Rep. Farnsworth), 385 (remarks of Rep. Baker), 406 (remarks of Rep. Eliot), 427 (remarks of Rep. Higby), 673, 1227–28 (remarks of Sen. Sumner) (1866); "The Constitutional Amendment," Boston *Daily Evening Transcript*, January 23, 1866, p. 2, col. 1; "Representation and Taxation," *Chicago Republican*, January 24, 1866, p. 4, col. 4; "The Basis of Representation," *Wisconsin State Journal*, February 3, 1866, p. 1, col. 1; "The Proposed Amendment," *Worcester Daily Spy*, January 24, 1866, p. 2, col. 1.
73. *See Congressional Globe*, 39th Cong., 1st Sess. 359 (remarks of Rep. Conkling), 431 (remarks of Rep. Bingham), 705, 1280–1281 (remarks of Sen. Fessenden), 1256 (remarks of Sen. Wilson) (1866). Both sides of the

argument were presented in "The Conkling Amendment," *Worcester Daily Spy*, March 9, 1866, p. 2, col. 1.

74. "The Proposed Amendment," *Portsmouth Journal*, February 11, 1866, p. 2, col. 1 (emphasis added).

75. See "A Double Report on the Constitutional Amendment," *Springfield Republican*, March 2, 1867, p. 4, col. 4.

76. See *Brevier Legislative Reports . . . of the Journals and Debates of the General Assembly of the State of Indiana*, IX (Indianapolis, 1867), 89 (remarks of Rep. Davis).

77. C. Hammond to Henry L. Dawes, May 2, 1866, Dawes Papers, Library of Congress, Washington, D.C.

78. *Congressional Globe*, 39th Cong., 1st Sess. 1755 (1866).

79. C. F. Tabor to John Sherman, March 19, 1866, John Sherman Papers, Library of Congress, Washington, D.C.

80. Rush R. Sloane to John Sherman, February 26, 1866, Sherman Papers, Library of Congress, Washington, D.C. (emphasis in original).

81. E. B. Sadler to John Sherman, March 23, 1866, Sherman Papers, Library of Congress, Washington, D.C. (emphasis in original).

82. William Sheffield to John Sherman, January 12, 1866, Sherman Papers, Library of Congress, Washington, D.C.

83. "The Conkling Amendment," *New York Evening Post*, March 7, 1866, p. 2, col. 1.

84. Silas Reid to John Sherman, February 28, 1866, Sherman Papers, Library of Congress, Washington, D.C.

85. E. Larned to Lyman Trumbull, March 10, 1866, Trumbull Papers, Library of Congress, Washington, D.C.

86. *Congressional Globe*, 39th Cong., 2d Sess. 64 (1866).

87. *Congressional Globe*, 39th Cong., 1st Sess. 3148 (1866).

88. R. P. L. Barber to John Sherman, March 12, 1866, Sherman Papers, Library of Congress, Washington, D.C. (emphasis in original). For a similar proposal, see "The People's Way," Johnstown *Tribune*, January 12, 1866, p. 2, col. 1.

89. See Kendrick, *Journal of Joint Committee*, 296–303.

90. *Id.* at 83–84.

91. *Congressional Globe*, 39th Cong., 1st Sess. 1095 (1866).

92. *Id.* at 87.

93. See "Reconstruction," San Francisco *Daily Alta California*, May 1, 1866, p. 2, col. 1.

94. See Kendrick, *Journal of Joint Committee*, 98–99. There is no regularity in patterns of voting on Bingham's language. For example, Reverdy Johnson, the respected Democratic Senator, first voted to include the language and then voted to delete it. All the Republicans who were present at the Committee concurred in the original inclusion of the language, but on the subsequent vote to delete it, the Republicans divided, with both radicals and moderates on each side of the division.

95. See *id.* at 100–107.

96. See *id.* at 114; *Congressional Globe*, 39th Cong., 1st Sess. 2265 (remarks of Sen. Fessenden), 2286 (remarks of Rep. Stevens).

97. 60 U.S. (19 How.), 393, 450 (1857).

98. *See Sears* v. *Cottrell*, 5 Mich. 251, 253 (1858) (opinion of Manning, J.) (dictum); *Wynehammer* v. *People*, 13 N.Y. 378 (1856); *Ervine's Appeal*, 16 Pa. State 256 (1851). *See generally* Edward S. Corwin, "The Doctrine of Due Process of Law Before the Civil War," *Harvard Law Review*, 24 (1911), 366, 460.

99. *See* Kendrick, *Journal of Joint Committee*, 116–117.

100. *See Congressional Globe*, 39th Cong., 1st Sess. 2545 (1866).

101. "Report of Reconstruction Committee," *The Right Way*, May 12, 1866, p. 1, col. 2–5.

102. *See Congressional Globe*, 39th Cong., 1st Sess. 2869, 3042 (1866).

103. *See id.* at 3148–3149.

104. E. B. Sadler to John Sherman, May 9, 1866, Sherman Papers, Library of Congress, Washington, D.C.

105. C. F. Noelting to Lyman Trumbull, June 22, 1866, Trumbull Papers, Library of Congress, Washington, D.C. *Accord*, "Reconstruction," *The Right Way*, June 9, 1866, p. 1, col. 2–3; "The Passage of the Constitutional Amendment," Boston *Evening Transcript*, June 14, 1866, p. 2, col. 1; "Congressional Reconstruction," *Memphis Daily Post*, June 15, 1866, p. 4, col. 2; "The Policy of Restoration — Conservative Action of the Senate," *New York Times*, May 31, 1866, p. 4, col. 3; "Reconstruction in the Senate," *Winona Daily Republican*, June 2, 1866, p. 2, col. 1.

106. "The Reconstruction Amendment," *Cazenovia Republican*, June 18, 1866, p. 2, col. 1.

107. Colin D. Mansfield to John Sherman, May 21, 1866, Sherman Papers, Library of Congress, Washington, D.C. (emphasis in original). *Accord*, "The Congressional Plan," *Rochester Democrat*, June 13, 1866, p. 1, col. 3.

108. George I. Bergen to Lyman Trumbull, June 15, 1866, Trumbull Papers, Library of Congress, Washington, D.C. (emphasis in original).

109. J. A. Chase to John Sherman, June 8, 1866, Sherman Papers, Library of Congress, Washington, D.C. *Accord*, "Coming into Line," *Worcester Daily Spy*, June 5, 1866, p. 2, col. 1.

110. *See Historical Statistics of the United States*, vol. 2, p. 1083.

111. "Governor Fenton's Message," *New York Commercial Advertiser*, January 2, 1867, p. 4, col. 1.

112. *Brevier Legislative Reports . . . of the Journals and Debates of the General Assembly of the State of Indiana*, IX (Indianapolis, 1867), 44 (remarks of Sen. Bennett).

113. "The Amendment: Speech of Hon. C. E. Dyer," *Milwaukee Sentinel*, February 11, 1867, p. 2, col. 3.

114. "Who attains Reconstruction?," *Paterson Daily Press*, January 11, 1868, p. 2, col. 1. *Accord, Brevier Legislative Reports . . . of the Journals and Debates of the General Assembly of the State of Indiana*, IX (Indianapolis, 1867), 61 (report of Special Committee on the Constitutional Amendment); [Pennsylvania] *Daily Legislative Record . . . of 1867* (Harrisburg, 1867), 14 app. (remarks of Mr. Bigham), 21 app. (remarks of Mr. Taylor).

115. [Pennsylvania] *Daily Legislative Record . . . of 1867* (Harrisburg, 1867), 69 app. (remarks of Mr. M'Creary).

116. *See* Joseph B. James, *The Ratification of the Fourteenth Amendment* (Macon, Ga.: Mercer University Press, 1984), 11–219.
117. *See id.* at 274–275.
118. *See id.* at 282–286. Oregon also rescinded its ratification in September 1868, after ratification had been completed. *See id.* at 300.
119. *See id.* at 294–298.
120. "Reconstruction," *The Right Way*, June 9, 1866, p. 1, col. 2–3.
121. Raoul Berger, *Government by Judiciary: The Transformation of the Fourteenth Amendment* (Cambridge, Mass.: Harvard University Press, 1977), 99–116, is the first book to suggest that the framers may have had a "conspiratorial purpose" to "conceal . . . future objectives that they dared not avow lest the whole enterprise be imperiled." *Id.* at 105. In making this suggestion, however, Berger claims merely to be rephrasing an earlier hypothesis advanced by Alexander Bickel and others that the framers rejected narrow in favor of broad language because they understood they were drafting a constitutional rather than a statutory provision. *See* Alexander M. Bickel, "The Original Understanding and the Segregation Decision," *Harvard Law Review*, 69 (1955), 1; Alfred H. Kelly, "The Fourteenth Amendment Reconsidered: The Segregation Question," *Michigan Law Review*, 54 (1956), 1049; William W. VanAlstyne, "The Fourteenth Amendment, the 'Right' to Vote, and the Understanding of the Thirty-Ninth Congress," in Philip B. Kurland, ed., *1965 Supreme Court Review* (Chicago, University of Chicago Press, 1965), 33. The point of Berger's restatement, of course, is to make the hypothesis appear less plausible.
122. An effort at clarification occurred in Tennessee, where a proposal was made that the amendment be ratified only on the condition that it not be construed to grant political rights to blacks or to authorize racial intermarriage. The effort was rejected on the ground the states had no power of conditional ratification. *See* "Tennessee Legislature," *Nashville Daily Press and Times*, July 12, 1866, p. 2, col. 3–4. A comparable effort in Indiana was rejected for the same reason. *See Brevier Legislative Reports . . . of the Journals and Debates of the General Assembly of the State of Indiana*, IX (Indianapolis, 1867), 72 (remarks of Reps. Honneus and Hughes).

IV. The Use of Antebellum Rhetoric

1. *See* Francis P. Weisenburger, *Ordeal of Faith: The Crisis of Church-Going America, 1865–1900* (New York: Philosophical Library, 1959), 2, 35–49, 61–79, 296–304.
2. Jesse Baldwin to John Sherman, March 19, 1866, Sherman Papers, Library of Congress, Washington, D.C. (emphasis in original).
3. Thomas Richmond to Lyman Trumbull, May 12, 1866, Trumbull Papers, Library of Congress, Washington, D.C.
4. Hobart Berrian to Salmon P. Chase, February 1, 1866, Chase Papers, Library of Congress, Washington, D.C.
5. S. Guiteau to John Sherman, February 27, 1866, Sherman Papers.
6. Thomas Richmond to John Sherman, February 27, 1866, Sherman Papers.

7. Smith Nichols to Lyman Trumbull, April 2, 1866, Trumbull Papers.
8. *The Right Way*, November 18, 1865, p. 1, col. 2. On the newspaper's distribution policy, *see id.* at p. 1, col. 1.
9. "Will the People Sustain Congress," New York *National Anti-Slavery Standard*, May 5, 1866, p. 2, col. 3–4.
10. "Principles, Not Men," Huntington *Long Islander*, February 16, 1866, p. 2, col. 4.
11. "Policy vs. Principle," Huntington *Long Islander*, March 23, 1866, p. 2, col. 1. On the "distance between policy and principle," *see also* "Will the People Sustain Congress," New York *National Anti-Slavery Standard*, May 5, 1866, p. 2, col. 3–4.
12. "Policy vs. Principle," Huntington *Long Islander*, March 23, 1866, p. 2, col. 1. *See also Congressional Globe*, 39th Cong., 1st Sess. 2798 (1866) (remarks of Sen. Stewart); "The Importance of Principles," *Washington Sunday Chronicle*, May 6, 1866, p. 2, col. 1–2.
13. "The Governor's Message," *Wisconsin State Journal*, January 10, 1867, p. 1, col. 2. *Accord*, "The Right Way," *Winona Daily Republican*, March 10, 1866, p. 2, col. 1. *See also Harper's*, 33 (1866), 671 (reporting speech of Benjamin F. Butler in Gloucester, Mass. in August, 1866); "Equal Rights," *Portland Transcript*, April 21, 1866, p. 30, col. 1.
14. "Republican Majority," Augusta, Ga., *National Republican*, July 23, 1866, p. 2, col. 2.
15. *Congressional Globe*, 39th Congress, 1st Sess. 340 (1866) (emphasis added). *See also* "Our Future Duty," *Bangor Daily Whig and Courier*, April 17, 1866, p. 2, col. 1.
16. *Congressional Globe*, 39th Cong., 1st Sess. 340 (1866).
17. *Congressional Globe*, 39th Cong., 1st Sess. 2542 (1866). *See also* "Our Madison Letter: Further Debate on the Constitutional Amendment," *Milwaukee Sentinel*, Feb. 9, 1867, p. 2, col. 2 (remarks of Assemblyman Kershaw); [Pennsylvania] *Daily Legislative Record . . . of 1867* (Harrisburg, 1867), 59 app. (remarks of Mr. Ewing).
18. Fragment of undated speech draft, p. 2, Thaddeus Stevens Papers, Library of Congress, Washington, D.C.
19. *Congressional Globe*, 39th Cong., 1st Sess. 322 (1866).
20. *Congressional Globe*, 39th Cong., 1st Sess. 500 (1866).
21. *Congressional Globe*, 40th Cong., 2d Sess. 351 app. (1868).
22. *Congressional Globe*, 38th Cong., 1st Sess. 1202 (1864).
23. *Congressional Globe*, 38th Cong., 1st Sess. 2990 (1864).
24. J. H. Martindale to John Sherman, May 12, 1866, in Sherman Papers (emphasis in original).
25. James Auten to John Sherman, December 31, 1865, in Sherman Papers.
26. Thomas Richmond to John Sherman, February 27, 1866, in Sherman Papers (emphasis in original).
27. Simeon Nash to John Sherman, January 27, 1866, in Sherman Papers.
28. Union League Club of New York, Resolutions of April 12, 1866, Library of Congress, Washington, D.C.
29. A. Nourse to Lyman Trumbull, February 22, 1866, in Trumbull Papers.
30. Thomas Richmond to Lyman Trumbull, May 12, 1866, in Trumbull Papers.

31. "Republicans and Democrats," *Rochester Democrat*, January 22, 1866, p. 2, col. 1. *Accord*, "The Free Negroes and the Naturalization Laws," *New York Times*, January 16, 1866, p. 4, col. 4.
32. "Principles, Not Men," Huntington *Long Islander*, February 16, 1866, p. 2, col. 5. *See also Harper's*, 33 (1866), 671 (reporting speech of Benjamin F. Butler in Gloucester, Mass., in August 1866).
33. "The Representative Basis," *Worcester Daily Spy*, January 6, 1866, p. 2, col. 1. *Accord*, "Shall the North Be United?," *Chicago Republican*, May 9, 1866, p. 4, col. 4; "The Constitutional Amendment," New York *Commercial Advertiser*, February 1, 1866, p. 2, col. 2.
34. "Equal Rights," *Portland Transcript*, April 21, 1866, p. 30, col. 1–2. *Accord*, "The Rights of Freedmen," *Rochester Democrat*, December 19, 1865, p. 2, col. 1.
35. Samuel Shellabarger to Lyman Trumbull, April 7, 1866, in Trumbull Papers.
36. James A. Doolittle to Horace Greeley, March 28, 1866, in Horace Greeley Papers, Library of Congress, Washington, D.C.
37. Fragment, August 29, 1866, in Sumner Papers.
38. "Some Remarks on Reconstruction," February 14, 1866, in Stevens Papers.
39. 6 Fed. Cas. 546 (C.C.E.D. Pa. 1823).
40. *Id.* at 551, quoted in *Congressional Globe*, 39th Cong., 1st Sess. 475 (remarks of Sen. Trumbull), 2765 (remarks of Sen. Howard) (1866).
41. *Congressional Globe*, 39th Cong., 1st Sess. 476 (1866). *See also id.* at 475 (remarks of Sen. Trumbull).
42. *Congressional Globe*, 39th Cong., 1st Sess. 504 (1866).
43. *Congressional Globe*, 39th Cong., 1st Sess. 1088 (1866). *See also* "Annual Message of Governor to Legislature," Springfield *Daily Illinois State Journal*, January 8, 1867, p. 3, col. 4; "The Veto of the Civil Rights Bill," *Providence Daily Journal*, March 29, 1866, p. 2, col. 1.
44. *Congressional Globe*, 39th Cong., 1st Sess. 2961 (1866). *See also id.* at 157 (remarks of Rep. Bingham), 1159 (remarks of Rep. Windom), 2511 (remarks of Rep. Eliot), 2766 (remarks of Sen. Howard); "The True Union Policy," *Worcester Daily Spy*, May 1, 1866, p. 2, col. 1.
45. "Governor's Message," *Cincinnati Commercial*, January 3, 1867, p. 2, col. 5.
46. *Congressional Globe*, 40th Cong., 3d Sess. 855 (1869).
47. "Principles, Not Men," Huntington *Long Islander*, February 16, 1866, p. 2, col. 4.
48. Thomas Richmond to John Sherman, February 27, 1866, in Sherman Papers.
49. *Congressional Globe*, 37th Cong., 2d Sess. 1639 (1862).
50. "Some Remarks on Reconstruction," February 14, 1866, in Stevens Papers (emphasis in original).
51. *The Pending Canvass! Speech of the Hon. Thaddeus Stevens, delivered at Bedford Pa., on Tuesday Evening, September 4, 1866* (Lancaster, Pa., 1866), 3.
52. Fragment, August 29, 1866, in Sumner Papers.
53. *Congressional Globe*, 39th Cong., 1st Sess. 1159 (1866).
54. *Congressional Globe*, 40th Cong., 3d Sess. 1004 (1869).
55. *Congressional Globe*, 39th Cong., 1st Sess. 1836 (1866) (remarks of Rep. Lawrence).
56. *Congressional Globe*, 39th Cong., 1st Sess. 157–158 (1866).

57. *Congressional Globe*, 39th Cong., 1st Sess. 2766 (1866). *See also id.* at 406 (remarks of Rep. Shellabarger), 1836 (remarks of Rep. Lawrence).

58. "Principles, Not Men," Huntington *Long Islander*, February 16, 1866, p. 2, col. 4–5.

59. "Manhood Suffrage," Boston *Daily Evening Voice*, December 28, 1865, p. 2, col. 1.

60. "Equal Rights," *Portland Transcript*, April 21, 1866, p. 2, col. 1.

61. *Harper's*, 33 (1866), 671 (reporting Butler's speech in Gloucester, Mass., in August, 1866). *See also* "Let There Be an Extra Session of the Legislature," Virginia City *Daily Territorial Enterprise*, June 16, 1866, p. 2, col. 2.

62. Jesse Baldwin to John Sherman, March 19, 1866, in Sherman Papers (emphasis in original).

63. C. H. Beekman to John Sherman, March 16, 1866, in Sherman Papers.

64. Thomas Richmond to Lyman Trumbull, May 12, 1866, in Trumbull Papers.

65. A. H. Wood to Thaddeus Stevens, February 3, 1866, in Stevens Papers.

66. Jesse Baldwin to John Sherman, March 19, 1866, in Sherman Papers (emphasis in original).

67. Thomas Richmond to John Sherman, February 27, 1866, in Sherman Papers. *See also* "Reconstruction," Leavenworth *Daily Times*, May 13, 1866, p. 2., col. 2.

68. J. H. Martindale to John Sherman, May 12, 1866, in Sherman Papers. *See also* "Justice to the Freedmen—The Suffrage Question," *New York Times*, March 13, 1866, p. 4, col. 4, which urged that "details of time and method" were "the only real questions left" in respect to black suffrage.

69. R. E. Fenton to Lyman Trumbull, April 9, 1866, in Trumbull Papers.

70. T. J. Pretlow to Lyman Trumbull, January 8, 1866, in Trumbull Papers.

71. T. J. Pretlow to Lyman Trumbull, January 19, 1866, in Trumbull Papers.

72. "Governor's Message," *Vermont Chronicle*, October 20, 1866, p. 2, col. 3.

73. Memorial to his Excellency Andrew Johnson, President of the United States, attached to Abner C. Twining to Lyman Trumbull, June 1, 1866, in Trumbull Papers (emphasis in original).

74. Petition. To the Honorable the Senate and House of Representatives of the United States in Congress assembled, undated ms., in Stevens Papers. *See also Congressional Globe*, 39th Cong., 1st Sess. 1272 (1866) (remarks of Sen. Howe).

75. Petition of William Marvin, Wilkinson Call, and Ferdinand M'Leod to Thaddeus Stevens, May 16, 1866, in Stevens Papers. *See also* "The Great Guarantee," *Memphis Daily Post*, June 2, 1866, p. 4, col. 1.

76. See text at note 73 above.

77. John Jay to Salmon P. Chase, January 5, 1867, in Chase Papers.

78. "The Proposed Amendment to the Constitution," New York *Commercial Advertiser*, January 23, 1866, p. 2, col. 3. *Accord*, "Capacity and Equality," *Cincinnati Commercial*, December 28, 1865, p. 4, col. 3. *See also* Hobart Berrian to Salmon P. Chase, February 1, 1866, in Chase Papers, which spoke of "the general good" as the object of government.

79. "Liberty, Union, and Order," Boston *Daily Evening Voice*, December 13, 1865, p. 2, col. 1–2.

80. "The Connecticut Election," Boston *Daily Evening Voice*, April 3, 1866, p. 2, col. 1.
81. "Congress and the Croakers," Huntington *Long Islander*, December 15, 1865, p. 2, col. 1–2 (emphasis in original).
82. "The Second Veto," *Portland Transcript*, April 7, 1866, p. 14, col. 1. *See also* "Speech of Judge Houk," *Nashville Daily Press and Times*, July 7, 1866, p. 2, col. 4.
83. "The Great Point," *Albany Weekly Journal*, March 31, 1866, p. 1, col. 1. *See also* "The Test Oath Not Sufficient—The Report of the Reconstruction Committee," *Bangor Daily Whig and Courier*, May 2, 1866, p. 2, col. 1; "The Duties of Congress," *Essex County Mercury*, April 4, 1866, p. 2, col. 1.
84. "Equality," *South Carolina Leader*, March 31, 1866, p. 2, col. 3.
85. *Congressional Globe*, 38th Cong., 1st Sess. 1203 (1864).
86. *Congressional Globe*, 40th Cong., 2d Sess. 40 (1867).
87. *Congressional Globe*, 38th Cong., 1st Sess. 2989 (1864) (emphasis in original).
88. *Congressional Globe*, 39th Cong., 1st Sess. 537 (1866).
89. "Some Resolutions of H. P. M. Bromwell during the Sessions of the Congress of Reconstruction, 1865–69," in Henry P. M. Bromwell Papers, Library of Congress, Washington, D.C.
90. *Congressional Globe*, 38th Cong., 1st Sess. 1482 (1864) (emphasis in original). *See also* "Mr. Shellabarger at Home: His Report to His Constituents of the Situation in Washington," *Cincinnati Commercial*, May 23, 1866, p. 4, col. 4–5.
91. *Congressional Globe*, 39th Cong., 1st Sess. 1291 (1866).
92. *Congressional Globe*, 39th Cong., 1st Sess. 158 (1866).
93. *Congressional Globe*, 39th Cong., 1st Sess. 431 (1866).
94. *Congressional Globe*, 39th Cong., 1st Sess. 1094 (1866).
95. *Congressional Globe*, 40th Cong., 2d Sess. 1971 (1868).
96. *Congressional Globe*, 40th Cong., 3d Sess. 558 (1869).
97. *Congressional Globe*, 38th Cong., 1st Sess. 838 (1864).
98. *Congressional Globe*, 39th Cong., 1st Sess. 2459 (1866) (emphasis in original).
99. *Congressional Globe*, 39th Cong., 1st Sess. 2502 (1866).
100. *Congressional Globe*, 39th Cong., 1st Sess. 2961 (1866).
101. *Congressional Globe*, 40th Cong., 2d Sess. 883 (1868).
102. "The Veto—What Next?," *Springfield Republican*, March 29, 1866, p. 2, col. 1.
103. Governor's Message, quoted in "The Reconstruction Plan," New York *Commercial Advertiser*, June 22, 1866, p. 2, col. 2. *See also* "Gone and Done It," *Paterson Daily Press*, February 21, 1868, p. 2, col. 1.
104. "New Hampshire Legislature," Concord *Independent Democrat*, July 12, 1866, p. 1, col. 3.
105. "Letter from Madison," *Milwaukee Sentinel*, February 7, 1867, p. 1, col. 2.
106. The statement in the text should not be taken as a harsh comment on modern political leaders. It may be that the accomplishment of Reconstruction was to identify and enact into constitutional law the bedrock principles of American nationality. As long as those principles continue, as they do, to

command wide support, the task remaining for politicians is to elaborate and apply them, with the result that the behavior of modern leaders has been determined by the success of their seemingly more principled predecessors.

107. *Congressional Globe*, 40th Cong., 3d Sess. 1004 (1869).
108. 6 Fed. Cas. 546 (C.C.E.D. Pa. 1823).
109. *Id.* at 551–552, quoted in *Congressional Globe*, 39th Cong., 1st Sess. 475 (remarks of Sen. Trumbull), 2765 (remarks of Sen. Howard) (1866).
110. *Congressional Globe*, 39th Cong., 1st Sess. 2765 (1866). *See also id.* at 41 (1865) (remarks of Sen. Sherman) for a somewhat different definition.
111. *Congressional Globe*, 39th Cong., 1st Sess. 605 (1866).
112. *Ibid.*
113. *Congressional Globe*, 37th Cong., 2d Sess. 1636 (1862).
114. *Congressional Globe*, 39th Cong., 1st Sess. 1294 (1866).
115. *Congressional Globe*, 40th Cong., 2d Sess. 350 app. (1868).
116. *Congressional Globe*, 40th Cong., 2d Sess. 1956 (1868).
117. *Congressional Globe*, 40th Cong., 2d Sess. 350 app. (1868).
118. *Congressional Globe*, 39th Cong., 1st Sess. 1088 (1866).
119. *Congressional Globe*, 39th Cong., 1st Sess. 1089 (1866).
120. *Congressional Globe*, 39th Cong., 1st Sess. 2890 (1866).
121. *Congressional Globe*, 39th Cong., 1st Sess. 1122 (1866).
122. *The Pending Canvass: Speech of the Hon. Thaddeus Stevens, delivered at Bedford, Pa., on Tuesday Evening, September 4, 1866* (Lancaster, Pa., 1866), 11.
123. *Congressional Globe*, 39th Cong., 1st Sess. 342 (1866).
124. *Congressional Globe*, 40th Cong., 3d Sess. 982 (1869) (emphasis in original).
125. E. J. Petre to Mr. and Mrs. Hopley, January 25, 1866, in Sherman Papers (emphasis in original).
126. Charles J. Raymond to John Sherman, April 25, 1866, in Sherman Papers (emphasis in original). *Accord*, E. J. Petre to Mr. and Mrs. Hopley, January 25, 1866, in Sherman Papers; *Congressional Globe*, 40th Cong., 3d Sess. 982 (1869) (remarks of Sen. Welch).
127. W. F. White to Lyman Trumbull, May 27, 1866, in Trumbull Papers. *Accord*, Charles F. Raymond to John Sherman, April 25, 1866, in Sherman Papers.
128. *Congressional Globe*, 40th Cong., 3d Sess. 1036 (1869).
129. Willard Warner to John Sherman, April 22, 1866, in Sherman Papers (emphasis in original). *See also* "Suffrage in the District of Columbia," *Hartford Daily Courant*, January 15, 1866, p. 2, col. 1; "Universal Suffrage," *Hartford Daily Courant*, February 8, 1866, p. 2, col. 1; D. M. Fleming to John Sherman, February 27, 1866, in Sherman Papers, who would "limit the right to those who are competent to wield the ballot;" M. French to Salmon P. Chase, February 7, 1867, in Chase Papers, who would grant "a qualified suffrage based on *intelligence*" (emphasis in original).
130. *See* John Binny to Thaddeus Stevens, February 13, 1866, in Stevens Papers.
131. *Congressional Globe*, 38th Cong., 1st Sess. 2244 (1864) (remarks of Sen. Wilson).
132. *See* "The Latest Radical Proposition," New York *Sunday Mercury*, April

22, 1866, p. 4, col. 3. *See also* C. H. Beekman to John Sherman, March 16, 1866, in Sherman Papers.
133. *Congressional Globe*, 39th Cong., 1st Sess. 179 (1866).
134. *Congressional Globe*, 39th Cong., 2d Sess. 103 (1866).
135. Jason Marsh to Lyman Trumbull, January 8, 1866, in Trumbull Papers. *Accord*, "The Question," *Chicago Republican*, May 16, 1866, p. 4, col. 4; "Congress," *National Anti-Slavery Standard*, December 2, 1865, p. 2, col. 4–5.
136. *Congressional Globe*, 40th Cong., 3d Sess. 982 (1869).
137. "The Case as It Stands," New York *Evening Post*, January 22, 1866, p. 2, col. 1.
138. Simeon Nash to John Sherman, January 27, 1866, in Sherman Papers.
139. D. Richards to John Sherman, March 20, 1866, in Sherman Papers.
140. W. F. White to Lyman Trumbull, May 27, 1866, in Trumbull Papers. *See also* "Congress," *National Anti-Slavery Standard*, December 2, 1865, p. 2, col. 4–5.
141. D. Richards to E. B. Washburn, May 7, 1866, in E. B. Washburn Papers, Library of Congress, Washington, D.C.

V. Objections to the Amendment

1. James D. Richardson, ed., *A Compilation of the Messages and Papers of the Presidents*, 6 (Washington, 1899), 353, 355, 361–362.
2. *Congressional Globe*, 39th Cong., 1st Sess. 1681 (1866) (emphasis added).
3. *Harper's*, 32 (1866), 668–669 (reporting Stephens' speech at Milledgeville, Ga., on February 22, 1866). *Accord*, "Improved Condition of Freedmen," New Orleans *Daily Picayune*, February 13, 1866, p. 6, col. 2; "The Status of Louisiana," New Orleans *Daily Picayune*, February 20, 1866, p. 6, col. 2.
4. *Congressional Globe*, 39th Cong., 1st Sess. 342 (1866).
5. "The Civil Rights Bill," *Little Rock Daily Gazette*, April 13, 1866, p. 1, col. 1. *See also* "The Freedmen's Bureau," New Orleans *Daily Picayune*, January 17, 1866, p. 2, col. 2; "The Georgia Freedmen," Raleigh *Weekly North-Carolina Standard*, January 24, 1866, p. 1, col. 2.
6. "Public Sentiment among the Negroes," *Memphis Daily Post*, January 27, 1866, p. 2, col. 1.
7. *See* "Who Shall Educate the Negro?," Jackson *Daily Clarion*, February 9, 1866, p. 2, col. 1. *See also* "Shall the Negro Be Educated?," *Memphis Daily Post*, January 26, 1866, p. 2, col. 1; "Education Among the Southern Freedmen," *Washington Sunday Chronicle*, January 28, 1868, p. 2, col. 1.
8. "Radical Premonitions," New York *Commercial Advertiser*, January 22, 1866, p. 2, col. 2.
9. "Reconstruction — The Radical Programme at Last," *New York Sun*, April 30, 1866, p. 2, col. 1.
10. "Passage of the Constitutional Amendment by the House," *Brooklyn Daily Eagle*, May 11, 1866, p. 2, col. 1. *Accord*, "The Constitutional Amendment," New York *Commercial Advertiser*, February 1, 1866, p. 2, col. 2.
11. "The Evils of Special Legislation and Their Cure," *New York Daily News*,

March 28, 1868, p. 4, col. 3. *See also Boston Post*, May 30, 1866, p. 1, col. 5.

12. "Salem Correspondence," Jacksonville *Oregon Sentinel*, September 29, 1866, p. 1, col. 3 (quoting remarks of Rep. Cox). *Accord, Brevier Legislative Reports . . . of the Journals and Debates of the General Assembly of the State of Indiana*, IX (Indianapolis, 1867), 46 (remarks of Sen. Sherrod); [Pennsylvania] *Daily Legislative Record . . . of 1867* (Harrisburg, 1867), 39 app.-41 app. (remarks of Mr. Jenks); "Governor's Message," *Louisville Daily Democrat*, January 5, 1867, p. 1, col. 7–8; "The Amendment Ratified," Concord *New Hampshire Patriot*, July 4, 1866, p. 2, col. 4 (reprinting report of minority of committee of national affairs); "Constitutional Amendment," Trenton *Daily State Gazette*, February 21, 1868, p. 2, col. 2–3 (reprinting part of argument by Sen. Winfield favoring recission of ratification of amendment); "Message of Gov. Orr," *Yorkville Enquirer*, November 29, 1866, p. 4, col. 3.

13. "Report and Resolutions of the Joint Standing Committee on the Constitutional Amendment," reprinted in "Georgia Legislature," Athens *Southern Watchman*, November 21, 1866, p. 1, col. 7–8.

14. "Constitutional Amendment," *Little Rock Daily Gazette*, December 13, 1866, p. 2, col. 1.

15. "The Constitutional Amendment," *Daily Richmond Enquirer*, January 10, 1867, p. 2, col. 1. *See also* "Robert Dale Owen's Plan of Reconstruction," New York *World*, April 25, 1866, p. 4, col. 1–2; "Georgia on the Howard Amendment: Extract from the Message of Gov. Jenkins to the Legislature of Georgia," *Weekly North-Carolina Standard*, November 14, 1866, p. 4, col. 2–3; "Report of the Select Joint Committee . . . on the proposition to adopt the Congressional Constitutional Amendment," *Weekly North-Carolina Standard*, December 19, 1866, p. 1, col. 6.

16. [Pennsylvania] *Daily Legislative Record . . . of 1867* (Harrisburg, 1867), 5 app. (remarks of Mr. Searight).

17. "Constitutional Amendment," *Little Rock Daily Gazette*, December 16, 1866, p. 2, col. 1. *Accord, Brevier Legislative Reports . . . of the Journals and Debates of the General Assembly of the State of Indiana*, IX (Indianapolis, 1867), 46 (remarks of Sen. Sherrod); "Report of the Select Joint Committee . . . on the proposition to adopt the Congressional Constitutional Amendment," *Weekly North-Carolina Standard*, December 19, 1866, p. 1, col. 6.

18. *See generally* "Lincoln Need Not Have Signed the Resolution Submitting the Thirteenth Amendment to the States," *Lincoln Lore*, no. 1604 (Fort Wayne, Ind.: Lincoln National Life Insurance, 1971).

19. *Congressional Globe*, 39th Cong., 1st Sess. 2938 (1866). *Accord, Congressional Globe*, 39th Cong., 1st Sess. 3041 (remarks of Sen. McDougall). *See also* "Secret Caucus," *Boston Post*, May 30, 1866, p. 1, col. 5–6. *See also Boston Post*, May 12, 1866, p. 1, col. 7.

20. *Congressional Globe*, 39th Cong., 1st Sess. 238 app. (1866).

21. "Proposed Changes in the Constitution," *Little Rock Daily Gazette*, December 28, 1865, p. 1, col. 4.

22. *Congressional Globe*, 39th Cong., 1st Sess. 426 (1866). *Accord, Brevier*

Legislative Reports . . . of the Journals and Debates of the General Assembly of the State of Indiana, IX (Indianapolis, 1867), 61 (report of minority of Special Committee on Constitutional Amendment); "The Report on Reconstruction," Baltimore *Sun,* May 2, 1866, p. 2, col. 1; "Reconstruction," New York *Commercial Advertiser,* April 30, 1866, p. 2, col. 1; "President Johnson," *Richmond Daily Dispatch,* March 29, 1866, p. 2, col. 1; "What They Contend For," *San Francisco Daily Examiner,* March 26, 1866, p. 2, col. 1.

23. *Congressional Globe,* 39th Cong., 1st Sess. 117 app. (1866).

24. "Negro Government — Louisiana," *Oswego Daily Palladium,* June 3, 1867, p. 2, col. 1.

25. "Report of the Reconstruction Committee," New York *World,* January 23, 1866, p. 4, col. 1. *See also* "The Reconstruction Committee Report," New York *Evening Post,* May 1, 1866, p. 2, col. 1; "The Latest Proposed Amendment to the Constitution," *Brooklyn Daily Eagle,* January 23, 1866, p. 2, col. 1.

26. "The Constitutional Amendment," *Daily Richmond Enquirer,* January 2, 1867, p. 2, col. 2.

27. *See* "Reconstruction," New York *Commercial Advertiser,* April 30, 1866, p. 2, col. 1. *Accord,* "The Reconstruction Plan," *Boston Post,* May 3, 1866, p. 1, col. 5.

28. "Tinkering the Constitution," New York *Commercial Advertiser,* February 6, 1866, p. 2, col. 2. *See also* "Tinkering the Constitution," San Francisco *Daily Alta California,* Jan. 31, 1866, p. 2, col. 1.

29. "Amending the Constitution," New York *Evening Post,* March 20, 1866, p. 2, col. 1.

30. "Tinkering the Constitution," New York *Sunday Mercury,* December 17, 1865, p. 4, col. 2.

31. "Amending the Constitution," New York *Sunday Mercury,* March 4, 1866, p. 4, col. 2.

32. "The Mania for Constitutional Amendments," *New York Daily News,* January 25, 1866, p. 4, col. 3. *See also* "The President upon Radical Measures," *National Intelligencer,* January 29, 1866, p. 2, col. 1; "Amending or Rending the Constitution," *Newburyport Daily Herald,* January 29, 1866, p. 2, col. 1; "The Amendment Ratified," Concord *New Hampshire Patriot,* July 4, 1866, p. 2, col. 4 (reprinting report of minority of committee on national affairs); "No More Negative Amendments," *Springfield Republican,* January 9, 1866, p. 2, col. 1–2; "Constitutional Amendments," Trenton *Daily State Gazette,* January 30, 1866, p. 2, col. 1. For other miscellaneous procedural objections, *see* "The Amendment Ratified," *New Hampshire Patriot,* July 4, 1866, p. 2, col. 4 (reprinting report of minority of committee on national affairs); "Proposition to Amend the Constitution of the United States without Consulting the People Thereof," San Francisco *Daily Alta California,* May 5, 1866, p. 2, col. 1. It is, indeed, impossible to report on the wide variety of objections offered to the amendment. All sorts of ideas outside the mainstream of political debate were expressed during the 1866–1868 period, including those of one Louisiana state senator who voted against ratification of the Fourteenth Amendment because "he believed that loyal Southern men should receive

compensation for their emancipated slaves." "State Legislature," *New Orleans Times*, February 7, 1867, p. 1, col. 5 (remarks of Mr. Egan).

33. "Negro Government—Louisiana," *Oswego Daily Palladium*, June 3, 1867, p. 2, col. 1.

34. "Negro Equality" *Newark Daily Advertiser*, May 21, 1866, p. 2, col. 1. *See also* "The Civilizing Effects of African Slavery," *Rochester Daily Union and Advertiser*, May 19, 1866, p. 3, col. 1.

35. *Congressional Globe*, 40th Cong., 3d Sess. 989 (1869). *Accord*, [Pennsylvania] *Daily Legislative Record . . . of 1867* (Harrisburg, 1867), 34 app. (remarks of Mr. McCandless).

36. *Congressional Globe*, 40th Cong., 2d Sess. 1973 (1868).

37. *Congressional Globe*, 38th Cong., 1st Sess. 1490 (1864). *See also* "Salem Correspondence," Jacksonville *Oregon Sentinel*, September 29, 1866, p. 1, col. 2–3 (reporting racist remarks by opponents of Fourteenth Amendment in Oregon legislature).

38. "The Future Prospects of England and the United States," *Newbern Daily Times*, June 9, 1866, p. 2, col. 1–2. *Accord*, "The Fate of the Negro," West Baton Rouge *Sugar Planter*, February 24, 1866, p. 2, col. 2.

39. *Daily Richmond Enquirer*, January 6, 1866, p. 2, col. 2. *Accord*, "The Colored People," *New Orleans Times*, December 24, 1865, p. 8, col. 2.

40. *Congressional Globe*, 39th Cong., 2d Sess. 79 (1866). *Accord*, "Miscegenation," Alexandria *Louisiana Democrat*, November 29, 1865, p. 2, col. 2.

41. *Congressional Globe*, 40th Cong., 3d Sess. 1310 (1869). *Accord, Congressional Globe*, 39th Cong., 1st Sess. 450 (1866) (remarks of Rep. Harding).

42. Resolution of Delaware Legislature, reported in "A Government for All Men," New York *Sun*, February 20, 1866, p. 2, col. 1. *See also* R. R. Collier to Salmon P. Chase, May 11, 1868, in Salmon P. Chase Papers, Library of Congress, Washington, D.C., which speaks of the *"ineradicable inadaptability* of the negro" (emphasis in original).

43. J. D. Cox to John Sherman, January 27, 1866, in John Sherman Papers, Library of Congress, Washington, D.C.

44. David Peck to John Sherman, March 19, 1866, in Sherman Papers.

45. *Congressional Globe*, 38th Cong., 1st Sess. 2141 (1864). *Accord, Congressional Globe*, 38th Cong., 1st Sess. 2240 (1864) (remarks of Senator Foster); "Unqualified Suffrage—Its Tendency," *New York Times*, March 17, 1866, p. 4, col. 3; "The Suffrage Question," *Rochester Democrat*, March 24, 1866, p. 1, col. 3.

46. *Congressional Globe*, 38th Cong., 1st Sess. 2248 (1864).

47. *Congressional Globe*, 39th Cong., 2d Sess. 56 (1866).

48. *Congressional Globe,* 39th Cong., 1st Sess. 3438 (1866). *See also Congressional Globe*, 38th Cong., 1st Sess. 2240 (1864) (remarks of Sen. Harlan); "Message of Governor Worth," *Weekly North-Carolina Standard*, November 28, 1866, p. 1, col. 6.

49. John Binny to Thaddeus Stevens, February 13, 1866, in Thaddeus Stevens Papers, Library of Congress, Washington, D.C.

50. D. Richards to John Sherman, March 20, 1866, in Sherman Papers.

51. *Congressional Globe*, 39th Cong., 2d Sess. 83 (1866) (remarks of Sen. Buckalew).

52. "Equal Suffrage—Where to Begin," *Springfield Republican*, February 19, 1866, p. 2, col. 1.

53. *Congressional Globe*, 39th Cong., 2d Sess. 84 (1866). *See also* "The Suffrage Question in Congress," *Springfield Republican*, January 24, 1866, p. 4, col. 1–2.

54. John Binny to Thaddeus Stevens, February 13, 1866, in Stevens Papers.

55. Simeon Nash to John Sherman, January 27, 1866, in Sherman Papers. *Accord, Congressional Globe*, 38th Cong., 1st Sess. 2140–2141 (1864) (remarks of Sen. Cowan); "The Suffrage Question," *New York Times*, February 13, 1866, p. 4, col. 5.

56. George Marsh to John Sherman, January, 1866, in Sherman Papers.

57. *Congressional Globe*, 39th Cong., 1st Sess. 1056 (1866) (remarks of Rep. Niblack).

58. *Congressional Globe*, 39th Cong., 1st Sess. 2890 (1866) (remarks of Sen. Cowan).

59. *Congressional Globe*, 39th Cong., 1st Sess. 497 (1866) (remarks of Sen. VanWinkle).

60. *Congressional Globe*, 40th Cong., 3d Sess. 287 app. (1869).

61. *Congressional Globe*, 39th Cong., 1st Sess. 2890–2891 (1866).

62. *Congressional Globe*, 40th Cong., 3d Sess. 939–940 (1869).

63. *Congressional Globe*, 40th Cong., 3d Sess. 1034–1035 (1869).

64. *Congressional Globe*, 39th Cong., 2d Sess. 84 (1866).

65. *Congressional Globe*, 39th Cong., 1st Sess. 2895 (1866).

66. *Congressional Globe*, 39th Cong., 1st Sess. 574 (1866).

67. *Brevier Legislative Reports . . . of the Journals and Debates of the General Assembly of the State of Indiana,* IX (Indianapolis, 1867), 81 (remarks of Rep. McFadden).

68. "Our Red Brothers," *San Francisco Chronicle*, April 1, 1867, p. 2, col. 2.

69. Amendment 14, sections 1 and 2.

70. *Congressional Globe*, 39th Cong., 1st Sess. 2897 (1866).

71. *Congressional Globe*, 39th Cong., 1st Sess. 1415 (1866).

72. *Congressional Globe*, 39th Cong., 1st Sess. 1414 (1866).

73. *Congressional Globe*, 39th Cong., 1st Sess. 478 (1866).

74. "Civil Rights Bill," Charlestown [W.Va.] *Virginia Free Press*, April 19, 1866, p. 2, col. 1.

75. "Constitutional Amendment," *Little Rock Daily Gazette*, December 13, 1866, p. 2, col. 1. *Accord*, "Report of the Select Joint Committee . . . on the Proposition to Adopt the Congressional Constitutional Amendment," *Weekly North-Carolina Standard*, December 19, 1866, p. 1, col. 7, and p. 2, col. 2. *See also* "The Special Session and the Constitutional Amendment," Nashville *Republican Banner*, June 26, 1866, p. 2, col. 2; "Congress and Restoration," New Orleans *Evening Picayune*, June 1, 1866, p. 6, col. 2.

76. "The Amendment Ratified," *New Hampshire Patriot*, July 4, 1866, p. 2, col. 4. *See also Brevier Legislative Reports . . . of the Journals and Debates of the General Assembly of the State of Indiana*, IX (Indianapolis, 1867), 46 (remarks of Sen. Sherrod); [Pennsylvania] *Daily Legislative Record . . . of 1867* (Harrisburg, 1867), 41 app. (remarks of Mr. Jenks); "Ohio Legislature," *Cincinnati Commercial*, January 13, 1868, p. 3, col. 1–2 (reporting

resolution of Ohio legislature rescinding ratification of the Fourteenth Amendment); "Ninety-Second Legislature," Trenton *Daily State Gazette*, March 6, 1868, p. 2, col. 2 (reprinting speech of Sen. Little).

77. *Congressional Globe*, 39th Cong., 1st Sess. 134 app. (1866).

78. "Governor's Message," *Mobile Daily Advertiser and Register*, November 13, 1866, p. 2, col. 8. *Accord*, "Message of Governor Worth," Raleigh *Weekly North-Carolina Standard*, November 28, 1866, p. 1, col. 6; "Message of Governor Orr," *Yorkville Enquirer*, November 29, 1866, p. 4, col. 3.

79. "The Civil Rights Bill," *Little Rock Daily Gazette*, April 13, 1866, p. 1, col. 2. *Accord*, "The Report of the Committee of Fifteen," *Newbern Daily Times*, May 31, 1866, p. 2, col. 1–2.

80. *Congressional Globe*, 39th Cong., 1st Sess. 598 (1866).

81. Richardson, *Messages and Papers of the Presidents*, v. 6, pp. 405, 409–410.

82. *Congressional Globe*, 39th Cong., 1st Sess. 1267 (1866). *See also* "The President's Objections to the Civil Rights Bill," Baltimore *Sun*, April 2, 1866, p. 2, col. 1; "The State Laws and the Civil Rights Bill in Indiana," *Charleston Daily Courier*, April 19, 1866, p. 2, col. 1; "The Civil Rights Bill," *National Intelligencer*, March 24, 1866, p. 2, col. 1. An eloquent and thoughtful defense of judicial independence appeared in "The Civil Rights Bill and the Judiciary," *New York Times*, March 31, 1866, p. 4, col. 5.

83. *See Congressional Globe*, 39th Cong., 1st Sess. 1291–1292 (1866).

84. *Congressional Globe*, 39th Cong., 1st Sess. 1758 (1866).

85. *See* Samuel Shellabarger to Lyman Trumbull, April 7, 1866, in Trumbull Papers.

86. *Congressional Globe*, 39th Cong., 1st Sess. 1270 (1866) (remarks of Rep. Kerr).

87. *Congressional Globe*, 39th Cong., 1st Sess. 2467 (1866). *Accord, Brevier Legislative Reports . . . of the Journals and Debates of the General Assembly of the State of Indiana*, IX (Indianapolis, 1867), 79 (remarks of Rep. Kizer); "Tennessee Legislature," *Nashville Daily Press and Times*, July 12, 1866, p. 2, col. 3 (protest of Sen. Frazier).

88. *Congressional Globe*, 39th Cong., 1st Sess. 1782 (1866).

89. *Congressional Globe*, 39th Cong., 1st Sess. 506 (1866).

90. "Radical Revolution — The Constitutional Amendment," *Daily Richmond Enquirer*, January 7, 1867, p. 2, col. 1–2.

91. *Congressional Globe*, 39th Cong., 1st Sess. 2538 (1866). For similar statements about the Thirteenth Amendment, *see Congressional Globe*, 38th Cong., 1st Sess. 2985–2987 (1864) (remarks of Rep. Edgerton); *Congressional Globe*, 38th Cong., 2d Sess. 125 (1865) (remarks of Rep. Cox); *Congressional Globe*, 38th Cong., 2d Sess. 242 (1865) (remarks of Rep. Cox). For a similar statement on the Civil Rights Act, *see Congressional Globe*, 39th Cong., 1st Sess. 182 app. (1866) (remarks of Sen. Davis).

92. "Radical Perplexities," *Brooklyn Daily Eagle*, December 29, 1865, p. 2, col. 1.

93. "The Evils of Centralization," New York *Evening Post*, December 6, 1865, p. 2, col. 1.

94. *Congressional Globe*, 39th Cong., 1st Sess. 1271 (1866) (remarks of Rep. Kerr).

95. *Congressional Globe*, 39th Cong., 1st Sess. 1065 (1866).
96. *See Congressional Globe*, 39th Cong., 1st Sess. 1809 (1866) (remarks of Sen. McDougall).
97. "Innovations on the Constitution," *New York Daily News*, March 24, 1866, p. 4, col. 2. *Accord*, "Radical Revolution — The Constitutional Amendment," *Daily Richmond Enquirer*, January 7, 1867, p. 2, col. 1; "The Crisis of the Republic and the Duty of the Hour," *San Francisco Daily Examiner*, January 3, 1866, p. 1, col. 6.
98. "The Only Issue," *San Francisco Daily Examiner*, May 4, 1866, p. 2, col. 1. *Accord*, "Open War," *Boston Post*, February 3, 1866, p. 1, col. 5.
99. "Stands Firm," *San Francisco Daily Examiner*, May 5, 1866, p. 2, col. 1.

VI. The Republican Rebuttal

1. *See Historical Statistics of the United States, Colonial Times to 1970*, 2 (Washington: Government Printing Office, bicentennial ed. 1975), 1140, showing that Union deaths alone were nearly as many as total American deaths in World War II.
2. "Civil Rights Bill," *The Right Way*, April 21, 1866, p. 1, col. 4–5. *See also*, "What Is the Civil Rights Bill?," *Norwich Courier*, April 12, 1866, p. 4, col. 3; *Wheeling Intelligencer*, April 11, 1866, p. 2, col. 1; "The Civil Rights Bill," *Worcester Daily Spy*, March 19, 1866, p. 2, col. 2.
3. *See generally* "Lincoln Need Not Have Signed the Resolution Submitting the Thirteenth Amendment to the States," *Lincoln Lore*, no. 1604 (Fort Wayne, Ind.: Lincoln National Life Insurance, 1971).
4. "Memorial to His Excellency Andrew Johnson, President of the United States," attached to Abner C. Twining to Lyman Trumbull, June 1, 1866, in Lyman Trumbull Papers, Library of Congress, Washington, D.C.
5. Jason Marsh to Lyman Trumbull, January 8, 1866, in Trumbull Papers. *Accord, Congressional Globe*, 40th Cong., 3d Sess. 982 (1869) (remarks of Sen. Ross).
6. *Congressional Globe*, 40th Cong., 3d Sess. 861 (1869) (remarks of Sen. Warner).
7. Thomas Richmond to John Sherman, February 27, 1866, in John Sherman Papers, Library of Congress, Washington, D.C. (emphasis in original).
8. *Congressional Globe*, 39th Cong., 1st Sess. 2891 (1866).
9. *Congressional Globe*, 39th Cong., 1st Sess. 2892 (1866).
10. "Centralization," Boston *Daily Evening Voice*, May 9, 1866, p. 1, col. 1. *Accord*, "The Reconstruction Committee and the Constitution," *New York Times*, February 19, 1866, p. 4, col. 3. One possible exception to these Republican protestations was a statement in a Nevada newspaper favoring adoption of the Fourteenth Amendment even though the paper thought it would "nationalize the States and forever destroy the dogmas of States' Rights." "Let There Be an Extra Session of the Legislature," *Virginia City Daily Territorial Enterprise*, June 16, 1866, p. 2, col. 2. *See also* "Reconstruction, No. 2," Eugene *Oregon State Journal*, December 16, 1865, p. 2, col. 3 (a letter to the editor arguing that each state should have "power to

legislate upon its local affairs" but favoring "[t]he same code of laws . . . in all parts of the Union," and further urging that "[t]he officers of each State, though elected by the people of the State should owe duty and obedience to the Federal Government and be amenable thereto, as other Federal officers"). Some readers might interpret these letters as favoring centralization. In my view, however, they exemplify the odd and confused statements, which simply defy classification, that were sometimes made during Reconstruction.

11. "The Last Veto," *Cincinnati Commercial*, March 30, 1866, p. 2, col. 4. *See also* "The Civil Rights Bill," *Cincinnati Commercial*, March 30, 1866, p. 4, col. 2.

12. *Congressional Globe*, 39th Cong., 1st Sess. 1065 (1866) (remarks of Rep. Hale). *But see* [Pennsylvania] *Daily Legislative Record . . . of 1867* (Harrisburg, 1867), 33 app., where Senator R. A. Browne commented that the states existed only "to conserve the rights of men" and that, "[w]hen a State becomes the oppressor instead of the protector of its citizens, it deserves to be destroyed."

13. *Congressional Globe*, 39th Cong., 1st Sess. 1088 (1866) (remarks of Rep. Woodbridge). *See also Congressional Globe*, 39th Cong., 1st Sess. 1832 (remarks of Rep. Lawrence), 3039 (remarks of Sen. Howard), 157 app. (remarks of Rep. Delano) (1866).

14. *Congressional Globe*, 39th Cong., 1st Sess. 2542 (1866). For other similar remarks by Bingham, *see Congressional Globe*, 39th Cong., 1st Sess. 1065, 1090 (1866).

15. *Congressional Globe*, 39th Cong., 1st Sess. 1760–1761 (1866).

16. *Congressional Globe*, 39th Cong., 2d Sess. 40 (1866).

17. *Congressional Globe*, 39th Cong., 1st Sess. 1117 (1866). *Accord, Brevier Legislative Reports . . . of the Journals and Debates of the General Assembly of the State of Indiana*, IX (Indianapolis, 1867), 80 (remarks of Rep. Ross).

18. *Congressional Globe*, 39th Cong., 1st Sess. 1832 (1866).

19. *The Pending Canvass! Speech of the Hon. Thaddeus Stevens, delivered at Bedford, Pa., on Tuesday Evening, September 4, 1866* (Lancaster, Pa., 1866), 11.

20. *Congressional Globe*, 40th Cong., 3d Sess. 559 (1869).

21. *Congressional Globe*, 39th Cong., 1st Sess. 1063 (1866).

22. *Congressional Globe*, 39th Cong., 1st Sess. 2766 (1866).

23. *Congressional Globe*, 39th Cong., 1st Sess. 174 (1866).

24. [Pennsylvania] *Daily Legislative Record . . . of 1867* (Harrisburg, 1867), 48 app. (remarks of Mr. Mann).

25. *Congressional Globe*, 39th Cong., 1st Sess. 1034 (1866).

26. *Congressional Globe*, 39th Cong., 1st Sess. 1090 (1866).

27. *Ibid.*

28. *Congressional Globe*, 39th Cong., 1st Sess. 2765 (1866).

29. *See, e.g.*, Charles Fairman, "Does the Fourteenth Amendment Incorporate the Bill of Rights?: The Original Understanding," *Stanford Law Review*, 2 (1949), 5, 81–126.

30. *See, e.g.*, Michael Kent Curtis, *No State Shall Abridge: The Fourteenth Amendment and the Bill of Rights* (Durham, N.C.: Duke University Press, 1986), 57–91, 131–153.

31. *Congressional Globe*, 39th Cong., 1st Sess. 2513 (1866).
32. *Congressional Globe*, 39th Cong., 1st Sess. 1089 (1866) (remarks of Rep. Bingham rephrasing the question of Rep. Hale).
33. *Congressional Globe*, 39th Cong., 1st Sess. 1089 (1866).
34. *Congressional Globe*, 39th Cong., 1st Sess. 1089 (1866).
35. *Congressional Globe*, 40th Cong., 3d Sess. 1003 (1869).
36. *Congressional Globe*, 38th Cong., 1st Sess. 2240 (1864).
37. *Congressional Globe*, 40th Cong., 3d Sess. 1003 (1869).
38. "Constitutional Amendments," *Rochester Democrat*, February 15, 1866, p. 1, col. 1.
39. An analog might be the practice under 42 U.S.C. sec. 1988 of turning to state law to fill in gaps, such as the absence of a statute of limitations, in federal civil rights statutes. *See generally* Theodore Eisenberg, "State Law in Federal Civil Rights Cases: The Proper Scope of Section 1988," *University of Pennsylvania Law Review*, 128 (1980), 499; Seth F. Kreimer, "The Source of Law in Civil Rights Actions: Some Old Light on Section 1988," *University of Pennsylvania Law Review*, 133 (1985), 601.
40. *Congressional Globe*, 39th Cong., 1st Sess. 2765 (1866).
41. 6 Fed. Cas. 546, 551 (C.C.E.D. Pa. 1823) (dictum).
42. *Congressional Globe*, 39th Cong., 1st Sess. 2765 (1866).
43. *See Congressional Globe*, 38th Cong., 1st Sess. 2240 (1864) (remarks of Sen. Morrill).
44. *Congressional Globe*, 39th Cong., 1st Sess. 3035 (1866) (remarks of Sen. Henderson). *Accord*, "What Is a Man," Augusta *Colored American*, December 30, 1865, p. 2, col. 2–3; "Prejudices of Race," *Rochester Democrat*, February 6, 1866, p. 2, col. 1.
45. *Congressional Globe*, 39th Cong., 1st Sess. 1118 (1866).
46. *Congressional Globe*, 39th Cong., 1st Sess. 1293 (1866).
47. *Congressional Globe*, 39th Cong., 1st Sess. 704 (1866).
48. *Congressional Globe*, 40th Cong., 3d Sess. 1033 (1869).
49. *Congressional Globe*, 39th Cong., 1st Sess. 2948 (1866).
50. *See* Michael Les Benedict, *A Compromise of Principle: Congressional Republicans and Reconstruction 1863–1869* (New York: W. W. Norton, 1974), 108–187; Raoul Berger, *Government by Judiciary: The Transformation of the Fourteenth Amendment* (Cambridge, Mass.: Harvard University Press, 1977), 52–68.
51. *Congressional Globe*, 39th Cong., 1st Sess. 1117 (1866) (remarks of Rep. Wilson).
52. *The Pending Canvass! Speech of the Hon. Thaddeus Stevens, delivered at Bedford, Pa., on Tuesday Evening, September 4, 1866* (Lancaster, Pa., 1866), 5. *See also* [Pennsylvania] *Daily Legislative Record . . . of 1867* (Harrisburg, 1867), 16 app.-17 app. (remarks of Mr. Bigham).
53. *See* "Governor's Address," *Bangor Daily Evening Times*, January 3, 1867, p. 1, col. 1. *See also* "Ninety-Second Legislature," Trenton *Daily State Gazette*, March 25, 1868, p. 2, col. 5 (reporting speech of Assemblyman Gage opposing recission of ratification of Fourteenth Amendment).
54. "Report of the Reconstruction Committee," *The Right Way*, May 12, 1866, p. 1, col. 6. *Accord*, "The Legislature," *Charleston Courier*, July 8, 1868, p.

1, col. 1; "South Carolina Legislature," *Charleston Courier*, July 9, 1868, p. 1, col. 5; Raleigh *North-Carolina Weekly Standard*, May 9, 1866, p. 1, col. 1; Montpelier *Vermont Watchman and State Journal*, May 18, 1866, p. 1, col. 2.

55. A. N. Rankin to Thaddeus Stevens, May 16, 1866, in Thaddeus Stevens Papers, Library of Congress, Washington, D.C. *See also* "The Proposed Constitutional Amendment," *Nashville Daily Press and Times*, July 10, 1866, p. 2, col. 1; *Nashville Daily Press and Times*, July 11, 1866, p. 2, col. 1.

56. Samuel Walker to Thaddeus Stevens, August 21, 1866, in Stevens Papers. *See also* A. Dewey to John Sherman, July 15, 1866, in John Sherman Papers, Library of Congress, Washington, D.C., "Nigro sufferage *we* could have carried. But it is best left where you left it."

57. *See* "The Legislature," *Worcester Daily Spy*, March 21, 1867, p. 2, col. 3. *See also* "Congressional Fraud," *National Anti-Slavery Standard*, June 23, 1866, p. 2, col. 3 (calling amendment "a flagrant, cruel cheat"); "Boutwell on Reconstruction—The Constitutional Amendment," *Daily Richmond Enquirer*, January 12, 1867, p. 2, col. 3 (reporting Rep. Boutwell's statement that Reconstruction without black suffrage was unsatisfactory).

58. *Congressional Globe*, 40th Cong., 3d Sess. 1003–1004 (1869).

59. *Congressional Globe*, 40th Cong., 3d Sess. 1003 (1869).

60. *Congressional Globe*, 39th Cong., 2d Sess. 185 (1866).

61. *Congressional Globe*, 40th Cong., 2d Sess. 2665 (1868).

62. "Massachusetts Legislature," *Boston Post*, March 13, 1867, p. 4, col. 4 (quoting remarks of Rep. Walker).

63. "Reconstruction in a New Aspect," *Worcester Daily Spy*, May 31, 1866, p. 2, col. 1. *Accord*, "Congress Surrenders," *National Anti-Slavery Standard*, May 29, 1866, p. 2, col. 4; "The Final Summing Up," *Springfield Republican*, May 26, 1866, p. 4, col. 1.

64. "Reconstruction," *Essex County Mercury*, May 2, 1866, p. 2, col. 1–2.

65. *Congressional Globe*, 40th Cong., 2d Sess. 352 app. (1868). *Accord*, "The Veto of the Civil Rights Bill," *Providence Journal*, March 29, 1866, p. 2, col. 1; "The One Only Right Way," *The Right Way*, December 2, 1865, p. 2, col. 2.

66. "The Proposed Amendment to the Constitution," *Newbern Daily Times*, June 15, 1866, p. 2, col. 2–3.

67. J. H. Martindale to John Sherman, May 12, 1866, in Sherman Papers (emphasis in original).

68. "The Congressional Plan," *Chicago Republican*, May 7, 1866, p. 4, col. 4.

69. [Pennsylvania] *Daily Legislative Record . . . of 1867* (Harrisburg, 1867), 6 app.

70. *Congressional Globe*, 39th Cong., 1st Sess. 2542 (1866).

71. *Congressional Globe*, 39th Cong., 1st Sess. 2766 (1866).

72. *Congressional Globe*, 40th Cong., 3d Sess. 1006 (1869).

73. *Congressional Globe*, 40th Cong., 3d Sess. 727 (1869) (remarks of Rep. Shellabarger).

74. *Congressional Globe*, 40th Cong., 3d Sess. 1004 (1869).

75. *Congressional Globe*, 39th Cong., 2d Sess. 450 (1867).

76. *Congressional Globe*, 40th Cong., 1st Sess. 543 (1867).

77. *Congressional Globe*, 39th Cong., 1st Sess. 298 app. (1866).
78. *Congressional Globe*, 40th Cong., 2d Sess. 2462–2463 (1868).
79. *Congressional Globe*, 40th Cong., 3d Sess. 1003 (1869).
80. *Congressional Globe*, 40th Cong., 3d Sess. 1006 (1869).
81. *Congressional Globe*, 40th Cong., 3d Sess. 1000 (1869).
82. *Congressional Globe*, 40th Cong., 3d Sess. 102 app. (1869).
83. *Congressional Globe*, 40th Cong., 2d Sess. 2609 (1868).
84. "Salem Correspondence," Jacksonville *Oregon Sentinel*, September 29, 1866, p. 1, col. 4 (quoting remarks of Rep. Humason). *Accord*, [Pennsylvania] *Daily Legislative Record . . . of 1867* (Harrisburg, 1867), 90 app. (remarks of Mr. Chalfant).
85. "Salem Correspondence," Jacksonville *Oregon Sentinel*, September 29, 1866, p. 1, col. 3 (quoting remarks of Rep. Chenoweth).
86. "Annual Message of Governor to Legislature," *Daily Illinois State Journal*, January 8, 1867, p. 3, col. 3.
87. "The Governor's Message," Alexandria *Louisiana Democrat*, February 6, 1867, p. 3, col. 1. *See also* "The Last Message," in *id.* at p. 2, col. 2. According to another paper, Wells, who supported the Fourteenth Amendment, had "the consummate impudence to advocate unqualified negro suffrage." Bellevue *Bossier Banner*, February 9, 1867, p. 2, col. 2. Governor Orr of South Carolina, who opposed ratification, also thought section one gave Congress power to alter voting rights. *See* "Message of Governor Orr," *Yorkville Enquirer*, November 29, 1866, p. 4, col. 3.
88. "Report of the Committee on Federal Relations," Dallas *Herald*, November 3, 1866, p. 1, col. 2. *Accord*, "Ohio Legislature," *Cincinnati Commercial*, January 13, 1868, p. 3, col. 2; "Report of the Select Joint Committee . . . on the proposition to adopt the Congressional Constitutional Amendment," *Weekly North-Carolina Standard*, December 19, 1866, p. 1, col. 7. *See also* "Reconstruction," *Galveston News*, May 3, 1866, p. 2, col. 2; "The Disunion Programme for Party Supremacy," Harrisburg *Patriot and Union*, May 1, 1866, p. 2, col. 1.
89. "Message of Governor Morton," *Indianapolis Daily Journal*, January 12, 1867, p. 2, col. 6.
90. *See Congressional Globe*, 40th Cong., 3d Sess. 336 (1869) (remarks of Rep. Nicholson).
91. *See Congressional Globe*, 39th Cong., 2d Sess. 154 (1866) (remarks of Rep. Stevens). *See also* [Pennsylvania] *Daily Legislative Record . . . of 1867* (Harrisburg, 1867), 7 app. (remarks of Mr. Searight); "Equalized Representation," *Hartford Daily Courant*, May 29, 1866, p. 2, col. 1.
92. *See* [Pennsylvania] *Daily Legislative Record . . . of 1867* (Harrisburg, 1867), 25 app., where Sen. Charleton Burnett, a Democratic opponent of the amendment, cited several cases that had construed the language used in section one and then observed that "the courts have taken both sides of the question, so far as the right of suffrage is concerned." It is likewise the case that the Fortieth Congress's adoption of the Fifteenth Amendment, explicitly granting blacks the right to vote, does not necessarily mean that the Fourteenth Amendment had nothing to do with voting or other political rights. One could support the Fifteenth Amendment, as did Sen. Richard

Yates, *see Congressional Globe*, 40th Cong., 3d Sess. 1004 (1869), not because he thought it was needed but because others thought so, because others had doubts, or out of a realization that there was some ambiguity in need of resolution. Moreover, as we have already seen in Chapter 3, the explicit references to suffrage for blacks in section two of the Fourteenth Amendment similarly does not exclude the possibility that section one also dealt with the issue.

93. *See* Earl M. Maltz, " 'Separate But Equal' and the Law of Common Carriers in the Era of the Fourteenth Amendment," *Rutgers Law Journal*, 17 (1986), 553, 558–567.

94. *See Congressional Globe*, 39th Cong., 1st Sess. 420 (1866) (remarks of Sen. Trumbull), 505 (1866) (remarks of Sen. Fessenden).

95. *Harper's*, 32 (1865), 395 (reporting Sumner's resolution of December 4, 1865).

96. "Legislature of North-Carolina," *Weekly North-Carolina Standard*, July 22, 1868, p. 4, col. 2 (remarks of Rep. Sweat).

97. *See* "The Colored Children," Huntington *Long Islander*, December 22, 1865, p. 2, col. 1.

98. "The Irrepressible African," Huntington *Long Islander*, January 5, 1866, p. 2, col. 4–5 (emphasis in original). It should be noted that the first paragraph quoted in the text was originally written by someone other than the author of the letter and then quoted by the author.

99. *Ibid.* (emphasis added). *See also Brevier Legislative Reports . . . of the Journals and Debates of the General Assembly of the State of Indiana*, IX (Indianapolis, 1867), 80 (remarks of Rep. Ross); "Working of the Civil Rights Bill," *Boston Post*, April 2, 1866, p. 1, col. 5; "The Civil Rights Law and its Effect with Us," *San Francisco Daily Examiner*, April 7, 1866, p. 2, col. 1; "The Civil Rights Bill," West Baton Rouge *Sugar Planter*, April 14, 1866, p. 2, col. 3.

100. *Hartford Daily Courant*, May 18, 1866, p. 2, col. 1.

101. *See* "The School Question," *Peoria Daily National Democrat*, April 21, 1866, p. 1, col. 1. *See also* Robert L. McCaul, *The Black Struggle for Public Schooling in Nineteenth-Century Illinois* (Carbondale, Ill.: Southern Illinois University Press, 1987), 67–72, 108–142.

102. *See* Baltimore *Gazette*, April 18, 1866, p. 1, col. 3; "An Irrepressible Darkey," Harrisburg *Patriot and Union*, May 28, 1866, p. 2, col. 1; "Practical Operation of the Civil Rights Act," *National Intelligencer*, May 16, 1866, p. 2, col. 1.

103. 59 Mass. (5 Cush.) 198 (1849).

104. *See* Alexander M. Bickel, "The Original Understanding and the Segregation Decision," *Harvard Law Review*, 69 (1955), 1.

105. 18 Stat. 335 (Pt. 3, 1875).

106. *Congressional Record*, 2 (1874), 4167.

107. *See ibid.*

108. *See Congressional Record*, 3 (1875), 945.

109. *See Congressional Record*, 3 (1875), 1010–1011.

110. Call for the Eleventh National Woman's Rights Convention, March 31, 1866, in Stevens Papers. *See also* "Radical Fallacies," New Orleans *Daily*

Picayune, February 4, 1866, p. 6, col. 2; "Why Not?," Washington *Evening Star*, December 27, 1865, p. 2, col. 1.

111. "The Progress of Reform," *Daily Richmond Enquirer*, May 16, 1866, p. 2, col. 1.
112. "The Wages of Women," *San Francisco Daily Chronicle*, April 3, 1867, p. 2, col. 2.
113. "The Employment of Women," *Cincinnati Commercial*, December 24, 1865, p. 4, col. 4.
114. *Congressional Globe*, 39th Cong., 2d Sess. 64 (1866).
115. *Congressional Globe*, 39th Cong., 2d Sess. 63 (1866).
116. *Congressional Globe*, 39th Cong., 2d Sess. 63 (1866).
117. *Congressional Globe*, 39th Cong., 2d Sess. 63 (1866).
118. *Congressional Globe*, 39th Cong., 2d Sess. 107 (1866).
119. "Woman's Rights," *National Anti-Slavery Standard*, December 30, 1865, p. 2, col. 3.
120. *Congressional Globe*, 39th Cong., 1st Sess. 116 app. (1866). *See also* [Pennsylvania] *Daily Legislative Record . . . of 1867* (Harrisburg, 1867), 21 app. (remarks of Mr. Davis).
121. *Congressional Globe*, 39th Cong., 1st Sess. 2767 (1866).
122. *Congressional Globe*, 38th Cong., 1st Sess. 2243 (1864).
123. *Congressional Globe*, 39th Cong., 2d Sess. 63 (1866). *Accord*, *Congressional Globe*, 39th Cong., 1st Sess. 2962 (1866) (remarks of Sen. Poland); "Female Suffrage," *Oregon State Journal*, December 30, 1865, p. 2, col. 2.
124. One question of theory that puzzled the Reconstruction generation was whether an interstate traveller was to have rights equal to those of his class in the state from which he came or those of the most favored class in the state to which he went. *See Congressional Globe*, 39th Cong., 1st Sess. 1269 (1866) (remarks of Rep. Kerr).
125. *Congressional Globe*, 39th Cong., 1st Sess. 1064 (1866) (emphasis in original).
126. *Congressional Globe*, 40th Cong., 2d Sess. 2609 (1868).
127. *Congressional Globe*, 39th Cong., 1st. Sess. 376 (1866).
128. *Congressional Globe*, 39th Cong., 1st Sess. 376 (1866). *Accord*, "Mr. Blaine's Proposed Amendment to the Constitution," Richmond *Daily Dispatch*, January 13, 1866, p. 1, col. 1.
129. "Suffrage in the District of Columbia," *Hartford Daily Courant*, January 15, 1866, p. 2, col. 1.
130. "The Voting Amendment," *Springfield Republican*, January 1, 1866, p. 2, col. 1.
131. "The Suffrage Question in Congress," *Springfield Republican*, January 24, 1866, p. 4, col. 1–2.
132. *Congressional Globe*, 39th Cong., 1st Sess. 3433 (1866).
133. *Congressional Globe*, 39th Cong., 1st Sess. 3433 (1866).
134. *Congressional Globe*, 39th Cong., 1st Sess. 3433 (1866).
135. *Congressional Globe*, 39th Cong., 1st Sess. 3433 (1866).
136. M. S. Isaacs to Lyman Trumbull, July 22, 1866, in Trumbull Papers.
137. *Congressional Globe*, 40th Cong., 3d Sess. 726 (1869).

138. *See Congressional Globe*, 40th Cong., 3d Sess. 728 (1869).

139. *See Congressional Globe*, 40th Cong., 3d Sess. 744 (1869).

140. *Congressional Globe*, 39th Cong., 1st Sess. 376 (1866). *Accord*, "Constitutional Amendments," *New York Times*, February 25, 1866, p. 4, col. 4–5.

141. *Congressional Globe*, 39th Cong., 1st Sess. 358 (1866).

142. *Congressional Globe*, 39th Cong., 1st Sess. 358 (1866).

143. *Congressional Globe*, 39th Cong., 1st Sess. 407 (1866).

144. *See Congressional Globe*, 39th Cong., 1st Sess. 1833 (1866).

145. *See Congressional Globe*, 39th Cong., 1st Sess. 1281 (1866).

146. B. R. Cowan to Salmon P. Chase, October 12, 1866, in Salmon P. Chase Papers, Library of Congress, Washington, D.C.

147. *See Congressional Globe*, 40th Cong., 1st Sess. 184 (1867). *See also Congressional Globe*, 39th Cong., 2d Sess. 42 (1866) (remarks of Sen. Wilson).

148. *Congressional Globe*, 39th Cong., 1st Sess. 3148 (1866).

149. [Pennsylvania] *Daily Legislative Record . . . of 1867* (Harrisburg, 1867), 7 app. (remarks of Mr. Landon).

150. *Congressional Globe*, 39th Cong., 1st Sess. 3010 (1866).

151. [Pennsylvania] *Daily Legislative Record . . . of 1867* (Harrisburg, 1867), 7 app. (remarks of Mr. Landon).

152. *Congressional Globe*, 39th Cong., 1st Sess. 1088 (1866).

153. *Congressional Globe*, 39th Cong., 1st Sess. 1095 (1866) (remarks of Rep. Hotchkiss). *See also Congressional Globe*, 39th Cong., 1st Sess. 1082 (1866) (remarks of Sen. Stewart, who understood the Bingham proposal to require Congress to make the laws of all states uniform).

154. *Congressional Globe*, 39th Cong., 2d Sess. 43 (1866).

155. *See Congressional Globe*, 39th Cong., 1st Sess. 527 (1866) (remarks of Sen. Trumbull), 572 (1866) (remarks of Sens. Henderson and Trumbull), 2894 (1866) (remarks of Sen. Trumbull).

156. *Congressional Globe*, 39th Cong., 1st Sess. 1120 (1866) (remarks of Reps. Loan and Wilson).

157. *Congressional Globe*, 38th Cong., 1st Sess. 1488 (1864). Senator John Sherman made the same point with reference to the Fourteenth Amendment. *See Congressional Globe*, 39th Cong., 1st Sess. 2986 (1866).

158. "The Civil Rights Bill," *Memphis Daily Post*, April 3, 1866, p. 4, col. 1–2.

VII. The Judicial Elaboration of Doctrine

1. *See* Civil Rights Act of 1870, 16 Stat. 140 (1870); Civil Rights Act of 1871, 17 Stat. 13 (1871); Civil Rights Act of 1875, 18 Stat. 335 (Pt. 3, 1875).

2. *See* chapter 6, pp. 129–131, 135–136 above for an analysis of the debates on the Fifteenth Amendment and the 1875 act. On the 1871 debates, *compare* Alfred Avins, "The Ku Klux Klan Act of 1871: Some Reflected Light on State Action and the Fourteenth Amendment," *St. Louis University Law Journal*, 11 (1967), 331; *with* Michael P. Zuckert, "Congressional Power under the Fourteenth Amendment—The Original Understanding of Section Five," *Constitutional Commentary*, 3 (1986), 123, 147–155.

3. *White* v. *Clements,* 39 Ga. 232, 259 (1869).
4. *Donnell* v. *State,* 48 Miss. 661, 677 (1873). *Accord, Charge to Grand Jury,* 30 Fed. Cas. 987, 988 (C.C.D.W. Va. 1870); *State* v. *Hairston and Williams,* 63 N.C. 451, 453 (1869).
5. *State* v. *Gibson,* 36 Ind. 389, 393 (1871).
6. *Donnell* v. *State,* 48 Miss. 661, 678 (1873).
7. *State* v. *Gibson,* 36 Ind. 389, 393 (1871).
8. *White* v. *Clements,* 39 Ga. 232, 263 (1869). *Cf. People* v. *Washington,* 36 Cal. 658, 670 (1869).
9. *See Clark* v. *Board of Directors,* 24 Iowa 266 (1868); *Smith* v. *Directors of Ind. Sch. Dist. of Keokuk,* 40 Iowa 518 (1875); *Dove* v. *Independent School District of Keokuk,* 41 Iowa 689 (1875). These cases, it should be noted, were decided without reference to the Fourteenth Amendment.
10. *See Coger* v. *North West Union Packet Co.,* 37 Iowa 145 (1873).
11. *Coger* v. *North West Union Packet Co.,* 37 Iowa 145, 158 (1873).
12. *See DeCuir* v. *Benson,* 27 La. Ann. 1 (1875), *rev'd on other grounds, Hall* v. *DeCuir,* 95 U.S. 485 (1878); *Donnell* v. *State,* 48 Miss. 661 (1873).
13. *See Ward* v. *Flood,* 48 Cal. 36 (1874).
14. *See Cory* v. *Carter,* 48 Ind. 327 (1874).
15. *See Marshall* v. *Donovan,* 73 Ky. 681, 693–694 (1874) (dictum).
16. *See Dallas* v. *Fosdick,* 40 Howard's Prac. Reps. 249 (N.Y. Sup. Ct. 1869); *People ex rel. Dietz* v. *Easton,* 13 Abbot's Prac. Reps. (new series) 159 (N.Y. Sup. Ct. 1872).
17. *See State ex rel. Garnes* v. *McCann,* 21 Ohio St. 198 (1871).
18. *See West Chester and Philadelphia R.R.* v. *Miles,* 55 Pa. 209 (1867).
19. *State ex rel. Garnes* v. *McCann,* 21 Ohio St. 198, 210 (1871).
20. 59 Mass. (5 Cush.) 198 (1849).
21. *Ward* v. *Flood,* 48 Cal. 36, 56 (1874).
22. *See Burns* v. *State,* 48 Ala. 195 (1872); *Hart* v. *Hoss,* 26 La. Ann. 90 (1874). The *Burns* case was expressly overruled in *Green* v. *State,* 58 Ala. 190 (1877).
23. *Burns* v. *State,* 48 Ala. 195, 197 (1872).
24. *See In re Hobbs,* 12 Fed. Cas. 262 (C.C.N.D.Ga. 1871); *State* v. *Gibson,* 36 Ind. 389 (1871); *State* v. *Hairston and Williams,* 63 N.C. 451 (1869); *Doc. Lonas* v. *State,* 50 Tenn. 287 (1871).
25. 39 Ga. 232 (1869).
26. *Green* v. *State,* 58 Ala. 190, 196 (1877); *State* v. *Gibson,* 36 Ind. 389, 393 (1871).
27. *See United States* v. *Anthony,* 24 Fed. Cas. 829 (C.C.N.D.N.Y. 1873); *VanValkenburg* v. *Brown,* 43 Cal. 43 (1872).
28. *Smith* v. *Moody,* 26 Ind. 299, 306 (1866).
29. *See People* v. *Washington,* 36 Cal. 658 (1869).
30. *See People* v. *Brady,* 40 Cal. 198, 199–207 (1870) (argument of counsel).
31. *Id.* at 211–212.
32. *See Roberts* v. *City of Boston,* 59 Mass. (5 Cush.) 198, 209 (1849). *See generally* Thomas M. Cooley, *A Treatise on the Constitutional Limitations which Rest upon the Legislative Power of the States of the American Union* (Boston, 1868), 182–187.

33. *In re Hobbs,* 12 Fed. Cas. 262, 264 (C.C.N.D. Ga. 1871).
34. *Van Valkenburg* v. *Brown,* 43 Cal. 43, 44 (1872) (argument of counsel).
35. *United States* v. *Hall,* 26 Fed. Cas. 79, 81 (C.C.S.D. Ala. 1871). The case is also reported as *United States* v. *Mall,* 26 Fed. Cas. 1147 (C.C.S.D. Ala. 1871). *See also Coger* v. *North West Union Packet Co.,* 37 Iowa 145 (1873), which took the familiar antebellum position that the "doctrines of natural law and of christianity forbid that rights be denied on the ground of race or color." *Id.* at 154.
36. *State ex rel. Garnes* v. *McCann,* 21 Ohio St. 198, 210 (1871).
37. *See Ward* v. *Flood,* 48 Cal. 36 (1874); *People ex rel. Dietz* v. *Easton,* 13 Abbott's Prac. Reps. (new series) 159 (N.Y. Sup. Ct. 1872); *State ex rel. Garnes* v. *McCann,* 21 Ohio St. 198 (1871).
38. *See Doc. Lonas* v. *State,* 50 Tenn. 287 (1871).
39. *See VanValkenburg* v. *Brown,* 43 Cal. 43 (1872).
40. 15 Fed. Cas. 649 (C.C.D. La. 1870).
41. *Id.* at 652.
42. *Id.* at 652–653.
43. *Id.* at 653.
44. 83 U.S. (16 Wall.) 36 (1873).
45. *Id.* at 100.
46. *Id.* at 101.
47. *Id.* at 93.
48. *Id.* at 109–110.
49. *Id.* at 105.
50. *Id.* at 97.
51. *Id.* at 95.
52. *Id.* at 95.
53. *Id.* at 95–96.
54. *Id.* at 97.
55. *Id.* at 105.
56. *Id.* at 97.
57. *Id.* at 111.
58. *Id.* at 60.
59. *Id.* at 62.
60. *Id.* at 61.
61. *See id.* at 64–65.
62. *Id.* at 61.
63. James Bradley Thayer, "Teaching Notes, Constitutional Law," in James Bradley Thayer (1831–1902) Papers, Box 2, Folder 2, Harvard Law School Library, Cambridge, Mass.
64. Anonymous, "One Notebook of Cases Used in JBT's Course on Const. Law," 34 (Harvard Law School Student Notebooks Collection) (undated ms. in Harvard Law School Library, Cambridge, Mass.)
65. *Id.* at 33–34. For another set of student notes reporting a similar statement on Thayer's part, *see* Clarence A. Bunker, "Constitutional Law Student Notes, 1890–1891," 48a (Harvard Law School Student Notebooks Collection) (ms. in Harvard Law School Library, Cambridge, Mass.).
66. 83 U.S. (16 Wall.) at 114.

67. *Id.* at 118.
68. *Id.* at 120.
69. *Id.* at 118.
70. *Id.* at 122.
71. *Id.* at 118.
72. If such was Bradley's view, he appears to have abandoned it within a year of *Slaughter-House*, when he ruled in *United States* v. *Cruikshank*, 25 Fed. Cas. 707 (C.C.D. La. 1874), that Congress had no power to legislate simply to protect basic civil rights, such as the right to personal security, from infringement by others; only states had such legislative power. Although he noted in an 1874 letter to Frederick T. Frelinghuysen, a Republican senator from New Jersey, that he continued to find "much force" in the contrary view that he had expressed in *Slaughter-House* and was "by no means certain that it is not the true view," he also recognized that to give Congress "the right . . . to legislate on all subjects of legislation whatever . . . would have the effect of establishing a duplicate system of government and law for all purposes—which, I cannot think was ever in the contemplation of a human being whilst the Amendments were under discussion." Thus he concluded that "the rights, privileges and immunities of a citizen" could not "embrace all the private rights. The rights of the individual and the rights of the citizen are not identical." He gave several examples to Frelinghuysen, the most telling of which involved "[a]n individual . . . entitled to demand a sum of money from another as a debt." As Bradley observed, "[t]his is his private right as an individual," but "[a]s a citizen," all he could demand was "the equal benefit of judicial proceedings for its collection." Joseph P. Bradley to Frederick T. Frelinghuysen, July 19, 1874, in Joseph P. Bradley Papers, New Jersey Historical Society, Newark, N.J. It thus appears that Bradley had come to agree with Field that, as long as a state protected all creditors equally, it gave due recognition to the rights of contract protected by section one and that the state could, if it wished, deny all creditors the right to collect their debts without thereby violating section one.
73. 83 U.S. (16 Wall.) at 123.
74. *Id.* at 123.
75. *Id.* at 124.
76. *Id.* at 129.
77. *Id.* at 128–129.
78. *Id.* at 77–78.
79. *Id.* at 82.
80. *Id.* at 81.
81. *Id.* at 79.
82. "Teaching Notes," 153, in James Bradley Thayer (1831–1902) Papers, Box 2, Folder 3 (ms. in Harvard Law School Library, Cambridge, Mass.).
83. 83 U.S. (16 Wall.) 130 (1873).
84. *Id.* at 139.
85. *Id.* at 140.
86. *Id.* at 141–142.
87. 85 U.S. (18 Wall.) 129 (1874).
88. *Id.* at 136–137.

89. *Id.* at 138–139.
90. Joseph P. Bradley to Frederick T. Frelinghuysen, July 19, 1874, in Joseph P. Bradley Papers, New Jersey Historical Society, Newark, N.J.
91. 85 U.S. (18 Wall.) at 133.
92. *Ibid.*
93. 88 U.S. (21 Wall.) 162 (1875).
94. *Id.* at 171.
95. *See id.* at 171–173.
96. *Id.* at 171.
97. 87 U.S. (20 Wall.) 655 (1875).
98. *Id.* at 662–663.
99. 96 U.S. 97 (1878).
100. *Id.* at 104–105. When sitting in review of a circuit court judgment, the Court under *Swift v. Tyson*, 41 U.S. (16 Pet.) 1 (1842), as it had come to be applied by the 1870s, could apply general principles of federal common law. *See* Tony Freyer, *Harmony & Dissonance: The* Swift *&* Erie *Cases in American Federalism* (New York: New York University Press, 1981), 45–100.
101. 41 U.S. (16 Pet.) 1 (1842).
102. 94 U.S. 113 (1877).
103. *Id.* at 124–126.
104. *Live-Stock Dealers' & Butchers' Ass'n* v. *Crescent City Live-Stock Landing & Slaughter-House Co.*, 15 Fed. Cas. 649, 653 (C.C.D. La. 1870).
105. Samuel Freeman Miller, *Lectures on the Constitution of the United States* (New York, 1893), 660.
106. *Id.* at 658.
107. *Id.* at 664.
108. *Id.* at 661. *See also id.* at 666.
109. 92 U.S. 542, 555 (1876) (dictum).
110. 94 U.S. at 140–141, 154.
111. *Id.* at 145–146.
112. *Id.* at 146.
113. 75 U.S. (8 Wall.) 603 (1870).
114. 79 U.S. (12 Wall.) 457 (1871).
115. *See* William E. Nelson, *The Roots of American Bureaucracy, 1830–1900* (Cambridge, Mass.: Harvard University Press, 1982), 65–72.
116. *Congressional Globe*, 39th Cong., 1st Sess. 57 app. (1866) (remarks of Rep. Julian).
117. E. L. Godkin, "Commercial Immorality and Political Corruption," *North American Review*, 107 (1868), 248, 253.
118. Henry Adams, *The Education of Henry Adams* (Boston: Houghton Mifflin, 1918), 280–281.
119. *See Bell's Gap R.R. v. Pennsylvania*, 134 U.S. 232, 237 (1890); *Plessy* v. *Ferguson*, 163 U.S. 537, 550 (1896).
120. 61 Mass. (7 Cush.) 53 (1851).
121. *Id.* at 95.
122. *Id.* at 85.

123. Many courts repeated the dictum about the impropriety of taking the property of A and giving it to B. *See, e.g., Legal Tender Cases,* 79 U.S. (12 Wall.) 457, 580 (1871) (dissenting opinion of Chase, C. J.); *Calder* v. *Bull,* 3 U.S. (3 Dall.) 386, 388 (1798) (opinion of Chase, J.); *Bradley* v. *New York & New Haven R.R.,* 21 Conn. 294, 306 (1851); *Taylor* v. *Porter,* 4 Hill 140, 143 (N.Y. Sup. Ct. 1843).

124. On class legislation, *see generally* Michael Les Benedict, "Laissez-Faire and Liberty: A Re-Evaluation of the Meaning and Origins of Laissez-Faire Constitutionalism," *Law and History Review,* 3 (1985), 293.

125. *Cf.* Peter Westen, "The Empty Idea of Equality," *Harvard Law Review,* 95 (1982), 537.

126. 60 U.S. (19 How.) 393 (1857).

127. 198 U.S. 45 (1905).

128. 410 U.S. 113 (1973).

129. Henry Brannon, *A Treatise on the Rights and Privileges Guaranteed by the Fourteenth Amendment to the Constitution of the United States* (Cincinnati: W. H. Anderson, 1901), 13.

130. *See* William D. Guthrie, *Lectures on the Fourteenth Article of Amendment to the Constitution of the United States* (Boston, 1898), 20–21.

131. Thomas M. Cooley, *A Treatise on the Constitutional Limitations which Rest upon the Legislative Power of the States of the American Union,* 6th ed. (Boston, 1890), 431, quoting Daniel Webster's argument in the *Dartmouth College* case.

132. *Id.* at 483.

133. *Id.* at 485.

134. *Id.* at 484.

135. *Id.* at 486.

136. *Id.* at 484.

137. Guthrie, *Fourteenth Article of Amendment,* 76.

138. Christopher G. Tiedeman, *A Treatise on State and Federal Control of Persons and Property,* 1 (St. Louis: F. H. Thomas Law Book, 1900), 5.

139. James Bradley Thayer, "Teaching Notes, February 17, 1890," 49, in James Bradley Thayer (1831–1902) Papers, Box 2, Folder 5 (ms. in Harvard Law School Library, Cambridge, Mass.) (emphasis in original).

140. Joseph Warren, "Constitutional Law Notes," v. 1, p. 267 (Harvard Law School Student Notebooks Collection) (ms. in Harvard Law School Library, Cambridge, Mass.) (emphasis in original).

141. Anonymous, "One Notebook of Cases," 41.

142. Henry Ware, "Lectures on Constitutional Law by James Bradley Thayer," December 5, 1895 (Harvard Law School Student Notebooks Collection) (ms. in Harvard Law School Library, Cambridge, Mass.) (emphasis in original).

143. Anonymous, "One Notebook of Cases," 40.

144. Warren, "Constitutional Law Notes," v. 1, pp. 254, 267 (emphasis in original).

145. Robert Young, "Examination upon Constitutional Law," 102 (ms. in Bentley Library, University of Michigan, Ann Arbor, Michigan).

146. Christopher G. Tiedeman, *The Unwritten Constitution of the United*

States: A Philosophical Inquiry Into the Fundamentals of American Constitutional Law (New York, 1890), 71.

147. *See id.* at 72–73.
148. Guthrie, *Fourteenth Article of Amendment*, 1–2.
149. Brannon, *Fourteenth Amendment*, 1.
150. 100 U.S. 303 (1880).
151. *Id.* at 310.
152. *Ibid.*
153. *Id.* at 306.
154. *Id.* at 308.
155. 100 U.S. 339 (1880).
156. *Id.* at 347.
157. *Ibid.*
158. *Id.* at 348.
159. It should be noted that during the early 1870s the Supreme Court was in the process of elaborating the doctrine of judicial immunity. *See* Jay M. Feinman and Roy S. Cohen, "Suing Judges: History and Theory," *South Carolina Law Review*, 31 (1980), 201, 243–249.
160. 163 U.S. 537 (1896).
161. 347 U.S. 483 (1954).
162. This statement is consistent with a new book on *Plessy* by Charles A. Lofgren, *The* Plessy *Case: A Legal–Historical Interpretation*, (New York: Oxford University Press, 1987), 174–175, 190–191, 195.
163. 103 Mo. 546 (1890).
164. *See* Herbert Hovenkamp, "Social Science and Segregation before *Brown*," *Duke Law Journal*, 85 (1985), 624, 627–634, 651–657.
165. 103 Mo. at 551–552.
166. 59 Mass. (5 Cush.) 198 (1849).
167. *Id.* at 209.
168. *Cummings* v. *Richmond County Board of Education*, 175 U.S. 528, 545 (1899) (dictum). The Court in *Cummings* would not consider closing the white school under such circumstances, however.
169. *Lehew* v. *Brummell*, 103 Mo. at 551.
170. *See* Meyer Weinberg, *A Chance to Learn: The History of Race and Education in the United States* (Cambridge: Cambridge University Press, 1977), 42–51. *But see* Horace Mann Bond, *The Education of the Negro in the American Social Order* (New York: Octagon Books, 1966), xiii, 37–115, suggesting that the most substantial black educational gains occurred during the 1870s when there was some integrated schooling.
171. *See* David L. Kirp, *Just Schools: The Idea of Racial Equality in American Education* (Berkeley: University of California Press, 1982), 283–302.
172. 113 U.S. 27 (1885).
173. *Id.* at 31.
174. *Id.* at 31–32.
175. 113 U.S. 703 (1885).
176. *Id.* at 710.
177. *Ibid.*
178. 118 U.S. 356 (1886).

179. *Id.* at 373–374.
180. *Id.* at 370.
181. *Ibid.*
182. 137 U.S. 86 (1890).
183. *Id.* at 94.
184. *Id.* at 89–90.
185. *Id.* at 91.
186. 123 U.S. 623 (1887).
187. *Id.* at 669.
188. 127 U.S. 678 (1888).
189. *Id.* at 685.
190. 127 U.S. 205 (1888).
191. *Id.* at 210.
192. 116 U.S. 307 (1886).
193. 118 U.S. 557 (1886).
194. 94 U.S. 113 (1877).
195. *Stone* v. *Farmers' Loan & Trust Co.*, 116 U.S. 307, 331 (1886).
196. *Chicago, Milwaukee & St. Paul Ry.* v. *Minnesota*, 134 U.S. 418 (1889). *But cf. Budd* v. *New York*, 143 U.S. 517 (1892), where the Court upheld a statute that did not provide for judicial review of rates in a case where the rate was set by the legislature instead of a commission, and where there was no explicit claim that the rate had been set arbitrarily.
197. *See* Nelson, *Bureaucracy*, 153; Benedict, "Laissez-Faire and Liberty," 301–305, 327–330.
198. 110 U.S. 516 (1884).
199. 137 U.S. 692, 697 (1891).
200. *Hurtado* v. *California*, 110 U.S. 516, 535–536 (1884).
201. *Caldwell* v. *Texas*, 137 U.S. 692, 697 (1891).
202. 109 U.S. 3 (1883).
203. *Id.* at 11.
204. *Id.* at 13.
205. *Id.* at 13–14.
206. *Id.* at 19.
207. *Id.* at 26.
208. 92 U.S. 542 (1876).
209. *Id.* at 555.
210. Joseph P. Bradley to W. B Woods, March 12, 1871, in Joseph P. Bradley Papers, New Jersey Historical Society, Newark, N.J. Woods was a circuit judge at the time he received the letter, and the opinion that Bradley communicated to him thus could well have become known to others. For dicta in *Cruikshank* suggesting this same approach, *see* 92 U.S. at 554, 556.
211. *See* Zuckert, "Congressional Power."
212. 165 U.S. 578 (1897).

VIII. The Transformation of the Amendment

1. 169 U.S. 366 (1898).
2. *Id.* at 389.

3. *Id.* at 387.
4. *Id.* at 398.
5. *Id.* at 395.
6. 198 U.S. 45 (1905).
7. *Id.* at 57.
8. *Id.* at 53.
9. *Id.* at 57.
10. *Id.* at 61.
11. See chapter 7, pp. 188–189 above.
12. 208 U.S. 412 (1908).
13. *See Coppage* v. *Kansas,* 236 U.S. 1, 14 (1915); *Adkins* v. *Children's Hospital,* 261 U.S. 525, 545–546 (1923); *Morehead* v. *New York ex rel. Tipaldo,* 298 U.S. 587, 610–611 (1936); Maurice Finkelstein, "From Munn v. Illinois to Tyson v. Banton: A Study in the Judicial Process," *Columbia Law Review,* 27 (1927), 769; Roscoe Pound, "Liberty of Contract," *Yale Law Journal,* 18 (1909), 454.
14. 198 U.S. at 73–74 (dissenting opinion).
15. *See* Paul Murphy, *The Constitution in Crisis Times, 1918–1969* (New York: Harper and Row, 1972), 146–151.
16. In *United States* v. *Carolene Products Co.,* 304 U.S. 144, 152 n.4 (1938), the Court declared that while it would defer to legislative judgments interfering with economic liberty, it would scrutinize more carefully acts impinging upon personal liberty. This approach differed markedly, of course, from the Court's late nineteenth century approach in Fourteenth Amendment cases — an approach that some of the liberal members of the Roosevelt Court may not have appreciated. But at least one member of the *Carolene Products* majority, Justice Brandeis, surely understood the older approach; indeed, he had used it successfully in *Muller* v. *Oregon. See* Philippa Strum, *Louis D. Brandeis: Justice for the People* (Cambridge, Mass.: Harvard University Press, 1984), 120–123. Nonetheless, for reasons that Strum and Lewis J. Paper, *Brandeis: An Intimate Biography of One of America's Truly Great Supreme Court Justices* (Englewood Cliffs, N.J.: Prentice-Hall, 1983), the two most recent biographers of Brandeis, do not attempt to explain, Brandeis joined *Carolene Products* without comment.
17. *See* Alpheus T. Mason, *Harlan Fiske Stone: Pillar of the Law* (New York: Viking Press, 1956), 515; Murphy, *Constitution in Crisis Times,* 146–166.
18. 304 U.S. 144, 152 n.4 (1938).

Index